Items should be returned on or before the last date shown below. Items not already requested by other borrowers may be renewed in person, in writing or by telephone. To renew, please quote the number on the barcode label. To renew online a PIN is required. This can be requested at your local library.
Renew online @ **www.dublincitypubliclibraries.ie**
Fines charged for overdue items will include postage incurred in recovery. Damage to or loss of items will be charged to the borrower.

Leabharlanna Poiblí Chathair Bhaile Átha Cliath
Dublin City Public Libraries

Baile Átha Cliath
Dublin City

Brainse Dhroimchonnrach
Drumcondra Branch
Tel: 8377206

920

Date Due	Date Due	Date Due

David Ryan was born in Galway and holds an MA degree in history from NUI Galway. His first book, *Blasphemers and Blackguards: The Irish Hellfire Clubs*, was published by Merrion Press in 2012. David currently lives in Dublin where he works as a television producer and scriptwriter.

BUCK WHALEY

IRELAND'S GREATEST ADVENTURER

DAVID RYAN

MERRION
PRESS

First published in 2019 by
Merrion Press
An imprint of Irish Academic Press
10 George's Street
Newbridge
Co. Kildare
Ireland

www.merrionpress.ie

© David Ryan, 2019

9781785372292 (Paper)
9781785372308 (Kindle)
9781785372315 (Epub)
9781785372322 (PDF)

British Library Cataloguing in Publication Data
An entry can be found on request

Library of Congress Cataloging in Publication Data
An entry can be found on request

Cover front: Portrait of Thomas Whaley
as a youth (Mervyn Whaley).

Cover back: Jerusalem from the north by David Roberts, 1839
(New York Public Library).

For Karla

'Know, my friends, that my father ... died whilst I was still a child, leaving me great wealth and many estates and farmlands. As soon as I came of age and had control of my inheritance, I took to extravagant living. I clad myself in the costliest robes, ate and drank sumptuously, and consorted with reckless prodigals of my own age, thinking that this mode of life would endure for ever.

It was not long before I awoke from my heedless folly to find that I had frittered away my entire fortune ... I sold the remainder of my lands and my household chattels for the sum of three thousand dirhams, and, fortifying myself with hope and courage, resolved to travel abroad.'

— The First Voyage of Sinbad the Sailor

CONTENTS

PART 3: DEBT AND DEATH

ACKNOWLEDGEMENTS

There used to be a nightclub called 'Buck Whaley's' on Leeson Street in Dublin. I never visited it, but I used to work just around the corner from it and I think that somehow 'Buck' himself would have approved of the flamboyant lettering on its sign. The nightclub is no more, but for around thirty years everyone who walked past it or stepped over its threshold must have realised that a character of this name existed – that is, if they didn't know already. But it wasn't this late-night venue or its sign that first drew my attention to Thomas Whaley, it was his alleged connection with the Dublin Hellfire Club, which consumed my attention for a while when I was writing my first book. At that time I got in touch with Mervyn Whaley, Thomas's descendant, who kindly invited me to his home to see the stunning oval portrait of his ancestor, the only individual likeness of him still in existence. Mervyn told me that there was quite a bit of primary source material on Whaley out there if I could get access to it. I realised that there was a book to be written and a story to be told, but I never imagined how extraordinary that story would turn out to be.

Many people have helped and encouraged me in the writing of this book and I'd like to say a special word of thanks to Marie Ryan, Karla Doran, Jimmy Doran, Joan Ryan and Aideen Keane for reading and commenting on drafts of different chapters. I would also like to acknowledge the staff of the different institutions in which I conducted research, in particular the National Library of Ireland, the Royal Irish Academy, Dublin City Library, the Public Record Office of Northern Ireland and the London Library.

I am very grateful to Ömer M. Koç for giving me permission to consult the manuscript journal of Hugh Moore in his collection in Istanbul, Turkey and to Özlem Çakar and Ayhan Kıbıç for arranging for me to visit the library where it is held. Thanks also to Ruth Ferguson for showing me around Thomas Whaley's family home, Newman House in Dublin, and to

Ted Cahill and Sue Chadwick for courteously welcoming me to two other buildings with which he is associated, Fonthill House and Fort Faulkner.

Thanks to Michael Berreby, Frances Coakley, Glenn Dunne and Ruth Ferguson for kindly giving me permission to reproduce a number of the images in the plate sections, and to Jim Butler, Vincent Hoban and Berni Metcalfe for supplying high-res versions of images. Very special thanks are due to Mervyn Whaley for giving me permission to reproduce the oval portrait of Thomas Whaley, which he recently had photographed, and the wax portrait of Richard Chapel Whaley and his family.

I am grateful to Conor Graham for his encouraging response when I first approached him with the idea for this book and for agreeing to publish it, and to Fiona Dunne for preparing it for publication. Sincere thanks also to the following persons for their help and advice: the late Nicola Gordon Bowe, Turtle Bunbury, William Butcher, Zoë Comyns, Patrick Conner, Leigh Crawford, Dorinda Evans, Nichola Goodbody, Karina Holton, James Kelly, Anthony Malcomson, Sami Malki, Jo-Anne Martin, Fonsie Mealy, Averil Milligan, Katie Milligan, Michael Monahan, Michael Ryan, Amanda Stebbings and Christina Tse-Fong-Tai. I am also grateful to my employer Stephen Rooke for allowing me to take a short period of leave to focus on finishing this book.

When you're immersed in researching and writing history it's easy to lose track of what life is really about and I'd like to thank our little boy Diarmuid for reminding me of the bigger picture and for being such a source of happiness in our lives. My wife Karla is my biggest supporter and I want to thank her for all her advice and encouragement and for indulging my fixation with Whaley over the past five years. This book is dedicated to her.

A NOTE ON THE TEXT

The text contains many quotations from manuscript and printed primary sources. In these quotations capitalisation has been standardised. For the most part spelling and punctuation have been left unchanged from the original, but in the case of quotations from manuscripts some minor alterations have been made: '&' is converted to 'and', and in the case of some words (e.g. 'distinguish'd') the modern spelling ('distinguished') is given for ease of reading.

A NOTE ON SOURCES, CITATIONS AND ABBREVIATIONS

Two of the main sources consulted are Thomas Whaley's own memoirs, written down *c.*1796–1797 and published in 1906 as Sir Edward Sullivan (ed.), *Buck Whaley's Memoirs* (London: Moring, 1906); and Captain Hugh Moore's *Narrative Journal of his Expedition to Constantinople and Jerusalem in the Company of Thomas Whaley*, an unpublished manuscript held in a private collection. Whenever a quotation from either of these sources is used in this book, the citation is given afterwards in parentheses: either W (to denote *Buck Whaley's Memoirs*) or M (to denote Moore's journal), followed by the relevant page number, e.g. (W, 43).

Occasionally reference is made to Sir Edward Sullivan's introduction and footnotes to *Buck Whaley's Memoirs* and in these instances the source is cited as Sullivan (ed.), *Memoirs*, [page number].

Many other sources are also used and these are referenced in the notes. In the case of printed sources, when a source is cited only once the full reference is provided in the notes. When a source is cited more than once an abbreviated form is given in the notes and the full reference is provided in the 'Works Cited' section at the end of the book. In the case of citations for letters and other documents, the names of the most common individuals are abbreviated as follows:

RC	Robert Cornwall
HF	Hugh Faulkner
SF	Samuel Faulkner
WN	William Norwood

AR   Anne Richardson

JR   John Richardson

RCW   Richard Chapel Whaley

TW   Thomas Whaley

WW   William Whaley

The following abbreviations are also used:

BNL	*Belfast News-Letter*
DEP	*Dublin Evening Post*
DIB	James McGuire and James Quinn (eds), *Dictionary of Irish Biography: From the Earliest Times to the Year 2002* (9 vols, Cambridge: Cambridge UP, 2009)
Faulkner Papers	Correspondence and papers of Samuel Faulkner, *c.*1721–1795 (in private ownership)
FLJ	*Finn's Leinster Journal*
FJ	*Freeman's Journal*
HJ	*Hibernian Journal*
NAI	National Archives of Ireland
NLI	National Library of Ireland
ODNB	H.C.G. Matthew and Brian Harrison (eds), *Oxford Dictionary of National Biography* (60 vols, Oxford: Oxford UP, 2004)
PRONI	Public Record Office of Northern Ireland
RCBL	Representative Church Body Library, Dublin
TW Manuscript Memoirs	Manuscript Memoirs of Thomas Whaley (2 vols), London Library, NRA 20043
SNL	*Saunders' News Letter*

Whaley Papers   Minor collection of correspondence and other material relating to Thomas Whaley (in private ownership)

WHM   *Walker's Hibernian Magazine*

PROLOGUE

In August 1792 an Anglo-Irish gentleman named Thomas Whaley stood in the Alpine village of Chamonix looking up at the snow-covered slopes of Mont Blanc. Known as the 'doomed mountain' it was once believed to be the abode of witches and sorcerers, but its sheer size and height made it even more daunting. At 15,780 feet it is western Europe's highest peak and in 1792 it had been summited by only a handful of climbers. Whaley was determined to clamber through the snow and ice to join their number. The fact that he had virtually no knowledge of the Alps and was completely devoid of climbing experience mattered not a jot to him. After all, he had faced much greater challenges in the past.

As a sport, mountaineering was still in its infancy in the late eighteenth century but a burgeoning community of climbers in the Chamonix area was steadily conquering the Alps. The most famous was Horace-Bénédict de Saussure, a geologist and physicist who had been fascinated by Mont Blanc since he first laid eyes on it in 1760. He decided that he would either conquer the mountain himself or direct the expedition that did so and in the end he succeeded in both objectives. Instructed by him, Jacques Balmat and Michel-Gabriel Paccard climbed to the top of Mont Blanc in August 1786, and a year later de Saussure accomplished the feat himself.[1] Any attempt to follow in their footsteps was not to be undertaken lightly but Whaley had resolved to give it a try. He knew that de Saussure had left a piece of paper with his name in a bottle at the summit and he wanted to pay 'homage to this great man, by placing my name next to this bottle'. (W, 293) To accompany him he recruited three Englishmen, one of whom, Lord Charles Townshend, he praised for 'his merit and distinguished virtues'. (W, 292) Conscious that local knowledge and expertise would be key to the success of the venture, he also assembled a team of around twenty local guides, one of whom was probably the seasoned climber Pierre Cachat. A man of huge stature, Cachat was renowned for his great strength and had been involved in several previous expeditions to Mont Blanc.[2] No doubt the expedition was reasonably well equipped by the standards of the day and wore, as de Saussure's team did, frock coats, hip-length boots and broad-brimmed hats. They would also have had ladders, ice axes and long poles.[3] And yet Whaley and his English companions were strangely nonchalant, seemingly unaware of the magnitude of the task that lay ahead. 'They thought that they were making an excursion as if they had been going to the Col de Balme or the Brévent, or making a pleasure trip,' the alpinist Marc-Théodore Bourrit observed. 'Alas! Their lightheartedness and lack of caution almost had deplorable consequences'.[4]

As they approached the lower slopes of the mountain Whaley and his team could see two glaciers separated by a dark tongue of rock. This was the ridge called the Montage de la Côte and they decided to ascend by it, hoping to reach the Gîte à Balmat, the two great boulders that stood at its crest. This was where Balmat and Paccard had bivouacked following their first day of climbing, but getting to it proved to be no easy matter. Although it was the climbing season, the conditions were not favourable and they had barely reached the snowline, around halfway up the ridge, when they encountered heavy rain and a thick, icy fog. Given the poor visibility, what followed was not surprising. Someone – it is not clear whether it was Whaley, one of the Englishmen, or one of the guides – missed his footing and dislodged a stone. 'It rolled down, set another much larger one in motion, & all came down into the path.' Some of the falling debris hit one of the guides, breaking his leg, while a stone struck another in the head and beat him 'almost to pieces, tho' without killing him'.[5] When they had recovered from the shock, the other guides paused for a moment in the freezing fog to take stock. The two injured men could not continue, the conditions were perilous, and the foreigners who had hired them clearly had no idea what they were doing. If they continued further disaster was inevitable. Their minds made up, the guides picked up their injured companions and began to descend.

Whaley later claimed that he and Townshend considered pressing on by themselves but 'after some deliberation we determined to join our cowardly attendants; as any attempt to proceed without them would be vain'. Feeling 'more or less roughly handled', they tottered back down the mountain. The guide with the broken leg recovered but the other man lingered between life and death for some time afterwards and eventually had to be trepanned. Despite Whaley's uncharitable description of the guides as 'cowardly', he and the others at least tried to make up for what an observer called 'the sad results of their foolhardiness' by generously compensating the men's families.[6] Whaley's hopes of placing his name in a bottle next to de Saussure's had been dashed. Hoping to have the unfortunate incident put down to the forces of nature rather than his own rashness, when he wrote his memoirs a few years later he claimed that they had been two thirds of the way to the summit when the accident happened, that it had been caused not by a rockfall but by an avalanche, and that the two guides had not been injured but killed outright. (W, 293)

Those who knew Thomas Whaley would not have been surprised to hear of his latest misadventure. It epitomised several of his defining characteristics: a tendency to set off on ill-considered escapades, an obsession with achieving what few or none had accomplished before, and a cavalier attitude towards danger. These traits made for an adventurous life, but they also encouraged an addiction that plagued him all his days. In an age notorious for its gamblers he was one of the worst. Born in Dublin in 1765 into an extremely wealthy Anglo-Irish family, he inherited close to £50,000 (around €19 million in today's money)[7] and estates worth almost £7,000 a year. Yet he squandered every penny of this, and many thousands besides, at the gaming tables. These catastrophic losses drove him into exile on the continent in the 1790s, but this did not cure him of his addiction. By the early summer of 1792 he had managed to redeem his fortunes somewhat by running his own casino in Paris before the turmoil of the Revolution forced him to relocate to Lausanne in Switzerland. It was from there that he set out to climb Mont Blanc (it is entirely possible that he did so on foot of a wager, though this is unknowable). Following his eventual return from the continent Whaley retired to the Isle of Man, where he wrote his memoirs. By this time (1796–7) he had accumulated monumental losses: 'in the course of a few years I dissipated a fortune of near four hundred thousand pounds, and contracted debts to the amount of thirty thousand more, without ever purchasing or acquiring contentment or one hour's true happiness.'[8] (W, 332) Indeed he was such a restless spirit that contentment eluded him until his dying day. 'Tis well known that Mr. Whaley was blessed with a good understanding,' read his obituary, 'but the whirl and blaze in which he lived, diminished its effect and force in an eccentricity of pursuits.'[9]

★★★

Why should we care about Whaley? He himself would have admitted that he was a wealthy spendthrift and playboy given over to self-indulgence. So why does he deserve attention, any more than the other rakes and libertines that crop up time and again in the annals of history? Perhaps because he was more than just a rich wastrel. Four years before the Mont Blanc debacle he had undertaken a much longer and more perilous expedition, setting out from Dublin for Jerusalem on the back of wagers amounting to £15,000. The journey had all but ended in disaster on many occasions. Whaley nearly suffocated in a cave in Gibraltar, was caught in a hurricane in the Sea of Crete, fell ill and almost died in Constantinople, had a close shave with pirates in the Dodecanese, was waylaid by bandits near Nablus and had a mesmerising encounter with an infamous Ottoman governor known as 'the Butcher'. When he returned triumphantly in the summer of 1789, having completed the journey in the allotted time, he became an overnight celebrity. He was feted in Ireland and Britain and mingled with luminaries such as the Prince of Wales and Charles James Fox until his gambling addiction caused his fortunes to spiral downward.

Since his childhood Whaley had wanted to explore far-off lands and exotic climes, and while he liked to give the impression that he undertook the Jerusalem expedition on a whim, in fact he planned it over a number of years. He was not fazed by the human and natural hazards or the complicated logistical challenges that lay in wait. And there were many, for he lived in a time when the world was a wider place than it is today and foreign travel frequently involved discomfort, disturbing realities and extreme danger. It was also an extraordinarily turbulent time. Ireland was about to descend into chaos, Britain was trying to maintain stability at home and abroad, France was on the brink of bloody revolution and the Ottoman Empire was creaking at the seams, embroiled in war with Russia and on the cusp of terminal decline. Whaley lit up this volatile world like a quick-burning candle, with a devil-may-care attitude and a strong self-destructive streak, but also an ability to recognise the absurdity of his own actions and the world around him. His travels also taught him something he might not have learned had he stayed at home. When he encountered hardship and danger on his travels he realised that his lavish life of privilege was a mere accident of birth. Survival required personal resilience: 'you are left to shift for yourself, with those advantages which nature and not any fortuitous circumstances may have bestowed on you'. (W, 96) Although this experience did not save him from his innate self-destructiveness, it did bring him closer to his essential humanity.

Whaley's Jerusalem odyssey earned him celebrity status in Britain and Ireland, a fame that persisted into later years. His great wager may even have given Jules Verne the idea for Phileas Fogg's bet in *Around the World in Eighty Days* (1872). Today he is remembered as 'Buck' Whaley, the flamboyant character who journeyed to Jerusalem on the back of a wager, and until recently a Dublin nightclub situated not far from his St Stephen's Green townhouse bore his name. Indeed his story is deeply resonant in the twenty-first century, a time when foreign travel has become commonplace. For those of us fortunate enough to live in first world countries it is usually a highly sanitised experience, involving strolls through shiny airport lounges, glitzy duty-free shopping, and a few hours airborne in a pressurised aircraft before we land, perhaps somewhat disorientated, in whatever place business or pleasure has ordained. Accommodation is constrained by budget, but normally we can expect some level of comfort. For Whaley and the adventurers of the past, travel was a far more complicated, protracted and visceral affair. For him it involved many days at sea, subject to the vagaries of the weather and encounters with pirates and hostile fleets, as well as gruelling overland expeditions and lodgings in whatever roadside shed or stable could be put to the purpose. His story puts the travel back into travel. It gives us a sense of what it must have once been like, long before the age of online booking.

***

This book is based on a number of manuscript and printed sources. One of these is Whaley's own memoirs, principally an account of the Jerusalem expedition. He died before he could publish the memoirs and they lay in obscurity for the next hundred years. Around 1900 the antiquarian Sir Edward Sullivan acquired the original manuscript, along with a copy which he claimed was 'to all intents and purposes a duplicate' of the original. Working from these volumes he published a version of the text in 1906 as *Buck Whaley's Memoirs*. This book has long been regarded as the best source for Whaley's life, but it is not the only one. The current whereabouts of the original manuscript are unknown[10] but the copy is now held in the London Library. It contains a fair amount of material, some of it risqué, that Sullivan saw fit to leave out of his published version. There is also an independent account of the Jerusalem expedition: a journal kept by Whaley's travelling companion Captain Hugh Moore. Now kept in a private collection in Istanbul, Moore's journal confirms most of Whaley's account while acting as an invaluable corrective to many of the latter's exaggerations. It also contains a great number of additional details and anecdotes.

The above sources focus mainly on the Jerusalem expedition. We would know comparatively little about the rest of Whaley's life were it not for one man: his land agent Samuel Faulkner, who carefully filed away virtually every letter he received concerning Whaley's estates, finances, expenses, near-continual gambling losses, and desperate attempts to clear or evade his debts. The correspondence includes many letters from Whaley's associates, friends and family members, not to mention the man himself. Although it is in private possession, the owners kindly allowed me to consult it while researching this book. Also, copies of many of the letters are held on microfilm in the Public Record Office of Northern Ireland and the National Library of Ireland. This material fills in many of the gaps in Whaley's life story while revealing a human side rarely glimpsed in the memoirs: the 17-year-old boy who thought he could replace missing teeth with substitutes purchased from a peasant, the hot-headed young gentleman ready to fight duels at the slightest provocation, the benevolent master who was kind to his servants, and the despairing fugitive on the run from yet another catastrophic gambling loss. Whaley was a human being like any other, and he freely admitted his own flaws, weaknesses and shortcomings. For his entire life he struggled with these deep human frailties, even as he hurled himself into one of the greatest adventures of the age. It is this, more than anything, that makes his story so appealing.

PART ONE
EARLY LIFE

1

MAKING A BUCK

I was born with strong passions, a lively imagination and a spirit that could brook no restraint. I possessed a restlessness and activity of mind that directed me to the most extravagant pursuits; and the ardour of my disposition never abated till satiety had weakened the power of enjoyment ... In the warmth of my imagination I formed schemes of the wildest and most eccentric kind; and in the execution of them no danger could intimidate, no difficulty deter me. (W, 335)

So wrote Thomas 'Buck' Whaley towards the end of his short life, evoking the powerful and wayward spirit that set his days ablaze, from the follies of his youth to the hare-brained schemes, remarkable adventures and crushing disasters of his adulthood. It was his sheer heedlessness, his willingness to do the unthinkable in the face of all sense and advice to the contrary, that made Whaley such an attractive character, not only to his contemporaries but also to us today, over 200 years after his demise. The same volatile and adventurous disposition that ignited his spectacular expedition to Jerusalem also set him on the road of calamity and financial disaster, a path he struggled on until his untimely death at the age of 34.

When Whaley was born in 1765[1] there was little to suggest that he was destined for such a reckless and dissipated life. His father, Richard Chapel Whaley, was a prominent Anglo-Irish landowner who had carefully consolidated and augmented the extensive landed wealth he had inherited from his forebears. Richard's great grandfather Henry Whalley had been a first cousin of Oliver Cromwell and a firm supporter of the parliamentarians during the English Civil Wars between King and Parliament in the 1640s. In 1649 Henry Whalley's brother Edward, along with Cromwell and others, signed Charles I's death warrant. Later that year Cromwell embarked on his conquest of Ireland, crushing and dispossessing the Irish Catholics who had sided with the king during the conflict. Many parliamentarians received grants of the confiscated estates and Henry came into substantial property in the Galway area.[2]

Over the generations that followed his descendants added to this landed fortune. In 1725 his great grandson Richard Chapel Whaley inherited the Galway lands, and some years later his uncle bequeathed him property in Armagh and Fermanagh.[3] Richard was a canny entrepreneur and in 1755 he invested 'to very great advantage' in a copper mine near Whaley Abbey, his home in the foothills of the Wicklow Mountains.[4] The money amassed from investments like this enabled him to acquire further estates in Dublin, Wicklow, Carlow and Louth. By this time he and his fellow upper-class Protestants had become a powerful elite in Ireland. Their victory in the Williamite War (1688–91) had enabled them to seize yet more property from the Irish Catholics and in the early-eighteenth-century Protestants, though a minority, owned some 80 per cent of the land in Ireland. They also controlled the Irish Parliament and the legislature. Determined to keep Catholics in a subordinate position, they introduced penal laws prohibiting them from practising their religion, owning land, voting or holding public office. The laws were only sporadically enforced but Richard Chapel Whaley was one of their firmest advocates, partly because he used them for his personal gain. When engaged in his mining venture he seems to have defrauded his business partner, a Catholic named Bolger: 'Whaley took advantage of the penal laws to rob him and prospered on the ill-gotten plunder.'[5]

Unsurprisingly given that he was the descendant of a Cromwellian, Whaley was also keen to enforce the penal laws for their own sake. The aftermath of the Jacobite Rebellion of 1745 saw the laws 'revived in Ireland without cause, and pursued by a few weak bigots with avidity; rewards were offered for apprehending priests, and the fellows who pursued this infamous avocation were termed *priest catchers*'. Whaley was said to be an ardent priest-catcher, leading expeditions into the countryside in search of his prey. At some point he became known as 'Burn-Chapel' Whaley: according to one tradition, he got the nickname when he fired his pistol at a Catholic chapel and set its thatched roof alight, burning it to the ground.[6] It seems the attack was motivated by Whaley's animosity towards a Father Byrne, a Catholic priest who lived at Greenan Beg near Whaley Abbey. Byrne's sister was married to a Protestant named Willis or Wills, and while dining with her one day the priest had given 'umbrage to a Protestant of the party by stating that Protestants would be lost'. In retaliation for this, and no doubt keen to deal with the Romish cleric in his midst, Whaley recruited a pair of thugs named Collins and Quinsey and set fire to the Catholic chapel at Greenan. The three men are said to have used a picture of the Virgin Mary for target practice, with Whaley exclaiming 'I shot the wh[or]e through the heart and she did not bleed.' Whatever the truth of the story, the 'Burn-Chapel' moniker stuck and would endure long after his death.[7]

It was not the only legacy he had to worry about. As the owner of estates scattered over seven counties – Dublin, Wicklow, Carlow, Galway, Armagh, Louth and Fermanagh – he needed to produce an heir who could carry on his name and property, but his first marriage, to Catherine Armitage, had been childless. When Catherine died in November 1758 Whaley, now in his late fifties, decided to remarry. Youth and good looks must have been among the qualities he sought in his new bride because she turned out to be Anne Ward, the 18-year-old daughter of the Rev. Bernard Ward, Rector of Knockbreda in County Down.[8] With her lustrous dark hair and prominent nose Anne was arrestingly beautiful. She also possessed 'captivating manners, a well-cultivated mind and the most incorruptible virtue'. (W, 9) The dramatist John O'Keeffe (1747–1833) described how she and Whaley met:

> [She] went to Dublin, on a visit, and with some female friends was one day walking about to see the fine buildings, as she had never been in town before. On viewing Stephen's Green, they stopped before a house, with a large carved stone dormant lion over the door; as they were admiring this, a person standing near, asked them to walk in and look at the house; they consented, and he led them all over the apartments, which were furnished in the first style, but they saw no one but their polite guide. They were much pleased, and, expressing

great admiration, were thanking him, and taking their leave, when, in a particular and pointed manner, he asked the country lady [i.e. Anne Ward] … whether she liked all she saw; with great pleasure she said she did. 'Then, madam', he replied, 'this house and all it contains is mine, and if you wish to make it yours also, you may have the house and the master of it;' – making her a low bow. A marriage followed.[9]

O'Keeffe claimed to have had the story from Anne's brother and it has the ring of truth, apart from one detail: Whaley had not yet started building the house with the lion over the door. When he met Anne he was living in 'prince-like magnificence' at No. 75 (now No. 85) St Stephen's Green and this must have been the dwelling he showed her around. Designed by the German architect Richard Castle, this stone-fronted townhouse is now part of Newman House, an administrative centre of University College Dublin. It has been carefully restored and boasts a lavishly decorated interior. Its front parlour, the Apollo Room, has magnificent stucco ornamentation, while the Great Room or Saloon is regarded as one of Ireland's finest eighteenth-century interiors.[10] Whaley must have seemed a decidedly eligible widower and Anne was sufficiently impressed to overcome whatever reservations she had about marrying a man forty years her senior. For his part he was besotted with his bride-to-be, who he described as 'my soul's darling'. The marriage took place in February 1759, just three months after Catherine's death, and Anne settled into the role of dutiful wife. Her son would later praise the 'undeviating rectitude of her conduct towards my father, notwithstanding the disparity of their age, which would have been sufficient to have excited the malevolence of slander against her, had she given the least opening for it, by any levity in her behaviour'. (W, 9)

The marriage was certainly successful if judged by the number of offspring it produced. The year 1760 saw the birth of a daughter, Mary Susanna, followed two years later by a son, named Richard Chapel after his father. Whaley was reported to be so delighted at the birth of his son and heir that he made his wife a present of £10,000, sending his banker a note in the form of a piece of doggerel:

Good Mr. Latouche,
Prithee open your pouch,
and pay my soul's darling
Ten thousand pounds sterling …[11]

With the arrival of a further two daughters, Anne and Frances Sophia in 1763 and 1764 respectively, Whaley decided that his present residence was too small to meet the needs of his growing family.[12] He set about building a new house on an adjoining plot of land. It was to be a huge mansion with five bays and four storeys over a rusticated basement and when completed it would dwarf No. 75 (see Plate 1).[13] Over the portico Whaley installed a lead statue of a lion by John Van Nost II (c.1710–1780), then Ireland's leading sculptor. Seemingly just awoken from its slumber, it gazes sombrely across at St Stephen's Green.[14] The mansion was similar in design to another great Dublin townhouse, Charlemont House, although its exterior was not as elegant. The interior was a different matter. Whaley hired skilled artists to produce some of the finest stuccowork in eighteenth-century Dublin. The stucco decoration on the walls and ceiling of the main staircase is breathtaking (see Plate 3). Many of the rooms also feature fine stuccoed ceilings, and in the ground floor drawing room there are two small portrait heads above the central wall panels, possibly representations of Richard Chapel Whaley himself.[15]

When not busy overseeing the construction and decoration of his palace Whaley concerned himself with the management of his estates, for which he relied heavily on his 'honest' and 'faithfull' servant and land agent, Samuel Faulkner. At this time Faulkner and his wife Catherine were living with the Whaleys, but they would later move into a place of their own a few doors down at No. 84 (now No. 96).[16] Born around 1721 near Cookstown, County Tyrone, Faulkner was a no-nonsense Ulsterman known for his blunt language. On one occasion, suffering from diarrhoea, he claimed to have been 'not less than 13 times at stool … at night[.] this would kill an elephant'.[17] Hard-working and meticulous, he also acted as agent for several other landowners and kept copies of all his correspondence.[18] Though his life was marred by tragedy – his wife and one of his nephews predeceased him – he was kindly, generous and well-liked. But Faulkner must also have had a ruthless edge to him; otherwise he would not have been able to perform the work of a land agent: letting property, collecting rents and arrears and, occasionally, carrying out evictions. In March 1765 Whaley gave Faulkner power of attorney to 'receive all moneys rents and arrears of rents' that were due to him while also instructing him to recover some property belonging to him 'by any means without blood shed or burning a house … do the thing with spiritt and I will support it'. The fact that Whaley referred to 'blood shed' and 'burning' at all suggests that he and Faulkner may have used these methods in the past.[19] They had known one another a long time and their relationship was one of friends rather than employer and employee.[20] For the Whaley children, who knew Faulkner from birth, he seemed more like an affectionate uncle than their father's agent.

★★★

On 15 December 1765, several months after work had begun on the new house, Anne gave birth to her fifth child. Thomas Chapel Whaley was baptised exactly two months later at St Peter's Church on Aungier Street.[21] Known to his family as Tom, this fair-haired blue-eyed boy captured his mother's heart, more so perhaps than any of his siblings, but she had little notion of the extraordinary life that lay ahead of him or the worry he would cause her. Nor was he the last child she would bear. Over the next couple of years a further two boys, John and William, arrived. Perhaps sensing that his family was now complete, Richard Chapel Whaley commissioned a sculptor, Patrick Cunningham, to commemorate them in an unusual portrait: a wax bas-relief intended for display on a chimneypiece in the new house (see Plate 2).[22] Here the ageing father appears as a kindly patriarch surrounded by his loving wife and children. He gazes devotedly at Anne as she tends to the seventh and youngest child, William, seated on her knee. To the left the eldest daughter, Susanna, sits seemingly preoccupied at a small desk, while to the right the eldest son, Richard, tugs at his father's sleeve, eager to show him something or involve him in a game. Beside him the second daughter Anne is dancing, anticipating her later career as a socialite. At the extreme right the third daughter, Sophia, plays with some fruit. Beside her the toddlers, 2-year-old Tom and 1-year-old John, play on the floor. Both are attired as girls: whether male or female, infants were dressed in floor-length gowns worn over stiffened bodices or stays. It was not until between the ages of 4 and 7 that boys were 'breeched', i.e. given male clothing. Tom holds a rattle in his hands, an inauspicious symbol of the 'play' he would devote himself to in later years: gambling.

Richard Chapel Whaley took great joy in the beautiful wife and children that came to him so late in life, but he did not enjoy their company for more than a few years. By the end of 1768 he had fallen ill and the following February he died.[23] After he had been buried in the Whaley family vault in Syddan, County Meath, his widow returned to St Stephen's Green. Not long afterwards the new house was completed under Faulkner's direction and the family moved into it. Now aged around 28, Anne faced bringing up her seven children without the support of a husband. Yet she was better placed than most widows to do so. She could rely on the help of the Faulkners (Catherine Faulkner acted as her maid) and her father, the Rev. Bernard Ward, who was guardian of the fortunes of the Whaley children. She also had the money to employ as many servants as she needed.[24] Many years later, Tom commended her for bringing her children up 'in the paths of religion and virtue … whatever follies any of us may have committed, the cause could never be imputed to her'. (W, 9)

Populated by a large family and a considerable staff of servants, the newly built mansion on St Stephen's Green must have been a lively place. The children would have played in the stately rooms and corridors, causing mischief and getting in the servants' way, while their mother or one of the Faulkners watched over and perhaps chided them. Over a century later, in his autobiographical *A Portrait of the Artist as a Young Man*, James Joyce hinted at feeling Tom Whaley's presence in these hallways: 'The corridor was dark and silent but not unwatchful … was it because he had heard that in Buck Whaley's time there was a secret staircase there?'[25] In the dining room, a large chamber with a richly stuccoed ceiling at the rear of the house, the family were served by a posse of attendants. French cuisine was in vogue and Anne and the older children may have tucked into a variety of exotic dishes such as lambs' ears ragoût, fricassée of frogs and badger flambé.[26] If so this influenced Tom's culinary tastes as he employed a number of French cooks later in life. At the close of day the family retired to sleep in their rooms at the top of the house. One of the bedrooms looked out onto the back yard and stables and beyond that a green area known as Lord Clonmell's Lawn (now the Iveagh Gardens). This may have been where Tom slept as a child. Over a hundred years later it was the bedchamber of the poet Gerard Manley Hopkins.[27]

It was unlikely that Anne would stay a widow. She was still young, attractive and fashionable and, as befitting a lady of her station, turned herself out in fine gowns and dresses, among them a Latin gown which she wore with a blond stomacher and 'sleeve knots with French flowers'.[28] More than a few gentlemen must have had their heads turned by this beautiful and wealthy widow and it was only a matter of time before she settled on a new husband. He turned out to be John Richardson, the son of a County Derry rector and a member of the Royal Dublin Society. A kind-hearted and affable man who would later enter politics as MP for Newtown Limavady, Richardson was the same age as Anne and seemed disposed to be a good stepfather to her children. They married at the end of 1770. It was a joyful union. 'You have no notion how happy I am,' Anne wrote to Faulkner a few years later, 'and it is not at all extraordinary that it shou[l]d be so, I am blest with the very best husband upon earth'.[29]

Yet she also suffered tragedy. On 12 August 1772 her eldest son, Richard Chapel Whaley Junior, died. He was 10 years old. We do not know what occasioned his passing but it must have caused his mother and siblings great sorrow. Yet for the next oldest brother, Tom, the event had special significance. Under the terms of his father's will, he had only stood to inherit leasehold lands in County Armagh. But now that he was the eldest surviving son he was also entitled to the extensive Carlow estates and the Dublin properties including, if he outlived Anne, the house on Stephen's Green.[30] The annual rental income from the Whaley estates came to £6,876 and Tom also stood to inherit the lion's share of his father's personal fortune of £43,630, which earned over £2,500 per annum in interest.[31] His mother and grandfather did not tell him the amount of his inheritance but he knew it was very large and henceforth he would wait impatiently for the day when this wealth would pass into his hands. This certainly spurred some of the extravagance and recklessness he manifested during his teens. We will never know if he would have led a more prudent life had his brother survived – what we know of his temperament suggests he would not have – but if nothing else he would have had less wealth to squander.

Around the middle of 1773 Anne went to live with Richardson in Ulster. She seems to have brought her daughters with her, leaving her three surviving sons in the Faulkners' care. Even though Richard junior's death the previous year must still have been on her mind, this was a blissful time for Anne and her new husband. For most of the ten years that she had been married to Richard Chapel Whaley her days had been consumed with bearing and raising children. Now, happily married to Richardson, she was enjoying new-found freedom and 'better health … than I have done for several years'. One suspects that she was also enjoying a break from rearing her boys. Tom, John and William were now aged 7, 6 and 5 respectively and must have been a handful. At the same time she missed them and at the end of the year she wrote to Sam Faulkner asking him to bring them to spend a month with her the following April or May.[32] During the summer months she and Richardson again took up residence at the house on St Stephen's Green, which was reportedly 'frequented by the first people in the kingdom … the proprietors are not only very rich, but have great interest [i.e. influence]'.[33] When Anne and her husband were absent, Faulkner had to keep the Whaley boys amused. Tom had a particular interest in exotic animals and Faulkner found himself bringing him to see the 'wild beasts': probably a private menagerie, as there were no zoological gardens in Dublin at the time.[34] Luckily, he did not have to keep him entertained indefinitely. The time had come for him to be sent away to school.

Portarlington in the Queen's County had been renowned for its boarding schools since the early eighteenth century. Most of them were run by Huguenots who had come to Ireland fleeing persecution in France. A large community of these immigrants had settled in the small town in the Irish midlands, where they filled a gap in the market for the education of upper-class Protestant children. By the middle of the century the number of schools in Portarlington ran well into double figures, with nobility and gentry from all over the country sending their children there to be educated. Tom probably attended Robert Hood's school, a boarding school where students learned writing, grammar, arithmetic, English, French, classics and dancing; or the Rev. Richard Baggs's public Latin school, 'from which many gentlemen of rank and fortune have entered the College [i.e. Trinity College Dublin] with particular credit'. Baggs's school taught writing, arithmetic, mathematics, geography, drawing, music and dancing.[35]

The writing master trained his pupils well, as is evident from the large neat calligraphy of a letter Tom wrote to Faulkner from Portarlington on 21 October 1775. By then his brothers had joined him at school, but he missed his mother and asked Faulkner 'please to let me know' when he expected her to arrive in Dublin as 'she told me in her last letter, that she would send for us then'.[36] But Tom was no shrinking violet, homesick and longing to be reunited with his loving mother. His thoughts wandered far beyond the bounds of home or school. Richard Baggs's school taught 'geography both antient and modern, as also the use of the globes'[37] and if he did go there, Tom would have paid attention during geography class as he had started drawing maps of exotic foreign regions. Earlier that year he had completed a map of southern Africa which he presented to his grandfather on 25 June ('dedicated to Mr. Ward by his dutiful gd. son Thomas Whaley'). Neatly and fairly accurately drawn, it is an impressive piece of cartography for a child of his age and was probably copied from a map by the London cartographer Herman Moll, which it closely resembles.[38] Tom planned to have 'a good many maps' ready to show to his mother and prepared several others, including 'a very large map of Spain and Portugal and the Mediterranean Sea'.[39] It was a formative time for the young boy. As he approached his tenth birthday he felt the stirring of an adventurous spirit and a burning curiosity about the wider world. Doubtless he hoped to visit at least some of the places he mapped, and while he would never make it as far as Africa, his early understanding of the geography of the Mediterranean would serve him well later in life.

Tom may still have been at his cartographic efforts over two years later: early in 1778 he wrote to Faulkner asking him to send him 'a couple of small pencil[s] and two or three brushes'. By this stage he and his brothers had moved to a new school, possibly in Armagh. Tom also asked after Faulkner's nephew Sam, who had been unwell.[40] It did not bode well. The Faulkner boy's health seems to have been poor and in September 1782 he died. The list of expenses for his funeral makes for poignant reading: a shroud sheet and cap, an oak coffin covered with black cloth, a hearse and horses to bring the body to St Peter's Church in Dublin, followed by a mourning coach. Tom later wrote to Faulkner to commiserate: 'one could not say but he [had] as good a life as I [I'll] drop this subject ... excuse me for calling to your mind a thing that must have distressed you very much but as he is happy I hope a manly firmness has reconsiled you'.[41] Having witnessed his own brother's passing ten years before Tom was well acquainted with the inescapable reality of death. Now, as he entered his late teens, he himself was starting to make his first moves towards manhood. His schooldays were over, and he was about to get his first taste of the wider world he had imagined so often while carefully marking out his maps.

★★★

'When I had attained my sixteenth year, my mother thought proper to send me to France in order to finish my education.' (W, 10–11) With this nonchalant statement Tom recalled the most formative and turbulent period of his early life: his grand tour. Travel on the continent was reckoned an indispensable part of the education of the sons of wealthy gentlemen. It was intended to broaden their minds, enhance their social accomplishments and enable them to acquire a range of useful contacts. But they did not always behave like the gentlemen they aspired to be.[42] Critics of the grand tour argued that the young men who went on it were too immature to appreciate its benefits and had too many opportunities for drinking, gambling and self-indulgence. Yet most felt that the benefits outweighed the dangers and hoped that under the guidance of their travelling tutors, known as 'bearleaders', grand tourists could avoid these pitfalls. As Tom Whaley's seventeenth birthday approached, his mother, assisted by his grandfather Bernard Ward, made arrangements to dispatch him to France.

It was around this time that Whaley sat for what was probably his first portrait. The only proper likeness of him that survives today, it shows a boy on the cusp of manhood (see Plate 4). Finely attired in a red coat and pink waistcoat, he stands with one hand on his hip, staring resolutely from the canvas. His face is well-nourished, slightly pudgy even, with the expression of a confident young gentleman readily embracing his life of wealth and privilege. But there is also a certain wildness in his blue-eyed gaze, as if he were liable to do something unwarranted and unpredictable at any time. Like the excitable adolescent he was, Whaley was enthusiastic about the new prospects and experiences that foreign travel would offer him. His grandfather proposed to send him off with a yearly allowance of £500, later increased to £600. This sum would have been sufficient to maintain a prudent tourist, but not a young man eager to be let loose on the world.

His mother trusted that his bearleader would provide wise and strict supervision. For this role she settled on an army veteran named William Wray, 'who had been recommended to her by some persons of distinction in Ireland'. (W, 11) The son of a County Donegal landowner, Wray had served as a lieutenant captain in the Thirty-ninth Foot, an Irish regiment that spent long periods stationed abroad. This old soldier with a penchant for books and smelling salts had spent much of his life on the continent and seemed a suitable individual to oversee Whaley's tour.[43] But had Anne looked more closely into his past she might have had second thoughts. Wray was a good-natured man but he was not good at managing money. In the army he had found his officer's salary insufficient to support his lifestyle and had had to sell his commission to pay off his debts. As well, he was in bad health – the result of youthful overindulgence – and he lacked the 'firmness of character necessary to superintend the conduct of a young man'. (W, 11) Wray hardly seemed a model of prudence and discretion. As a contemporary writer put it, he 'was supposed to be a fit person to undertake the direction of young Whaley's studies. It soon however appeared that the tutor had not the ability'.[44]

It was arranged that Bernard Ward would accompany Whaley to Bath, where they would rendezvous with Wray. The young grand tourist and his bearleader would then leave for Paris, where the grand tour would commence. But neither Anne nor Ward nor Wray could have anticipated the series of disasters that would unfold in the course of Whaley's travels. He set out brimming with energy and optimism, but he would return a year and a half later distressed and disarrayed, having abandoned his tutor and endured a remarkable series of misfortunes that left him physically shattered and thousands of pounds in debt.

2

THE GRAND TOUR

Ward and his grandson arrived in Bath sometime in November or early December 1782. This was one of Whaley's first trips out of Ireland and while he had little time to admire the famous spa town's elegant streets and ancient remains, he knew he would soon visit more exotic places. He seems to have been impressed to meet Wray, with the genial old soldier perhaps regaling him with tales of derring-do from his days in the army. As they were stepping into their coach to depart a thought struck Ward and he stopped them for a final word. 'Mr. Wray my G[ran]d. Sons allowance is five hundred,' he reminded him. 'But should you go beyond [this] weel suppose it was laid out properly and your bills shall be honoured.' The old man did not know it, but he was opening the first crack in the floodgates. Whaley would not be of age for another four years but already he was musing on how to get hold of and spend his inheritance. 'I know [I'll] have a good fortune and a good deal of ready money [which] I have found out is in my disposal should any thing happen between this and that time.'[1]

Soon afterwards Wray and Whaley reached Paris. The French capital was a popular and attractive destination on the grand tour, offering 'an enormous range of cultural and social activities that tourists could participate in, an active artistic life, and a large number of splendid sights'.[2] While these no doubt interested Whaley, he was also keen to sample the city's other attractions. One evening Wray went alone to the theatre, returning later to find his pupil in the arms of a prostitute. Without taking much notice, the older man went straight to bed. The next morning Whaley faced Wray with 'all the awkward bashfulness attendant on a first offence' but was surprised to find him 'treating the matter as a bagatelle. He told me that the love of the fair sex was a natural passion, particularly at my time of life, and concluded by giving me some general cautions respecting the prudence to be observed and the choices to be made in those connexions'.[3] Wray's relaxed attitude set the tone of the relationship, but in time Whaley would find that this laid-back approach was not to his advantage.

At the end of December they relocated to Auch in the south of France where Whaley was to learn French and refine his riding, dancing and fencing skills. Boasting an imposing gothic cathedral, the ancient Gascon town is sited prominently on an escarpment overlooking the River Gers. Visiting it in 1787 the agriculturist Arthur Young found Auch to be 'almost without manufactures or commerce, and ... supported chiefly by the rents of the country'. Farmsteads were scattered throughout the surrounding countryside instead of being gathered in towns, as elsewhere in France.[4] This rustic region may have seemed a strange place for Whaley to work on refining his character, but Wray had reasons of his own for choosing it: he had once lived in Auch and had many friends there who welcomed him and his young charge with open arms. 'This place is Mr Wrays home,' Whaley observed, 'and the people here of the first rank quite court him ... by which means I will get into the best company'. He continued to take more than a passing interest in the opposite sex. His experience with the prostitute had probably been his first sexual encounter, and though initially bashful he soon became more confident. Whaley did not care for the appearance of most of the Auch women, who were 'as yellow as saffron' and, he thought, 'the uglyest creatures I ever saw'. Yet he found them 'nevertheless very ingageing[.] they have a great deal of wit and are very agreeable'. He did find a few of the girls pretty. One in particular caught his eye: the 20-year-old niece of the Archbishop of Auch, who invited him to attend to mass with her. 'I would you may be sure have been glad to go,' he wrote to Faulkner, 'but unfortunately [on] the day appointed I was seized so violently with the tooth ach[e] I really thought I should have dyed.'[5]

It turned out that Whaley had to have a tooth pulled. It was no doubt an uncomfortable procedure: eighteenth-century dentistry could be excruciating. A couple of years later his lawyer Robert Cornwall complained of being 'in the greatest torture these three days with a pain in my jaw, I went yesterday to have one of my teeth drawn, but the fellow has left the stump behind after cutting away great part of my gum and at this moment [I] am in great agony'.[6] Whaley's dentist was not so ham-fisted, but it seems that he impressed upon his patient the fashionable notion that teeth could be transplanted from one individual to another. Keen to find replacements, Whaley 'gave three guineas to a peasant for one of his that fitted and it was put in the place of mine immediately and I am in hopes it will do. In a day or two I am to get another put in as soon as the one is fast'.[7] But he was to be disappointed. Teeth cannot be transplanted and the ones he got from the peasant must have fallen out soon afterwards.

Despite his dental issues Whaley was not long in making himself at home in Auch, where he rented a stylish house and set himself up with servants, horses and dogs. He also acquired residences in several nearby towns, alternating between them as it suited him. Wray's hands-off approach to his pupil's tuition suited both parties and for a while they lived together amicably. 'I am very happy with Mr. Wray,' Whaley declared. 'He is a real gentleman.'[8] But in time they started living apart. 'I found that we generally agreed better asunder, and therefore his visit at one of my residences was always a signal for me to remove to the other.' (W, 13) Wray, in any case, had other things to occupy his mind. Whaley had noticed that in Auch women would 'come lepping into Mr Wrays room before he is well out of bed in the morning and taulk pollyticks for two hours'.[9] It is not clear whether talking 'pollyticks' was a code for something else, but in any event it was not long before the bearleader took up with a female companion.

***

As time went on Whaley found his funds running low. The rentals on his houses and his other outgoings could not be maintained on an allowance of £600 a year and in June 1783 he had to undertake a costly excursion. His tutor was ailing and so, 'for my amusement and for poor Wrays health', they travelled to the Pyrenean town of Bagnères de Luchon, famous for its thermal baths and medicinal waters. Bagnères was 'one of the most expensive towns in France, [and] after Spa the most fashionable water drinking place'. It attracted upper-class visitors from all over Europe and Whaley met many young Irish and English gentlemen. He soon found his money running away from him as he tried to keep up with them. 'When they gave one a dinner, or supper [they] thought it odd if I did not entertain them in return, which I did and certainly did what was proper.' Within a month he spent £150, a quarter of his allowance, accumulating large debts into the bargain. To add further pressure, his new friends declared themselves shocked 'at the pittyfulness of my scanty allowance'.[10]

Whaley was convinced that his relatives were treating him shabbily. His allowance, he felt, did not reflect his status or his fortune. In late June he wrote to Samuel Faulkner asking him 'if you think *six hundred* a year a compatency equal to *my fortune* and what a young man on his travels should have when within three years of being of age'. Faulkner, of course, did not decide the amount of Whaley's allowance, but as his land agent he did have access to the income from his estates and the young man knew he was his best chance of getting money. Insisting that 'I neither play [i.e. gamble] nor whore' he asked Faulkner to send him £300 to offset the expenses of his horses, his munificence to the locals ('a young man in a small town abroad is esteemed and respected principally by his gennerous manner of treating the inhabitants'), and his excursions to places like Bagnères 'where the acquaintance may well merrit cultivation'. While admitting that he was fond of pleasure 'as is natural at my age', he reiterated that he had 'not the least desire to play'.[11] The young gentleman, it seemed, protested too much: probably he had already lost a fair bit of money gambling. Faulkner forwarded the requested amount, but it was insufficient to answer Whaley's demands. He was also annoyed to find his tutor spending with abandon: 'Mr. Wray instead of saveing his income to my knolege spends every farthing of it.'[12] Meanwhile he discovered that in France debtors were not permitted to leave town until they had paid everything they owed. When some of his creditors stopped his phaeton (a lightly sprung open carriage, the eighteenth-century version of a sports car) in the street in front of several of his compatriots, from whom he borrowed the money to pay them, he was mortified. 'Now sure,' he reasoned, 'every person of common sense must see the impropriety and bad polliticks of sending me abroad when I am not allowed sufficient to live like a gentleman.' His letters to his mother contained similar protestations, which eventually had the desired effect: from April 1784 his allowance would be doubled to £1,200 a year.

Shortage of money was not the only trouble Whaley had to contend with. At some point during his stay in Bagnères his horse fell on top of him, bruising him so badly that he decided to move further into the Pyrenees to another spa town, Barèges, where 'the waters are better for wounds'.[13] Though he recovered from the injury he did not see fit to tone down his excessive lifestyle and soon he was engaging in 'all the folly and extravagance peculiar to our countrymen abroad'. (W, 13) Some of it involved the opposite sex. After leaving Barèges to return to Auch, probably during the autumn of 1783, he started pursuing romantic intrigues in earnest.

On a visit to Tarbes, around forty miles from Auch, Whaley made the acquaintance of an aristocratic couple: Henri Louis de Rohan, Prince of Guéméné, and his wife Victoire-Armande. The pair had once stood at the glittering apex of Parisian society: Henri Louis belonged to a noble house that claimed descent from the dukes of Brittany, while his wife was a favourite of Marie Antoinette and had been governess to the royal children. In 1782 Henri Louis had 'managed to set the entire nation in an uproar by playing the starring role in one of the country's most resounding bankruptcies'.[14] His wildly extravagant lifestyle had resulted in an astronomical debt of 33 million livres and he and his wife were forced to flee to the south of France. Whaley was a regular visitor to their chateau in Tarbes and became a particular favourite of Victoire-Armande. He learned that she was contemplating a match between him and a female relative he believed to be her daughter. 'At first I looked upon this as a feint; as I had conceived the idea that the Princess did not regard me with indifference herself. But on her persisting in the proposal, I expressed my acknowledgment in the warmest terms.' (W, 15) In fact, Victoire-Armande could not have proposed such a match: her only surviving daughter, Marie-Louise, was already married. It may be that the noblewoman actually suggested that Whaley marry a niece or other female relative. But Whaley's relatives in Ireland were vehemently opposed to the idea on the basis that the two parties were of different religions and they instructed Wray to take the young man away from Auch as soon as possible. This might have proved difficult had Whaley not become caught up in another romantic entanglement. This one had a much more troubling outcome.

This affair arose out of his acquaintance with the young female cousin of an Auch nobleman he named only as the Count V—. Whaley's efforts to seduce her 'in a short time succeeded to the utmost extent of my wishes' (W, 15), but things became more complicated when it transpired that the girl was pregnant. Hoping to hush the matter up Whaley tried to keep her concealed in his house 'till such time as it might be thought proper for her to appear again in the world'. (W, 16) Unfortunately a local abbé discovered what had happened and lectured the young woman harshly. Whaley responded to this interference by subjecting the priest to a thrashing. This was an era when gentlemen frequently met perceived slights or insults with violence and Whaley, though still a minor, certainly considered himself a gentleman. Even so, to attack a priest was nothing if not reckless and the local magistrate arrested him and threw him into prison without even the formality of a trial. Luckily the Archbishop of Auch, who was friendly with Wray, intervened on his behalf and he was released. It afterwards transpired that the 'abbé' was no such thing. 'This fellow only wore the dress of a Priest, and had never been ordained.' (W, 17)

While this meant that Whaley would not be prosecuted for attacking a priest,[15] it did not signal an end to his troubles. If it was shown that he had abducted a female he would face the full rigours of French law. Whaley managed to get the young woman away from Auch and to Montpellier, where she gave birth to a daughter. The child died not long afterwards and as soon as the unfortunate mother had recovered Whaley had her committed to the care of a religious order.[16] Although she had joined willingly with him in their liaison, its outcome had destroyed her life as she knew it. For eighteenth-century females such experiences were not uncommon. The law offered women a degree of protection, but in general men used them as they saw fit and few gave much thought to female suffering. Whaley probably regarded the fate of his erstwhile lover as unfortunate but not much more than that. And while he no doubt regretted his daughter's death, she was only the first of several children he would father out of wedlock. He was living in a man's world and fast becoming an adept player in it.

Whaley had now been in France for around a year. In that time he had lurched fecklessly from mishap to misadventure but had come off relatively unscathed. He had survived a dangerous accident and a spell in prison and his debts, while significant, were not prohibitive.[17] He had also managed to escape any lasting consequences from his ill-fated liaison. His letters home carefully avoided any mention of this affair but in one, probably written early in 1784, he hinted at it. Describing himself as 'a *quarrelsome* dog' (a possible reference to his thrashing of the 'abbé') he mentioned that he had 'been such a wild fellow of late that I have neither heard nor wrote to any one'. He knew that the time was approaching for him to leave Auch. His sister Sophia and her husband Robert Ward, formerly MP for Wicklow, had moved to France after Ward failed to get returned in the election of 1783. Having already met them in Aix, Whaley decided to join them in Lyons, where they had relocated.[18] It was there that his luck finally ran out.

★★★

Accompanied by Wray, who seems to have offered little in the way of guidance during the pregnancy crisis, Whaley set out for Lyons in May 1784. Unimpressed by the city's attractions, he decided to make his own entertainment and footed the bill for 'sumptuous entertainments' for all and sundry. 'Magnificent balls and suppers to the ladies, extravagant and expensive dinners to the gentlemen, succeeded each other in quick rotation.' (W, 19) Lavish displays of this kind were bound to attract hangers-on and opportunists and before long Whaley took up with 'a set of wild young men' among whom were two Irish gentlemen.[19] He was no doubt glad to make the acquaintance of these fellow countrymen and he enjoyed their company so much that before long they were inseparable.

Not long afterwards he received an anonymous note warning him that the men were a pair of swindlers who planned to make him 'the dupe of their execrable trade'. (W, 20) Recognising this as sincere and valuable advice, Wray begged Whaley to ditch his new friends – to no avail. This was the extent of the bearleader's guidance and when Whaley accepted an invitation to dine with the Irishmen, Wray inexplicably failed to accompany him to the soiree. On arrival Whaley found that 'a handsome company of female beauties' were present and with their encouragement he drank so much wine 'that before the dessert was introduced the glasses seemed to dance before me. Nothing would then satisfy them but we must drink champagne out of pint rummers, which soon completed the business.' Getting a gambler drunk was and is among the oldest tricks in the book and with Whaley now 'in a proper state for them to begin their operations' his 'friends' proposed that they gamble. Within a short time they had extracted no less than £14,800 from him, 'exclusive of my ready money, carriage, jewels, etc. I know not why they even stopped here; for I was in such a state that they might have stript me of my whole fortune.' (W, 21)

Still just 18 years old, Whaley had been efficiently and remorselessly defrauded by two of the most predatory sharpers he ever had the misfortune to encounter. He immediately drew up a bill instructing his banker in Dublin to pay the amount, but even in his drunken state he must have known it would be returned protested, which it was in due course. With his allowance and any monies he had obtained from Faulkner long since spent, there seemed to be little hope of his raising the huge sum needed to pay his 'friends'. But soon an opportunity to do so seemed to present itself, in the form of a mad scheme to abduct a wealthy young heiress.

3

WILD SCHEMES

Even as he reeled from the worst gambling loss he had ever suffered, Whaley somehow got his hands on a sum of money: two thousand louis d'ors (around £2,000), possibly advanced by Faulkner, to whom he may have written and given a hint of what had happened. If so, he swore him to secrecy. Under no circumstances were his mother and stepfather to be told and indeed they would not find out for several more weeks. Whaley used some of the £2,000 to clear his less significant debts: the lavish parties he had thrown in Lyons had not paid for themselves. The remainder fell well short of what he owed the Irishmen, but they were not deterred and proposed that he go to London 'where, upon my fortune being made known, I should find no difficulty in getting my bills discounted to any amount I thought proper'. (W, 22) If he would do this, they promised, they would halve the amount of the debt. There was just one catch: one of them, John Ryan,[1] would accompany him.

Wray advised against the London trip but Whaley dismissed the older man's protestations and agreed to the plan.[2] Wray had not been much of a bearleader. Having given Whaley little in the way of guidance in Auch and the spa resorts of the Pyrenees, he had failed to protect him from being monumentally defrauded in Lyons. Admittedly, Whaley had not been the easiest pupil. Headstrong and impulsive, he had refused to listen to sensible advice or be swayed in his resolutions, however foolish. But by allowing him to go unaccompanied to London, Wray was exposing him to whatever further machinations the swindlers might choose to employ. With Ryan in tow, Whaley set out for Paris. He spent long enough in the city to have a fling with 'an intriguante … whose business it was to entrap young men by such artifices, in which the courtezans are much more expert … than they are in London'. The lady knew her business well, and after Whaley had spent 'a most delicious time' in her company she informed him that she needed a large sum to settle a gambling debt.

Ignoring his own precarious financial situation he handed her £500.[3] To be fleeced twice in such a short space of time looked like carelessness, and the episode would take its toll on more than just his purse. Following this latest debacle he and Ryan continued on to London, arriving there around the middle of May 1784.

This was to be Whaley's first extended stay in the British capital. Home to some 700,000 people, it was a massive city by the standards of the time and as notorious for its poverty and squalor as it was famous for its wealth and elegance. With money still in his pocket (though he was going through it fast), Whaley avoided the squalor and stayed in the West End, home to luminaries like the Prince of Wales and the Duchess of Devonshire. He checked into the Royal Hotel on St James's Street[4] while Ryan, determined to keep his prey within arm's reach, took lodgings just up the road on Albemarle Street. Somehow, Whaley had to raise the money needed to get the sharper off his back. Almost certainly his first recourse was Leslie Grove, an Irish merchant-turned-banker based at 4 Crosby Square in Bishopsgate.[5] Grove was friendly with Wray and had managed finances for Whaley's family in the past, but getting the required sum out of him proved more difficult than anticipated. Although the banker would have been well aware that the young man stood to inherit a large fortune, he either could or would not advance the money: probably he did not want to do so without first conferring with Whaley's relatives.

His attempts to get hold of the money elsewhere came to nothing. But soon afterwards he received a proposition that seemed to promise an end to his troubles. A man had arrived from Paris with a message from a Miss Duthrey, an heiress who had been confined in a convent there. Claiming to having heard of Whaley while he was in Paris, she had written asking him to rescue her. 'From what I have heard of your character I have conceived the flattering hope that you will exert your utmost endeavours to deliver me from this captivity.' The letter-bearer said that he was married to the heiress's governess 'and that if I would go back he and the governess had agreed to let me carry off Miss Duthrey'. Always susceptible to flattery, Whaley was ready to believe that the heiress was 'in love with me who she never saw'. He doubtless saw himself a knight-errant about to save a distressed maiden, but what really attracted him was the young woman's enormous inheritance: a lump sum of £100,000 along with an annual income of £12,000.[6] As a proof of her gratitude, Miss Duthrey avowed, she would 'be happy to lay myself and [my] fortune at your feet'. (W, 27) If Whaley could but get her to Ireland, they would be free to marry, he would have untold wealth and his troubles would be at an end.

He told Ryan, who was 'in raptures at the prospect of such a good fortune, and confirmed me in the design of repairing immediately to Paris'. With only ten guineas now left to his name, Whaley turned to Grove to obtain money for the journey. He was surprised when, instead of rebuffing him, the banker joined enthusiastically in the scheme. He promised to supply the required finance and even offered to accompany Whaley to Paris. Grove's lack of caution in this matter seems extraordinary, but he was credulous and generous to a fault.[7] 'Without guile himself, he suspected none in others'. (W, 29) Even when Miss Duthrey's messenger absconded with £150 he had borrowed from Grove, ostensibly in order to pay a creditor, the banker was not deterred. But just as they were about to set out for France, Whaley found that his skin had broken out in an unpleasant rash.[8] In return for his money the Parisian courtesan had given him his first dose of the pox (syphilis).[9] As a popular rhyme put it,

> All alone, yet in Her Lap,
> The Temple Beau may get a Clap,
> Where, Pox'd, & Poxing, they shall own
> The Pains of Love, are Pains alone.[10]

Whaley felt too unwell to go outdoors, let alone contemplate another trip to France, but he and Grove decided to press ahead with the plan regardless. Grove hired a French-speaking lawyer to deal with the legalities and left for Paris, 'determined to carry [Miss Duthrey] off and bring her to Ireland'.[11]

★★★

Even as he languished in his sickbed Whaley was conscious of Ryan watching him with hawklike vigilance 'lest I should slip through his fingers'. (W, 30) It was then that he made his first sensible move for weeks and wrote to his stepfather John Richardson to tell him how things stood. 'You will I dare say be much surprized to hear from me from London', he began. Richardson would have been even more surprised at the sorry sequence of events that had brought him there. Whaley admitted that while gambling in Lyons he had made 'a very considerable and serious loss', though he did not dare to mention the amount, and confessed to having 'very unfortunately … got poxed'. In an attempt to soften the bad news he proceeded to reveal 'the good': his planned abduction of and marriage to Miss Duthrey and the financial windfall he believed would accompany it. 'I am getting rich fast', he assured Richardson, 'and if I was perfectly so could set out for Ireland but must hear from these [i.e. Grove and the lawyer] from Paris first … I just leave it to yourself to come over to me or not as you think it necessary … I shall be impatient to know how I am to act.'[12] Richardson's reaction to this bolt from the blue is not hard to imagine. Whaley's evident naïveté and recklessness was not so surprising; after all he was still only 18. Much more worrying was the news that he was heavily in debt, dangerously ill and at the mercy of a ruthless swindler. As if his massive loss in France was not bad enough, he had also embroiled himself in a crazy scheme to abduct an heiress. Richardson knew he had no option but to leave for London at once and drag him back from the edge of the precipice.

When Richardson received the letter his wife was away in the spa town of Swanlinbar, County Cavan, attempting to cure an upset stomach and a dose of gout. When her son was in France he had written to her regularly, mentioning some of the debts he had racked up, but thus far this had caused her only mild concern. She informed Faulkner that 'Toms demands will I fear be much higher now than we coud wish and yet what can you or I do.' He had assured her he would not gamble again until he came of age and she blithely trusted that this would be the case: 'God grant he may keep his resolution.'[13] She then wore her pen 'to an actual stump' writing him a nine-page letter, the contents of which leave little doubt that he was her favourite son: 'it is very good of you my dearest boy to write so constantly to me, your letters are the delight of my heart'. She urged him to 'keep but your resolution with respect to play, and my anxietys about you will from this moment be at an end, except those which a doating mother must always feel when the darling of her heart is at such a distance'.[14] Instead, Anne's anxieties were about to increase. Soon she would discover not only that Whaley's 'demands' were far greater than she thought, but also that he was dangerously ill.

Leslie Grove's Paris mission did not go as hoped. When he and the lawyer arrived at the convent they presented the letter Whaley had received to the heiress and her governess. They, however, knew nothing about it: it was, unsurprisingly, a complete forgery. Miss Duthrey 'burst into a violent fit of laughter in which she was joined by her companion, to the manifest confusion of the two adventurers, who ... slunk away and made the best of their way back to London'. (W, 30) It later transpired that John Ryan and his associates had cooked up the whole story. Since Whaley had failed to raise any money in London, they had hoped to lure him back to France to get him arrested for the bill his banker had returned protested and 'pursue their further operations and schemes on me with greater security'. (W, 31)

Whaley's illness had saved him from this fate but it threatened to consign him to a worse one. With his condition deteriorating rapidly he had no option but to seek medical advice, even though the likely treatment was far from appealing. Many doctors treated syphilis using a method known as 'salivation', whereby sufferers took doses of mercury that not only poisoned them but also produced large amounts of black saliva.[15] It is not known if Whaley's physician, Cuthbert Potts of Pall Mall, used this method: he was after all said to be 'skilful and humane in his profession'.[16] But whatever treatment he employed, it was not to his patient's liking and Whaley informed him that he would be seeking a second opinion. Offended, Potts replied that he was as well qualified as any physician in London to treat him 'and had you treated me with the respect due to a gentleman who is in the practice of a liberal profession, surely I could never object to your consulting whome you pleased'.[17] By this time Whaley was probably not in an entirely reasonable frame of mind. He would have found salivation, if he underwent it, both mentally and physically debilitating.[18] Meanwhile he was still fending off the avaricious Ryan, who by now had been weaving webs around him for several weeks. Alone, vulnerable and lacking even Wray's feeble guidance, he was in sore need of a friend. Richardson could not come soon enough.

Whaley had a high opinion of his stepfather, commending him as an 'incomparable man ... at once the tender husband, the warm friend and generous benefactor'. (W, 31) In a surviving portrait Richardson looks kindly and good-natured (see Plate 5) and indeed he seems to have been universally liked.[19] The man that Anne esteemed as 'the very best husband upon earth' had proven himself a true friend to his stepchildren and she assured Tom that 'were you his own son I am confident he coud not be more anxious for your welfare'.[20] When Richardson finally reached London early in July, he and his stepson had not seen one another for over a year and a half and their reunion was an emotional one. 'I was much afflicted at the sight of this sincere friend,' Whaley confessed. Richardson's first action was to bring him 'to his lodging, where I should be better accommodated than at a public Hotel, and at the same time be at some distance from a society to whom I might impute the greatest part of my misfortunes'. (W, 32) As soon as he had lodged his stepson in a safer place, Richardson set about dealing with his troublesome creditor.

The failure of the Duthrey ploy and Richardson's presence in London meant that John Ryan's chances of getting money out of Whaley were fast diminishing. In a last-ditch effort he seems to have reduced his demand to £1,000 but found he could not obtain even this. On 13 July he wrote requesting the money urgently as he had 'occasion for it immediately and conceives it must be very easy for Mr Whaley to get it from Mr Richardson'.[21] Richardson, however, refused to give him a penny and took him to task 'for the atrociousness of his conduct in pillaging a young man and enticing him away from his tutor'. (W, 32) Though the criticism was well warranted, Ryan saw fit to call Richardson to account for it and a duel might have ensued had some unknown third parties not made peace between the antagonists. Whaley, meanwhile, slowly recovered. By the end of July he was well enough to set out for Ireland.

★★★

On 30 July Whaley set out for Holyhead[22] and soon afterwards he reached Dublin, pox-scarred and all but penniless. On the whole it was not surprising that his grand tour had turned out thus. He had been barely 3 years old when his father died and had lacked a firm hand to instil discipline and responsibility. His mother doted on him and neither she, Richardson nor his grandfather Bernard Ward (who died before he returned) seems to have done much to rein him in. While Samuel Faulkner had taken care of Whaley as a child, he was not his guardian and he lacked the authority to refuse his demands or check his wilder impulses. William Wray had been vested with this authority but had been incapable of exerting it. As a result, Whaley had all but gone off the rails during his grand tour and was lucky to survive it. He had shown himself to be volatile, careless and irresponsible, but after all he was still only 18 and perhaps he had learned something from the experience.

On his return Whaley was 'received and treated like the Prodigal Son' (W, 33), no great surprise given his mother's partiality to him. She hoped he would open a new leaf and 'let unnecessary superfluitys alone, not only now but during your whole life ... prove your self a man of sound principles and good sense, setting such a value on every thing, as a man of success ought, and not letting your self be carried away by fashion or the very natural love of pleasure inherent almost in every young breast'.[23] No doubt such advice filled Whaley with good intentions, but only time would show if he would take the lessons of his grand tour to heart and henceforth live a responsible life. The events of early 1785 seemed to suggest he would. Like many other young men he was attracted by the idea of a political career and the prestige and opportunities that went with it. In February 1785 he stood for election to Parliament and was returned as MP for Newcastle, County Dublin.[24] This encouraged him 'to apply myself, for some time, to the study of the constitution, laws and commerce of the country, with that degree of attention and assiduity, which so important and arduous a pursuit required'. (W, 276) Standing on the cusp of manhood, he seemed to have acquired a new sense of purpose and responsibility.

Whaley had chosen an exciting time to enter politics. Dublin was the administrative and parliamentary capital of Ireland, boasting a parliament house that was architecturally far more impressive than that at

Westminster.[25] For a long time the Irish Parliament had been technically subordinate to the British and its legislation had had to be approved in Westminster before it could be enacted, but in 1782 the Irish Parliament had won a degree of legislative independence and over the years that followed various groups clamoured for further political change. Political reformers known as 'patriots' angled for greater political independence, while Catholics, having seen some of the penal laws repealed, pursued further concessions. Whaley, like his future brother-in-law, the Attorney General John Fitzgibbon, was more concerned with preserving the British connection and the authority of the Crown. But his fledgling career in parliament never took off because he, like a number of other MPs, had little or no interest in politics. Mostly avoiding the proceedings of the House of Commons, they spent their time pursuing pleasure. Those with whom Whaley socialised included Arthur Saunders Gore (known as Lord Sudley), George Frederick Nugent (styled Lord Delvin), and the dashing revolutionary-to-be Lord Edward Fitzgerald. The dissolute life he threw himself into in the company of these gentlemen threatened to extinguish his political career 'and every other serious and laudable application'. (W, 276)

***

'Nothing can be so gay as Dublin is,' a correspondent insisted in 1782. 'The Castle twice a week, the opera twice a week, with plays, assemblies and suppers to fill up the time.'[26] Certainly, if one had money the city had a lot to offer. There were two fashionable districts, one centred around Rutland Square (now Parnell Square) to the north of the Liffey, and the other around St Stephen's Green and Merrion Square to the south. Both were known for their streets of fine terraced houses and their wealthy inhabitants, who enthusiastically pursued comfort, fashion and pleasure. Whaley resided in the house his father had built on St Stephen's Green. Technically the property was owned by his mother, but he stood to inherit it and seems to have treated it like it was his own, at least while he was living there.[27] Although he had not yet come into his legacy (and would not until 15 December 1786) he was known to be one of the city's richest young gentlemen and he did not mind flaunting his wealth. Whaley maintained an extensive domestic staff, including a coachman, footmen, a groom, a nurse, a French cook and a sedan chair manned by two chairmen. He kept a pack of hunting dogs and a small pet dog, a black and yellow female terrier named Vixen.[28] He must have been a reasonably decent master as his coachman, Denis Lennard, later declared that 'there is no gentllman in Ir[e]land I would [serve] before my master as he was so good to me when I was with him'.[29]

Whaley's pastimes, normal enough for a young upper-class male, included attending the theatre, music, drinking, gambling, hunting and yachting.[30] The last of these became a passion. Like many other young gentlemen Whaley liked racing boats along the coast, especially when wagers were involved. Yet he also had a much grander project in mind. 'I conceived the strange idea of performing, like [Captain] Cook, a voyage round the world; and no sooner had it got possession of my imagination, than I flew off at a tangent ... in order to put my plan in execution'. (W, 34) The impracticality of sailing around the globe must have been pointed out to Whaley and he modified his plan, but it remained an ambitious one. In August 1785 Anne Richardson caught wind that he, 'tho' he has not as yet told it to me himself', was 'on a very wild scheme of building a ship to take him up the Mediterranean'. He intended to sail 'through the Straights of Gibraltar ... visiting all the noted places bordering on the Mediterranean sea, whether in Europe, Africa, or Asia'.[31] Of course, to realise this dream Whaley needed money and he decided he would borrow £1,500 from his mother or his sister Anne, who had by then inherited her share of the Whaley fortune. His mother urged Samuel Faulkner to 'try to put him off and shew him the impossibility of his getting the cash from us ... or ... his sister'. Tom pressed ahead regardless and by October he had hired a shipbuilder on the Isle of Wight to start building a yacht.[32] The money problem now became more pressing, as he found that the tradesmen working on the ship were 'calling every minuet for the amount of their bills and how to pay them he knew not ... he then exclaimed of his own doings and said he had no one to blame but himself'. Faulkner found the money to pay some of the men,[33] but further demands would inevitably follow.

The ship was not the only drain on Whaley's finances. On one of his periodic trips to London he had visited a brothel and fallen for one of the girls, 'a *fille de chambre*, who had not only the character of being chaste, but had actually remained so during three years service with her mistress'. Apparently Whaley had had to resort to 'the assistance of a bank note and gold watch [to] beat her virtue out of the field ... a circumstance which has made many believe, that she never before was offered what she esteemed an adequate price for it'.[34] This girl was later depicted alongside Whaley in the *Town and Country Magazine*, a London society publication (see Plate 6). She may have been the woman he brought from London to Dublin to be his lady companion, as described in his memoirs. Her name was Harriet Heydon, and it is unlikely that she was 'chaste' as she was, or had been, a married woman. Though she was 'neither distinguished for wit or beauty,' she was not as aggressively greedy as other courtesans he had visited. (W, 33) Perhaps this was what attracted him. He lodged Harriet in a house he had rented on Holles Street and spent lavishly on her.[35] This was also where Whaley 'kept my midnight orgies, and saw my friends, according to the fashionable acceptation of the word'. (W, 34)[36]

Alarmed at the rate with which Whaley's expenses and debts were piling up, his mother urged him to join her at Somerset (or Summerseat), a country house near Coleraine that her husband had inherited. 'When we get him here we will not part with him again if we can possibly keep him here,' she insisted. 'I wish I knew how much money he has got or drawn for, in short how much he has expended ... a very great deal I fear.'[37] Whaley seems to have been reluctant to go, as this meant leaving Harriet in Dublin, but his mother was insistent and around the middle of November he arrived at Somerset. He would stay there for several weeks while the Richardsons distracted him with various amusements such as hunting and theatre.[38] 'We shall keep down his expenses as much as possible,' Anne resolved, while admitting that it was 'very hard to accomplish it for the money vanishes without my being able to find out how it goes'.[39] This was not surprising: Whaley was secretly sending money to Harriet.[40] By the New Year (1786) he was unable to stay away from her any longer and he returned to Dublin. Almost resignedly, Anne wrote to Faulkner asking him to 'manage him as well as you can till I come'.[41] While she knew he would continue spending money on Harriet she was probably more concerned about the cost of his ship and the wagers it would inevitably give rise to. By the summer of 1786 the vessel was ready to sail. She was commodious enough, with space below decks to accommodate a cabin and a 'state room,'[42] but how would she bear up on a lengthy sea voyage, namely the planned expedition to the Mediterranean? To try her out Whaley decided to sail to Milford Haven in Wales before pressing on to Brighton and Le Havre. Harriet, his brother John and his fellow MP Lord Sudley agreed to accompany him.[43]

Before they departed Faulkner's nephew and clerk William Norwood sat down with Whaley to go through his accounts with 'his boatmen, tradesmen &c I mean those that have done any work for the boat'. Unsurprisingly he had not kept track of his outgoings and Norwood estimated that he had paid the tradesmen £200 more than was owed. 'I showed him clearly how much he was cheated. he seemed something troubled. and was satisfied it was so. but all that he said … was not to let on to Faulkner his mother or anyone for fear it should be knowen.' No doubt they knew already and harboured serious misgivings about the mooted voyage to Le Havre. Whaley was down to his last 150 guineas, and Norwood did not believe there was 'a farthing more remaining' of £1,000 he had received 'the other day' – probably an advance of funds from his inheritance, secured through Faulkner.[44] Anne was unwell and had reached the end of her patience with her son's continual spending. 'Her little fitt of sickness has altered her for the worse very much,' Norwood observed. 'She says she never will whilst she is Mr. Whaley's guardian [i.e. the guardian of his inheritance] accept a bill of his that may be on acc[oun]t of his house or girl.'[45]

Norwood, for his part, could only dream of the kind of money Whaley was splurging. His father Jack had worked at the Faulkners' linen bleaching yard near Cookstown, County Tyrone, where he lived in 'a house built of mud … 42 feet long'.[46] This was where William had grown up, a far cry from the magnificence of St Stephen's Green. He knew that he and Whaley had little in common ('moderate and immoderate youth are no companions') and he was inclined to be sanctimonious, stating confidently that if he moved in 'a higher sphere' he would not be seduced into extravagance or do anything to 'hurt and shame' himself: 'folly and disapation [dissipation] is a lesson I realy do not wish to learn'.[47] Meanwhile he dismissed Harriet as Whaley's 'whore'. Yet it is not hard to feel some sympathy for Norwood. All he hoped was to someday improve his circumstances by obtaining a lease on a small farm, and he insisted that no one wished Whaley better than he did. The latter, for his part, did not look down on the humble clerk and invited him to dine with him on several occasions. 'I did not wish to go oftimes as he has always such great folks with him,' Norwood confessed, 'but realy he made no distinction between any one that was there and me.'[48] Whaley had his faults, but snobbery does not seem to have been one of them.

He and his companions sailed from Dublin Bay at midnight on 12 August. There followed a few weeks' of nervous anticipation as his family and associates waited for news of the voyage. Almost on a daily basis, Norwood reported to Faulkner that he had received no word.[49] Finally, on 4 September a letter arrived. Whaley had reached Plymouth, where he was staying with John Macbride, a captain in the Royal Navy. Macbride was 'an exceedingly troublesome, busy, violent man' but it seems that he and Whaley were on friendly terms. The young adventurer was 'much pleased with the part of England he has seen' and planned to continue his voyage.[50]

Norwood passed the news on to Faulkner, but the land agent was about to receive a devastating blow. A few days later his wife Catherine died at the age of 76. They had no children and her passing hit him hard: 'Lov'd in they Life Lamented in they End,/The Loving Wife and Faithful Friend' read part of the headstone inscription he drafted.[51] His friends and family rallied round. 'I hope that your verey great distress has not impeared your health as I much dread it', wrote one, but Faulkner was made of stern stuff. In the course of a voyage from Dublin to Holyhead just over a month later the pain of his loss seemed not to trouble him as much as the tempestuous crossing: 'I dont ever remember to have felt such a rowl and swell in the sea,' he exclaimed. 'All the pasangers were most monsterously sick I never was so sick in all my life I streained and reached [retched] so much that the discharge from my stomack was tinctured with blood.'[52] Hard-bitten and resilient, Faulkner battled through his grief and would continue to manage Whaley's affairs for almost another decade. But the Irish Sea had not done with him.

Whaley, meanwhile, resumed his voyage but like Faulkner he ran into bad weather and cancelled his plans to sail to Brighton and Le Havre. In early October he reached Bristol and decided to return to Ireland from there. Around the middle of the month he landed at Waterford and headed north, planning to join his mother at Somerset House.[53] Thus far he had not managed to undertake his voyage to the Mediterranean and it seemed unlikely that it would happen. After all, he had failed to even make it as far as Brighton in his yacht. But within a few days he would find himself embroiled in an affair that threatened to put an end not only to the planned expedition, but to his very life.

4

JERUSALEM SYNDROME

On the evening of 21 October 1786 Tom Whaley entered the Phoenix Park near Dublin with feelings of excitement, indignation and fear churning in his stomach. He and an attorney, identified in reports only as a Mr O—r, had agreed to meet near the Castleknock Gate at the park's north-western fringe to settle a quarrel. This was to be Whaley's first duel, and although such encounters rarely ended in fatalities, there were exceptions. Just five days before two gentlemen, Robert Keon and George Nugent Reynolds, had kept a rendezvous in Sheemore, County Leitrim. Before the duel had formally commenced – 'the seconds had neither measured the ground … nor requested the principals to take their positions' – Keon had shot Reynolds in the head, killing him instantly.[1] This murderous act was a flagrant breach of the code of honour, but it showed how tempers could flare during duels and how easy it was for them to end fatally, adding to the tension that surrounded Whaley's encounter. However, on this occasion the proper formalities were observed and the two antagonists 'behaved with the greatest honour and coolness at the ground'. With the seconds having agreed that the principals should discharge their pistols simultaneously on a 'word of command', Whaley and O—r took up their positions and prepared to fire.[2]

The incident that occasioned the meeting had happened only that morning, when Whaley was approaching Dublin in his carriage. On the road near Chapelizod a chaise – a two-wheeled, one-horse carriage – overtook him and while it is unclear what exactly happened, it seems the two vehicles either collided or narrowly missed one another. The mishap was sufficient to provoke an outburst of road rage, a phenomenon that has existed for as long as there have been roads. Fiery words passed between Whaley and the chaise's occupant, Mr O—r. The two men met again that afternoon at Daly's Chocolate House in Dublin where they tried and failed to make up the quarrel. Agreeing to settle their differences in another manner, they appointed seconds and arranged to meet that same day in the Phoenix Park.[3]

Although duelling was illegal, for decades gentlemen had resorted to it to settle even trivial and imagined slights. By the late eighteenth century the idea that one's honour could only be defended by sword or pistol had become extraordinarily popular and there were many earnest advocates of the practice. In 1777 a number of self-proclaimed experts drew up a list of twenty-seven rules designed to ensure that duels were fought fairly and with some level of regulation. In the years that followed, several high-profile encounters between prominent politicians gave the practice increased respectability and legitimacy and a new breed of aggressive gentlemen known as the 'fire-eaters' emerged. Whaley was about to join their ranks.

The word was given and the pistol shots rang out in the evening air. Whaley's shot missed, but 'the ball of Mr. O—r's pistol … entered the thick part of his antagonist's thigh and lodged in the other'.[4] A surgeon who was present attended the stricken duellist and 'probed the muscular part to a considerable depth, but the ball … eluded his search'. Despite the excruciating pain Whaley managed to keep his composure and even shake hands with his opponent. The ball was successfully removed the next day and a few days later Whaley was said to be 'in a fair way of recovery'.[5] Samuel Faulkner's brother Hugh, perhaps with the Keon–Reynolds encounter in mind, believed that Whaley was fortunate to escape with his life. In his opinion he had been most to blame for the duel: 'I am astonished that a gentleman who has seen so much of the world and good company would behave in such a manner that he must quarrel with a man because his chaise drove past him on the publick road,' he expostulated. 'Sure he can't think that because he has got more money than another, that he has a liberty to insult all who has less than himself.'[6]

Whether this was true or not, for the next few weeks Whaley was laid up and in no position to quarrel with anyone. For his mother and stepfather this was a silver lining: now they had an opportunity to try and talk some sense into him and dissuade him from further dangerous escapades. They were also anxious to somehow stem his financial excesses: on 15 December Whaley would turn 21, at which time he would have full control over his inheritance. By late November he was well enough to travel and Anne was expecting him at Somerset. 'I am sure the country will be of service to him after his long confinement,' she anticipated, 'and will soon restore him to his strength and flesh, and I am in hopes that his presence will be of use to Mr Richardson.' Her husband was in bad health and low spirits, probably partly as a result of worry over his stepson's antics.[7] He had not rescued him from a hazardous situation in 1784 to watch him throw his life away two years later and he resolved to act.

Samuel Faulkner had calculated the total amount of Whaley's fortune at £48,674, eighteen shillings and ten pence halfpenny, in addition to the annual rental income from the estates.[8] On paper the young man was due to come into this impressive inheritance on 15 December 1786, but for years he had been borrowing heavily on the strength of it, even selling one of his Carlow properties, Castletown House, to Faulkner earlier that year to raise money.[9] Richardson insisted that Whaley examine the state of his fortune and when he did he 'found it still more diminished by the variety of my dissipation and extravagance'. (W, 35) Even more worrying, it seemed that the money that remained was insufficient to clear his outstanding debts. Richardson now made a valiant attempt to rein in Whaley's spending, warning him that 'the way of life in which I was engaged, must inevitably lead me to ruin ... and that at the rate I proceeded, I must in a short time be reduced to indigence'. (W, 35) 'With tears in his eyes' he urged his stepson to relinquish his two greatest indulgences: Harriet, on whom he was spending an 'extraordinary, not to say scandalous' (W, 35) amount, and the yacht. Each was costing him in the region of £5,000 a year.[10] Though genuinely touched by his stepfather's concerns, Whaley found it impossible to give up both of his 'favourite hobby-horses'. Eventually he agreed to sell the ship rather than part ways with Harriet, to whom he was 'now really attached'. (W, 37) He later confided to Faulkner that he would 'rather have her happy than any other woman in the world'.[11]

★★★

Offloading the yacht meant that Whaley's planned voyage to the Mediterranean would be put on hold, though he still hoped to one day undertake it and perhaps even make money by betting on it. It was not surprising that gambling or 'play' continued to use up much of Whaley's time and money: in the eighteenth century it was a near universal pastime. 'This obsession of the age played itself out most ferociously ... in the drawing rooms and private clubs', where members gambled feverishly over cards and dice.[12] The most famous Irish club was Daly's Club on Dame Street, a 'mecca for gamblers'.[13] Daly's was frequented at all hours and its candles burned behind drawn blinds even in the daytime. It had become one of Whaley's favourite haunts and his losses there were such that his brother John, hardly a paragon of restraint himself, declared himself 'very sorry' that 'Tom's itch for gambling' continued. 'I think if he goes on much longer he will not have a farthing left.'[14] Yet even in the midst of his money worries Whaley showed compassion for others, notably his one-time bearleader William Wray, whose health and fortunes had declined steadily in the two years since the grand tour. In May 1786, when Wray was destitute and near death, Whaley had contributed a significant sum to support him. Then, in December, he provided a Miss Katherine Wray (probably William's daughter or sister) with an annuity which he insisted on renewing even when he himself was in financial distress.[15]

The following year did not bring much change in Whaley's fortunes. He was now in control of what was left of his inheritance but as expected it did not meet his needs and he still required around £2,000 to pay off his debts. Frustrated that rents due on his Carlow and Armagh estates had not been collected, he blamed Faulkner for procrastinating: 'I cannot help remarking that those things are generally the agents faults.' He even tried to borrow £1,000 from his sister's father-in-law, Sir Annesley Stewart, who turned down the request unequivocally: 'I could no more raise a £1,000 at present than I could a million. I was in hopes you were free from all embarrassments except the ship and am very much concerned indeed to find it otherwise.'[16] Then, in May, there came a reprieve: all but one of his creditors agreed to give him 'time sufficient, to raise the mon[e]y' to pay them. Welcome as this was, the constant anxiety was making Whaley despondent. 'Would to God, I were as *old* and as *fat* as you', he remarked to Samuel Faulkner, in not altogether complimentary terms. 'I am sure I should then be as happy[.] at present I am poor and miserable.'[17] If he remained in Dublin frequenting places like Daly's he would only add to that poverty and he decided, or allowed himself to be persuaded, to spend the summer with Harriet at Faulkner's country retreat, Fort Faulkner in County Wicklow.

The three-bay Georgian house still stands in an idyllic stretch of rolling countryside near the small village of Ballinaclash.[18] Faulkner had acquired the house and adjoining lands around 1780 and placed them in the care of his steward, John Donnelly. By early 1787 William Norwood had moved to Fort Faulkner, hoping the country air would help him recover from a bad cough (in fact he was in the early stages of consumption).[19] Around the middle of May Whaley and Harriet arrived with an entourage of servants. Favoured by a spell of particularly fine weather, they were much taken with the place. On 22 May Tom reported that he and Norwood had gone 'a ferreting, and we kill[e]d 6 brace of rabbits, and … all the trout in the river'. On another occasion he claimed to have 'had the best sport I have yet had in the river', catching 'one trout eleven inches long'. It is easy to picture him holding up the trout in a classic fisherman's pose, his still boyish (though pox-scarred) face radiant with pride. Harriet, too, was enchanted by Fort Faulkner, preferring it 'even to London' and on 2 June Whaley declared that they were getting comfortable there. 'I think upon my soul that I have not been so happy these many months.'[20] He seemed to be reaping the benefit of the improved diet and surroundings. 'He takes the goats whey every morning and exercises greatly after it', Norwood reported to Faulkner, 'so that you would almost already say he has got a look quite different from that you have seen him have this five years past'. Even the habitually dour clerk conceded that 'we all seem as happy as we could wish ourselves.'[21]

These blissful days would not last. At least one person was not happy: John Donnelly. The steward was irked by the damage that Whaley's servants, horses and livestock (the servants seem to have brought along a cow) did to the land and complained that 'the lawn is very much hurt with dogs and p[e]ople trampling it. also I have a most damnable heavy stock on my little pasture[.] theirs two mare … and one cow of Mr. Whaleys two horses and two cow of yours that is eight head all on the gorse bogg for I may be damd. if I suffer them in the waste land'.[22] He also had little time for Harriet, who he referred to as 'the English whore'. Whaley, however, had more serious things to worry about than the irascible steward. On 6 June he found himself suffering from 'a very great pain in his head',[23] and soon afterwards he was laid up with a fever. Though he was prone to bouts of illness throughout his life, this was one of the worst. Following a prolonged period of indolence and self-indulgence, his system may have reacted to the sudden change in lifestyle and diet.

At first Whaley's condition gave serious cause for concern. After someone wisely treated him with Peruvian bark, a powerful anti-fever medicine,[24] he improved and by early July had 'every favourable appearance of a speedy recovery'. Harriet hoped he would be able to leave his sickbed: 'this day we mean to get him up, and have got an arm chair for that purpose … I am happy to say I believe all danger is now over.' At first Harriet had not known that Whaley was ill: somehow, and for some reason, his 'friends' (meaning, presumably, Norwood, acting on instructions) had contrived to keep her in the dark about it. 'What reason I was not inform'd of it I cannot tell,' she exclaimed. 'But … it hurt me much as Mr. Whaley is my only friend.' She knew he was the only reason his family and friends tolerated her presence, and she was understandably exasperated that they saw her as his 'whore' and nothing else. 'Had anything bad happen[e]d him, they need not have been allarm'd[.] I should not have been any trouble to them while I had my own free country to go to, where the people are not quite so illiberal in their ideas as they are in Ireland.'[25] Harriet was a kind-hearted soul. She knew well what it was to be a woman in vulnerable circumstances and had tried to help others less well-off than herself. Before leaving for Wicklow she had asked Faulkner to look out for her maidservant, 'a very sober honnest woman and the best servant I ever had in Dublin', who for some reason had suffered opprobrium from the other domestics.[26]

Whaley recovered slowly and hung on at Fort Faulkner for a few more months, indulging himself at his agent's expense. Despite this he believed that the salary of £300 a year he was paying Faulkner to look after his estates was too generous, and in August he told Norwood he was determined to reduce it. The clerk reported to Faulkner,

I asked him did he know what it was he paid you he said he did answering £300 a year. To which I replied Sir. look through all your accounts and see has my uncle ever charged you a farthing for traveling expences. and which every agent in Ireland is allowed. Now Sir said I considering all this he has not over £100 a year for his trouble. We have had a great deal of conversation on this subject and I find he is determined to deduct something off the am[oun]t. of what you have at present by the receipt of the rents. Now my dear uncle who is at the bottom of this I cannot say, nor is it possible for you or I to find out at present…

Norwood was convinced that some 'deceitfull and ill minded people', determined to harm Faulkner, had put Whaley up to this. 'I realy am of opinion there is some one at his elbow underminding you.' He advised his uncle to hold the agency even at a reduced rate rather than satisfy their malice. 'Poor young man he is foolish and ill advised at present but that will have an end.'[27] Whether it would or not remained to be seen, but Norwood was right about one thing: Whaley was indeed susceptible to the wiles of the 'deceitfull and ill minded', and they would cause him considerable distress in the years that lay ahead.

For the present, Fort Faulkner had given him a taste for the rustic lifestyle and he began planning to settle down as a country gentleman. Within the coming couple of years he hoped to put aside 'ten or twelve thousand pounds with which please God I will settle at home and laugh at the world.'[28] Anne Richardson was delighted to hear of her son's new plan and hoped that he would start farming 'and lead the life of an honest country gentleman, he will find more real satisfaction in it, than in all the scenes of dissipation he has already been engaged in'. She dreamily anticipated that he might 'turn his thoughts to matrimony and get some thousands with a good wife'.[29] Indeed Whaley seemed to be transforming into a responsible and charitable member of society. In November he cancelled his membership of several Dublin clubs (including, possibly, Daly's), suggesting that he had turned his back on gambling. He also showed sympathy for others who had suffered losses. The following month he and a friend, Mr Singleton, donated money to the inmates of the Four

Courts Marshalsea, a debtors' prison, professing themselves 'shocked at so many slaves in bondage, fallen victims to the folly of wrong-headed creditors'.[30]

At this time Whaley and Harriet were settling into a new property he had purchased in County Carlow: Font Hill, a country house and estate adjacent to the River Barrow.[31] The house boasted several showpiece rooms including a scarlet room, a green room, a drawing room, a parlour and a billiard room. There were fine views across the country to the south, which along with the Barrow offered ample opportunities for hunting and fishing. However, Font Hill was in sore need of refurbishment and Whaley and Harriet were greatly discomfited by its 'deplorable' condition. Holes in the roof let in the rain and the walls were 'running down with water'. There was only one dry room, in which the couple were sleeping, but this did not prevent them from catching bad colds. By the end of December work was underway, though Whaley was still waiting for the lead needed to repair the roof to arrive.[32] Meanwhile he was keen to go hunting on his new estate and he asked Faulkner to send him cock shot, duck shot, partridge shot, snipe shot and buckshot.[33] He also indulged a sweet tooth: the groceries ordered in by Harriet from Dublin included 'three loafs of house keepers lump sugar ... two stone of common brown sugar and three pound of the best chocolate and two pound of brown sugar candy'.[34] But life at Font Hill was too sedate for Tom. Before long his mind was wandering elsewhere and soon his body would follow.

★★★

Thus far in his life Whaley had not done much to earn a place in the annals of history. He had gone on a chaotic grand tour, indulged in a series of liaisons, fallen prey to swindlers, become an MP, fought a duel, accumulated large debts and made a belated effort to settle down to the quiet life. While he had certainly had some adventures, his career was not so different from that of other moneyed and wayward young men in Ireland and Britain. But things were about to change. For years Whaley had longed to travel, not simply to the usual grand tour destinations of France and Italy, but to more remote and exotic lands. As a boy he had spent long hours drawing and colouring in maps of foreign regions and he seems to have immersed himself in tales of Captain James Cook, Sinbad the Sailor and other real or legendary explorers. Now, in early 1788, he began planning in earnest for his long-anticipated trip to the Mediterranean. Although he no longer owned a ship, that need not prevent him from securing a berth on a vessel. He had also decided to do more than simply visit the Middle Sea and its ports. He dreamt of travelling beyond its shores to a great walled city, the home of some of the world's most ancient and sacred shrines. Like thousands of pilgrims, travellers and soldiers before him, Whaley was unable to resist the lure of Jerusalem.

Going by his own account, the whole thing originated in a simple quip over a meal 'with some people of fashion' at Leinster House, the Duke of Leinster's magnificent townhouse on Kildare Street (see Plate 7):

> the conversation turned upon my intended voyage, when one of the company asked me to what part of the world I meant to direct my course first, to which I answered, without hesitation, 'to Jerusalem.' This was considered by the company as a mere jest; and so, in fact, it was; but the subject still continuing, some observed that there was no such place at present existing; and others that, if it did exist, I should not be able to find it. This was touching me in the tender point: the difficulty of an undertaking always stimulated me to the attempt. I instantly offered to bet any sum that I would go to Jerusalem and return to Dublin within two years from my departure. I accepted without hesitation all the wagers that were offered me ... (W, 34–5)

When exactly this happened is uncertain: it may have been as early as 1786, when the *Freeman's Journal* remarked that 'it would be well worth his while to undertake a voyage, even to Judea' if he could get others to join in a wager with him.[35] In July 1787 he had told his mother that he intended to set off for Jerusalem that autumn, but she feared he was too weak following his illness and hoped he would postpone the trip until the following year.[36] She had got her wish, but by 1788 the expedition was back on the agenda with a vengeance and betting began in earnest.

The precise terms of the wager are unclear, but it seems that the odds were placed at two to one against Whaley completing the trip, so that he stood to gain £2 for every pound he staked.[37] Also, the expedition had to be completed within a certain time. Whaley himself put it at two years (W, 35) but other reports suggest a more limited timeframe: twelve months, fourteen months,[38] or that 'he should visit Jerusalem in the space of 12 months ... there is no limitation as to the time of his return.'[39] The patrons of Daly's Club were the heaviest subscribers to the wager but many other members of the gentry and nobility also put their names down, among them the Earl of Grandison. Known for turning himself out in fine velvet embroidered with jewels, Grandison was said to be 'very ingenious in the art of wasting the most possible money in the least possible time.'[40] Under the terms of his bet with Whaley, made on 22 February 1788, he promised to pay him £455 'upon his return to Dublin from Jeruzalem.'[41] This was just one of many individual wagers and when all were added up the amount Whaley stood to gain ran into five figures. He put the total at around £15,000, but other reports specify a larger sum: anything between £20,000 and £40,000.[42] Whatever it was, it was a huge amount, at least €6 million in today's money. But then gambling was one of the great obsessions of the eighteenth century. Wagers were laid on all sorts of sporting events, from prize-fighting to horseracing, but in theory one could bet on the outcome of almost anything. 'There were bets on lives ... on politics, on others' bets, on every vagary of public and private life.'[43] The famous dandy Richard 'Beau' Nash (1674–1761) had once ridden naked on a cow for a wager, and in 1785 Lord Derby undertook to pay Lord Cholmondeley 500 guineas 'whenever his lordship fucks a woman in a balloon one thousand yards from earth.'[44] Whaley himself claimed that he once jumped from the second-floor window of a Dover hotel 'over the roof of the mailcoach that was then standing near the door. By laying mattresses in the street to break the fall, I performed the feat and had the honour of winning the wager.'[45] (W, 326–7)

Eccentric as these bets were, gambling on something as dangerous and unpredictable as a journey to Jerusalem was all but unheard of. This was despite the fact that the Holy City, once thought to be the centre of the world, had exerted a powerful magnetism for centuries. Christian pilgrims had flocked there since the early Middle Ages, and the Crusaders had captured and held the city for nearly a hundred years. But by the early fourteenth century the Crusaders were a spent force and over the centuries that followed the flow of European pilgrims to the Holy Land slowed dramatically. By the eighteenth century few Europeans – and even fewer Irish[46] – were travelling to Jerusalem. In the present age of online booking it is hard to conceive just how out of bounds most people regarded Jerusalem. One might almost as well have proposed a trip to the South Pole. To travel there for a wager was unthinkable, but as ever Whaley was galvanised by the thought of doing something that had not yet been accomplished. Indeed it was a seminal moment in his life: had it not been for the bet and the expedition that followed, it is unlikely he would be remembered today. But his track record of shambolic misadventure and profligacy did not inspire confidence, and the journey that lay ahead was so fraught with hazards that many reckoned his chances of winning the bet to be slim indeed. They 'never imagined that a young man of his volatile disposition, would seriously engage in such a distant expedition.'[47]

Other than his volatility and unreliability, there were plenty of reasons for expecting Whaley to fail. The most efficient way to get to Jerusalem was to sail through the Straits of Gibraltar and down the Mediterranean, but a voyage would take several weeks and was likely to be hindered by unfavourable weather. Violent storms were frequent and could easily wreck a ship and drown its occupants, while adverse winds and dead calms could hold up the progress of a vessel for days on end. Apart from that there was the lurking possibility of attack by pirates or the naval fleets of hostile powers. Even if Whaley survived the perils of the sea, dry land presented hazards of its own. As well as visiting Jerusalem he planned to make overland detours to other places of note, in particular the city of Constantinople (Istanbul). But most land routes were ill-equipped to accommodate travellers. Unfavourable terrain, bad roads and bad weather were to be expected, along with accommodation that ranged from poor to abysmal to non-existent. Meanwhile there was an ever-present risk of attack by bandits or other hostile parties.

The political situation in the Near East was another cause for concern. The region Whaley planned to visit was part of the Ottoman Empire, the greatest power in the Muslim world and a place of 'mystery, anxiety and fantasy'.[48] Following its emergence in Turkey in the fourteenth century, the Empire had grown to become one of the largest and most formidable on earth, comprising Turkey, Greece, the Balkans, the Caucasus, Syria, Palestine and large parts of Arabia and northern Africa. The Ottoman sovereign, the Sultan (also known as the 'Grand Seignior' or 'Grand Seigneur'), was based in Constantinople as was the central government, the Porte. In the late eighteenth century, just as European imperial ambitions were increasing, the Ottoman Empire was in decline. Riven by internal turmoil, the Porte was losing control of some of the outlying regions, where local governors had become almost like autonomous rulers.[49] Simultaneously, ongoing wars with the great powers of Europe threatened to result in the loss of other territories. For years Russia and Austria had been aggressively pursuing plans to carve up the European part of the Ottoman Empire between them, and in 1787–8 their belligerence lured the Sultan into the latest of a series of costly wars. On the eve of Whaley's departure news was filtering through of clashes between Ottoman and Austrian armies on the Danube. Meanwhile the Russians were besieging the Ottoman-controlled city of Ochakov near the Crimea, a protracted engagement in which the Turks would ultimately come off the worst. The land war between the Ottomans and the Austrians was unlikely to hinder Whaley, but he risked being caught up in the hostilities with the Russians if they spread further south. In previous conflicts, much of the fighting had taken place in the Aegean, for instance at Çeşme near Smyrna (now Izmir), where Russian ships had destroyed an Ottoman fleet in 1770.

Whaley would be sailing directly through these seas. Commenting on his planned route, one newspaper referred ominously to 'the disturbance which affects the scenes thro' which he is to pass'.[50] Also, those in authority would have to be dealt with and perhaps placated. Worryingly, the road to Jerusalem led through the Ottoman province of Sidon, the domain of a ruthless governor known as al-Jazzar, 'the Butcher'. In addition, the cultural differences between the West and the Ottoman world had to be taken into account. As a European Christian travelling in lands that were predominantly Muslim, Whaley would inevitably attract curiosity, if not hostility. If he could find ways to blend in with the locals, or at least make himself less conspicuous, so much the better. Whaley did take the time to apprise himself of many of these realities by reading the accounts of Europeans who had recently travelled in the Ottoman lands, among them Francois Baron de Tott's *Memoirs ... Containing the State of the Turkish Empire and the Crimea* (1785) and Constantin de Volney's *Travels Through Syria and Egypt in the Years 1783, 1784, and 1785*, an edition of which was published in Dublin in 1788. Volney's work was full of useful information on the places, people and dignitaries Whaley expected to encounter.[51]

Yet there was one final, unpredictable force that threatened the success of his expedition: an epidemic disease whose very name inspired terror. The plague had killed millions in Europe before being all but eliminated there through improved sanitation, healthcare and the use of quarantines. But it remained rampant in the Near East and visited Constantinople almost every year. A particularly virulent outbreak in 1778 may have wiped out a third of the city's population.[52] These facts were not unknown to Whaley and while the other dangers of the journey and the ongoing wars and disturbances did not concern him much as he prepared to embark, he was terrified of falling victim to the plague.

By the summer of 1788 almost everything was ready for Whaley to begin his great undertaking, but shortly before his date of embarkation he stumbled once more on his Achilles heel. Early in August he took a trip to Brighton and predictably found himself seated once more at the gaming tables. This time he would prove more alert to the wiles of sharpers and cheats and even help expose one of them. Yet the affair would have serious consequences for his pocket, and as a result of these 'accidental circumstances'[53] he would face imprisonment. Those who had anticipated that Whaley's much vaunted journey to the Holy Land would come to nothing looked to have been proven correct. The Jerusalem expedition, it seemed, was over before it had even begun.

PART TWO
THE JERUSALEM PILGRIM

5

LIGHTNING AND THE MOON RISING

Towards midnight on 10 August 1788 Thomas Whaley found himself in an all too familiar setting. The scene: a private room in the Castle Inn, Brighton. The company: Whaley, a friend identified only as Mr Cr—r, and various gamblers and chancers, among whom was a Major Gardner, 'a man of good breeding, fortune, and apparent honour'.[1] The game: hazard, a dice game, here being played for very high stakes. As the dice rattled the flickering candlelight illuminated the players' flushed and sweaty faces. Playing with the same company the night before, Whaley and Cr—r had both lost heavily and they were keen to make good their losses, but there seemed little chance of this as they looked to be roaring drunk. When it came to Gardner's turn to throw, Whaley and Cr—r immediately staked large sums, which the Major eagerly accepted. Just as he was about to roll the dice Cr—r seized his hand and attempted to force the fingers open. Turning to the shocked company, Whaley shouted that Gardner was concealing false dice and that he and his friend were 'ready to stake our lives upon the issue of a strict examination'. (W, 273) The Major, however, had no intention of opening his hand and the three men struggled violently, crashing to the ground near a laden sideboard. Grabbing a knife, Whaley warned Gardner that if he did not unclench his fist he would cut it open. This, the Major realised, was no idle threat and with great reluctance he succumbed. When the two dice in his hand were examined it was found that one had two fours, two fives, and two threes, while the other had two sixes, two fives, and two ones.[2] Such are the rules of hazard that rolls resulting from such dice will always hand victory to the caster. Major Gardner had been fleecing the company.

Whaley and Cr—r were now as hard pressed to protect the cheat from the gamblers' fury as they had been to unmask him. Most of those present wanted to defenestrate him, a not-uncommon punishment for gambling cheats. The Major himself was petrified. Expecting 'instant destruction' (W,

274), he begged for mercy. Whaley managed to secure him permission to depart unharmed, though his reputation was in tatters. Whaley and Cr—r then had the dice sealed inside a piece of paper and sent for examination by the Jockey Club, the body that superintended horseracing and, by extension, tried to ensure that gambling took place fairly and above board. As the disgraced fraudster prepared to flee the country, the Jockey Club commended 'the merit of the gentlemen to whose spirit the world is so much indebted'.[3]

Whaley and his friend had resolved to expose Gardner the previous night after Cr—r confided that he believed him to be cheating. The pair had then feigned drunkenness in order to take their adversary off guard.[4] Incidents like this give a sense of the crookery and double-dealing that went on in gaming houses across Britain and Ireland. In fact Gardner's false dice were so common that they had a nickname, 'The Dispatches',[5] presumably because by using them a gambler could easily 'dispatch' his opponents. With such widespread trickery at play it is little surprise that Whaley lost heavily so many times while gambling. Even though he managed on this occasion to uncover the deception, it did not save him from another bruising loss. The large sum he had staked to expose the Major had vanished from the table in the course of the uproar, and when this was added to his other losses in Brighton he found himself all but penniless. Ordinarily this would have been bad enough, but the timing of this particular setback, just before his planned departure for Jerusalem, made it particularly serious. To be clapped on the back by the Jockey Club was all well and good but it did not save him from the fervent attentions of his creditors, one of whom had him arrested in London soon afterwards for non-payment of £1,500. The possibility of incarceration in a debtors' prison now loomed large. In London the most notorious such institution was the Marshalsea, later vividly described by Charles Dickens in *Little Dorrit*. The Marshalsea's inmates faced starvation and even torture if they could not support themselves. As many as fifty could be crammed into a single room, sanitation was non-existent and disease was rife. There was now a very real possibility that Whaley would end up in this hellish place.

He immediately sent to a Dublin gentleman 'whose snuff is much admired' requesting a loan of £2,000 to pay the debt and 'some other trifling demands'.[6] The snuff manufacturer was Lundy Foot, a larger-than-life character who was renowned for his 'Blackguard' snuff, which was popular throughout Britain and Ireland: the poet Robert Burns was said to be particularly fond of it. A keen property speculator, Foot owned large estates in four counties and was not short of cash. As a sideline he lent money at substantial rates of interest, and Whaley had already borrowed large sums from him on several occasions; indeed he may have been one of the main sources of finance for the Jerusalem expedition. Foot saw no reason to refuse this latest request and 'directly sent' the required £2,000 back to London.[7] Having eluded prison, for the time being at least, Whaley resumed his preparations to embark for Jerusalem. But a time would come when Lundy Foot would seek to recoup what he was owed.

***

Whaley arranged to leave Dublin on 20 September 1788. His friend Dudley Loftus agreed to lend him his yacht to sail to Deal in south-east England, where he would seek a berth on a vessel bound for the eastern Mediterranean. News of the extraordinary wager had spread through Ireland and Britain and as the date of departure approached public interest intensified. A contemporary ballad entitled 'Whalley's [sic] Embarkation' has it that he embarked from George's Quay in Dublin amid extraordinary scenes:

> One morning walking George's-quay,
> A monstrous crowd stopp'd up the way,
> Who came to see a sight so rare,
> A sight that made all Dublin stare ...
> BUCK WHALLEY lacking much some cash,
> And being used to cut a dash,
> He wager'd full Ten thousand Pound,
> He'd visit soon the Holy Ground

According to the ballad Whaley, watched by a 'blackguard throng' of onlookers, proceeded to the quayside at the head of a motley crew of well-wishers, hangers-on, servants and exotic beasts. Harriet Heydon, 'with paint and ribbons smile and glee', was said to be present as were many well-known figures including several MPs, Whaley's neighbour Lord Gillford, Loftus, Lundy Foot and the famous courtesan Peg Plunket. Also supposedly in attendance was an extraordinary collection of exotic animals, including a bear, a baboon, a monkey, a black Newfoundland dog and two lap-dogs; and several servants: a Swiss, leading the baboon on a chain, and four French valets ('By Garlick you'd have smelt the crew'). This, the ballad claimed, was the retinue to accompany him to Jerusalem:

> And now behold upon the strand,
> This Cargo for the holy Land,
> *Bears, Lap-dogs, Monkies, Frenchmen, Whores,*
> *Bear-Leaders,* and *dependents poor*

Published in a collection of humorous verse entitled *Both Sides of the Gutter*, 'Whalley's Embarkation' is not what might be called a true-to-life account.[8] Its author, a journalist named William Paulet Carey, specialised in satirical ballads and political pamphlets,[9] and his aim was to poke fun at various celebrities and politicians rather than provide a literal account of Whaley's departure. No doubt some of the named individuals did turn out to see him off, but the notion that he was accompanied by an entourage of French and Swiss servants and a menagerie can only be an invention for comic purposes.[10] It pandered to the growing public interest in the man who would become known as the 'Jerusalem Pilgrim', a tongue-in-cheek allusion to the fact that his journey was not religiously motivated.

Whaley's actual going away was more low-key. Apart from Harriet, who was only to accompany him to England, he brought just one servant with him. He had also recruited a travelling companion, Captain James Willson, who would join him in Deal. The short voyage was uneventful and once they had landed Whaley sent Harriet back to London with an allowance of £200 a year, 'which was regularly paid her till all my property was sold'. (W, 37) We know nothing of the words that passed between them at this time, but it seems that neither regarded it as a final parting and Whaley would write to her several times over the course of the expedition.

He then rendezvoused with James Willson. Then in his mid-50s, Willson was a former captain in the Marines whose father had, for some reason, disinherited him. In 1776 he had been elected MP for County Antrim, a constituency which, according to a contemporary report, he represented with 'much honour to himself, and credit to his electors'.[11] In reality Willson was so corrupt that he alienated his constituents and was not returned in the election of 1783.[12] Five years later he decided to throw his lot in with Whaley for the trip to Jerusalem. They made an odd pairing: Willson was the older of the two by more than thirty years, he had a wife and four children, and it is not clear why he decided to join an impulsive young gambler in what must have seemed a madcap enterprise. However, he may not have intended to go all the way to Jerusalem: he had business of some kind in Constantinople, a city that Whaley also wanted to see, and this is probably why the travellers decided to sail first to Smyrna rather than a port on the coast of Syria or Palestine.

Now they had only to find an appropriate vessel. The *London*, a merchant ship under the command of a Captain Neil, was then docked in Deal and due to embark for Smyrna.[13] She had a number of cannon and was a fast, well-weathered vessel, while Neil was an experienced skipper who had sailed to Smyrna on at least two previous occasions.[14] He was also prudent and modest and happy to seek advice from other captains if he thought they knew a body of water better than he did. Whaley was impressed by this level-headed seafarer and decided to hire the cabin of the *London* for the voyage to Turkey.[15] She would make only one stop en route at the small British colony of Gibraltar. With the agreement concluded, Whaley and Willson embarked aboard the *London* on 7 October.[16]

***

The voyage got off to an unsettled start, with the ship weathering a rough storm in the Bay of Biscay. But as she continued south along the coast of Iberia calm conditions set in, bringing home an unavoidable reality of travel by sea: boredom and long days with nothing much to do, surrounded by the featureless swells of the ocean. Whaley discovered that 'in order to live pleasantly at sea, two qualifications were absolutely necessary: in the first place, a man must possess an uncommon share of philosophy, and in the next a good stock of patience'. (W, 40–1) He had to endure the ship's physical constraints, 'the confined bird-cage-like space which seamen are obliged to live in'. [17] But there were sources of diversion. Whaley and Willson fished, on one occasion catching a large albacore, and in the evenings they drank Madeira wine.

Unfavourable sailing conditions made progress difficult and nineteen days into the voyage the *London* was still in the Atlantic. Adverse winds delayed the ship off the south-western tip of Portugal until at last, on 27 October, she approached the Straits of Gibraltar. But now human forces threatened her progress. Off the coast of Morocco they encountered six frigates, some of which had as many as thirty-six guns. When the closest ship began to lower a boat the captain decided enough was enough. 'We crowded all the sail we could' (W, 43) and within two hours the *London* had distanced her pursuers. Whaley later learned that discretion had indeed been the better part of valour. The frigates belonged to Mohammed III, the Sultan of Morocco. Locked in a sort of cold war with Gibraltar's British garrison, the Sultan had ordered his fleet to disrupt ships going to and from the naval base. [18] Had the Moroccans boarded the *London* they would surely have detained the vessel and its occupants.

For now, at least, Whaley and his companions had escaped danger and a strong tide was hurrying them towards the Straits, overlooked by high ground on both the Spanish and Moroccan sides. As the *London* entered the narrow passage a powerful and dramatic scene unfolded. Whaley was transfixed:

> The immense height of the rocks ascending perpendicularly from the surface of the sea strikes the imagination with sublime though awful ideas … in the midst of that immense body of water which washes a shore of no less than three thousand miles, even in a direct course, to the head of the Black Sea, I discovered so many new, interesting and variegated scenes, which were much heightened by the reverberation of the sound of cannon through a chain of mountains, and the setting sun plunging itself into the Atlantic directly central to our situation. (W, 44–5)

At the eastern end of the Strait stand two great promontories, Jebel Moussa to the south and the Rock of Gibraltar to the north. The Greek demigod Heracles was said to have created these peaks when he broke apart a mountain that connected Africa and Europe. Traditionally, they marked the western extremity of the classical world and on reaching them Whaley must have felt that he was leaving one world and entering into another. He was now in the Middle Sea and the Levant, with its spellbinding sights, haunting sounds and intoxicating smells, somehow seemed more within reach. But he knew that a long sea voyage still lay before him and before continuing he looked forward to a few days' rest at the most striking and contentious of all British naval bases.

★★★

Gibraltar's strategic setting and impressive natural defences make it an ideal location for a sea fortress and over the centuries various powers have laid claim to it. An Anglo-Dutch force captured Gibraltar in 1704 and nine years later Spain formally ceded it to Britain. Since then it had been an important British naval base, guarding the only entrance to the Mediterranean from the Atlantic. The towering ridge of limestone and shale known as 'the Rock' symbolised the naval power of the nation that claimed to rule the waves. Spain, never at ease with the loss of this prized possession, made several attempts to win it back. Most dramatically, a combined Spanish and French force had laid siege to Gibraltar in 1779 while the British were distracted by the American Revolutionary War (1775–83). The siege dragged on for over three years, the decisive moment coming on 13 September 1782 when the attackers bombarded the Rock from ships and floating batteries. Thousands of Spanish onlookers crowded the nearby hills hoping to see the garrison pounded into dust, but the British counter-attacked with lethal effect. They showered the enemy positions with over 40,000 rounds of red hot shot (heated cannonballs), annihilating several of the floating batteries. The French and Spanish were forced to call off the bombardment and a few months later they lifted the siege.[19] As a youth Whaley would have been enthralled by news of this dramatic encounter and he was keen to visit the scene of the heroic defence. He could be sure of a warm welcome at Gibraltar: not only did he know many of the officers serving in the garrison, having attended school with some of them, he was also personally acquainted with the acting governor, Major-General Charles O'Hara.

On disembarking Whaley was struck by the civilians of different nationalities that milled around him and 'the odd and confused noise resulting from a dozen different languages spoken at once'. (W, 46) Around 3,000 British, Spanish, Portuguese, Jewish, Genoese and Moroccan civilians lived in the colony, working variously as shopkeepers, brokers, traders, gardeners, sailors and fishermen.[20] Accompanied by Willson, Whaley went to meet Major-General O'Hara (see Plate 8).[21] Known in Gibraltar as 'Old Cock of the Rock', O'Hara was a veteran of the Seven Years War and the American Revolutionary War, in which he had been second-in-command to the British general Lord Cornwallis.[22] It was probably while O'Hara was serving under the Lord Lieutenant of Ireland a few years later that Whaley made his acquaintance. The two were kindred spirits: O'Hara loved dining and drinking, and he too had had his troubles with money, having been forced to flee to Italy in 1784 to escape his creditors.[23] Whaley was 'certain of meeting with excellent cheer' when he called to see him and he was not disappointed: the governor entertained him and Willson with food, drink and good-humoured conversation.[24] O'Hara had possibly already heard about Whaley's expedition and the reason for it, which would have amused him. The wager had long been a hot topic in society and news of it had no doubt reached Gibraltar ahead of his arrival.

The next day Whaley and Willson climbed the Rock to explore the Great Siege Tunnels, the passages that had been blasted out of the limestone to accommodate cannon,[25] and the King's Bastion, where the red hot shot had been fired during the siege. That evening they dined with the officers of the Eighteenth Foot, an Irish regiment that had been stationed at Gibraltar since 1783.[26] For Whaley it was an auspicious gathering, perhaps even key to the expedition's chances of success. One of the officers was Captain Hugh Moore, the son of a County Down land agent (see Plate 9).[27] Whaley found himself regarding this dark-haired, resolute-looking young man with interest. When he learned that Moore was about to take leave of absence he had an idea 'which I thought of much importance'. (W, 54) Having another active and reliable companion by his side would greatly enhance his chances of success. Willson was enthusiastic enough, but he was in his fifties and lacked Whaley's youthful energy. Moore, on the other hand, was twenty-five, strong and fit. Having downed a few glasses of wine to fuel his powers of persuasion, Whaley took the officer aside. Instead of returning to London, would he consider joining the expedition to Jerusalem? Moore seems to have agreed without hesitation. Unmarried, he had no immediate obligations and he embraced this once-in-a-lifetime chance to visit the Levant and the Holy Land.

Moore was also a more mature and level-headed individual than Whaley. Having been a soldier since the age of sixteen, when he joined the Eighteenth Foot as an ensign,[28] he brought dynamism and discipline to the venture, along with a swift and decisive manner. A friend later told him that as a military man he was 'so full of celerity that compared with a mercantile man it is lightning and the moon rising'.[29] Moore was also fatalistic, a predestinarian in the Presbyterian tradition. On the face of it he was a very different man to the whimsical and reckless Whaley but he would prove to be a faithful and steadfast companion to him, never leaving his side even in his darkest moments. 'From this moment we considered ourselves as embarked in one common cause, in which we felt equally interested.' (W, 54)

It was now nearly time to resume the voyage, but Whaley was not content to go without indulging a dangerous and rather pointless ambition. He had heard of St Michael's Cave, a labyrinth of caverns that extended deep into the bowels of the Rock, and was 'determined to go to the bottom … or at least, as far as any other person had ever been'. (W, 54–5) This had no relevance whatsoever for his wager, but Whaley had a recurrent compulsion to go further, deeper or higher than others, even if there were no tangible benefits beyond being able to say that he had done so. With Moore busy making preparations for his departure, he and Willson set out for St Michael's Cave the following morning. O'Hara had provided them with a guide, a twelve-man escort and 200 fathoms of rope. When the party reached the cave entrance high on the upper Rock they boosted their courage with a few swigs of fortified wine, lit their torches and ventured inside.

Entering the first cavern, Whaley was mesmerised by the profusion of stalactites, stalagmites and 'different crystallizations … [in] this great ante-chamber'. (W, 55) Descending to a lower level they lighted piles of straw, revealing 'reversed pyramids of petrified water, thirty and forty feet in length, hanging from the ceiling everywhere, and reflecting the light in different colours'. (W, 55–6) Illuminated by the flickering firelight, the cave must have appeared even more atmospheric than it does today. A painting by the Rev. Cooper Willyams, who visited it around twelve years later, evokes the awe the explorers felt (see Plate 10). With bats flapping around them O'Hara's men clearly felt they had done enough and returned to the surface, but Whaley and Willson were determined to continue their subterranean adventure. Accompanied by the increasingly reluctant guide, they climbed a hundred feet down to a deeper cavern.[30] Already tired from the first descent, Whaley 'began to find my body rather heavy for my arms to support' and on reaching the bottom he took some time to recover, 'panting for breath and much exhausted'. (W, 56) He had arrived in the sub-system of caves that later became known as Leonora's Cave. Some believed it led to a subterranean passage linking Gibraltar and North Africa, and that the Barbary macaques that inhabited the Rock had come there by this route. From time to time, members of the garrison had undertaken expeditions to discover the supposed tunnel and some had not returned.

The air was thin and difficult to breathe and the explorers found their torches were going out. Whaley noticed that the guide was trying to conceal a small opening from his view and when he asked why, he replied that the only ones ever to enter it had been two soldiers, doubtless in search of the passage to Africa. They had succeeded in squeezing into the opening but had been unable to get back out and had perished. On investigating the hole, Whaley

thought it sufficiently large for the dimensions of my body. I thrust my head and shoulders into it, and perceived that at the distance of five or six feet it took a different direction, and appeared to go perpendicularly downwards. I ascertained this fact by throwing my torch into it, which disappeared suddenly: we heard it for some seconds falling with a hollow noise, which at last subsided, and on looking into the hole, I perceived a very clear light at a great distance. (W, 57)

Nothing would do for Whaley now but to lower himself into this awful abyss. Securing what was left of the rope around his shoulders, he began to let himself down. As he descended the hole narrowed to a point where it was almost impossible to proceed, but Whaley forced his way through and reached the bottom. Willson attempted to follow, but he proved to be too large a man for the bottleneck and he got stuck fast, completely blocking the only outlet for the smoke from Whaley's torch. If they could not free the passage, he would suffocate.

Whaley does not say precisely how he managed to escape this predicament, only that he was determined that 'my courage and presence of mind should not forsake me … I struggled like a person in the last agonies of death, and in a little time found myself returned to the spot where I had left the guide.' (W, 58) Presumably he climbed back up to Willson and the two used their combined strength to free the passage. The guide had by now abandoned them. Both were exhausted, and they still had the task of hauling themselves back up through the caverns with the rope. After several hours of severe exertion they reached the cave entrance, where Whaley promptly fainted. In total, he and Willson had spent five hours in the cave. Whaley admitted that had it not been for the 'ridiculous vanity' of saying they had gone to the bottom, half an hour would have sufficed to see the place. He believed he had reached a greater depth than any other explorer.[31] The episode demonstrated his reckless determination to go to extremes – a propensity that had actuated his greatest wagers and that would manifest itself again in the course of his travels.

★★★

The *London* embarked from Gibraltar on the evening of 6 November with Moore now a committed member of the expedition. It was exactly nine years to the day since he had enrolled in the Eighteenth Foot, a fact that may not have been lost on him as he sailed off to begin a new chapter in his life. He brought with him a large half calf-bound journal in which he planned to record his experiences 'as a future gratification to myself, by enabling me to recollect the occurrences of a long tour', though he had no thought of his journal 'ever appearing more publickly than within the small circle of my most particular friends'. (M, preface) Nor did he know that it would survive to corroborate Whaley's own memoirs and act as a yardstick for his more exaggerated claims and statements.

The *London* left Gibraltar with a fair wind, but an error in navigation caused her to veer slightly north of her course. A week later she docked off Sardinia. After downing a couple of bottles of port, Whaley and his friends 'went on deck to admire the beauties of the setting sun, and there renewed our conversation till the rising moon brought forward other pleasing and interesting sensations'. (W, 63) The placid scene was deceptive. Turbulent seas lay ahead. Several days later, on 22 November, the *London* came in sight of the Peloponnesian coast. Struck by its barren and uncultivated appearance, Whaley disparaged its Greek inhabitants. He believed that under Ottoman domination they had become 'mean, cruel, cowardly, ignorant, dishonest, and embracing contentedly the fetters of slavery, to which their ancestors would so much rather have preferred death!' (W, 65–6) Harsh criticism indeed, but it was not uncommon among western travellers. Such impressions were largely based on hearsay. At no point during the voyage to Smyrna did Whaley venture onto the Greek mainland or any of the islands. He seems to have been unaware of the rise of Greek nationalism, which would culminate in the 1820s in an uprising against Ottoman rule.

As the *London* entered the Sea of Crete, an event occurred to make Whaley turn his thoughts from Greek 'degradation' to self-preservation. The sky had begun to wear 'a very threatening aspect' (W, 67), and Captain Neil was pleased when a French merchant ship was sighted. The French knew the eastern Mediterranean well owing to their extensive trade in the Levant, and Neil hailed the ship to ask advice of her captain. He told him a storm was in the offing and advised him not to approach the islands, but instead follow his example and lay to. Neil ordered the sails to be furled and the ship to remain stationary facing the wind. Scarcely had this been done when forked wires of lightning began pulsing over the sea. By late evening they were in the midst of 'a true hurricane, accompanied by the most dreadful thunder and lightning'. (W, 67) The black night made the storm more terrifying, with the rain pouring 'down in such torrents as rendered it impossible for the men to keep their feet'. (W, 67–8) Every movable object on deck was washed away and the binnacle, used for holding compasses, was smashed to pieces. The crew could do nothing but let the *London* drift at the mercy of the storm. Moore described the conditions vividly:

> the tempest was attended with ... more thunder than I had ever heard, and lightning so bright that it entirely eclipsed the inferior lustre of our candles ... never had I seen a ship so violently agitated, nor a ship so much tossed about at the will of the waves. The total darkness of the night ... was only interrupted by the continued chains of lightning that illuminated the horizon, and our knowledge of our situation, greatly augmented our apprehensions; almost surrounded by islands and low rocks which would only be distinguished when the effulgence of the lightning shed brightness on the water. (M, 5)

Disregarding Neil's advice to remain in his cabin, Moore ventured on deck and was shocked by what he saw: 'I never beheld any thing equal to the scene of horror and confusion ... all hands were on deck, expecting every moment to go to pieces, and the ship was so violently strained, that several of the seams had opened.' (M, 6) The *London* was shipping so much water that her cabins were flooded, though the pumps were continually active. With the vessel so perilously close to the rocks shipwreck seemed inevitable, but Whaley's fear that he would lose his wager surmounted his concern for life and limb: 'had I gone to the bottom ... I would in my last moments have regretted not having been permitted by providence to perform my journey, and to win the bets which these gentlemen were confident they had laid with so great odds in their favour.' (W, 68)

Fortunately providence was not yet ready to halt Whaley's progress. As the night wore on the tempest abated and by five o'clock in the morning the wind was slackening. With the coming of day they found that the *London* had not drifted too far off course. The storm was the worst Neil had experienced in twenty years at sea, and as they scanned the watery wastes around them they could see no sign of the French ship. Whaley feared the worst and quoted solemnly from Virgil: '*haud ignarus mali, miseris succurrere disco*' ('not unacquainted with misfortune, I learn to aid the wretched').[32] (W, 68) Having survived the dreadful storm, he was feeling more disposed to help the less fortunate, just as the French had helped him. His travels in the Ottoman lands would give him the opportunity to put this resolution to the test.

Fine weather set in and the *London* proceeded idly northwards, reaching the Cyclades two days later. On 1 December she entered the Gulf of Smyrna. By midday the great port itself was in sight. The setting was magnificent, the bay like a huge amphitheatre enclosed by rugged arms of mountain. All kinds of merchant ships crowded the harbour, their flags and pennants fluttering in the wind, while the houses of the city could be seen strung out along the quayside (see Plate 11). In the evening the *London* fired one of her cannon to salute the town, receiving in return a salute from 'above fifty ships of different nations'. (W, 71) It was an electrifying moment: Whaley, Willson and Moore had completed the first and longest part of their journey. Now that they had arrived in Turkey, Jerusalem somehow seemed more attainable.

But Whaley's mind was not at ease: Ralph Sneyd, a British midshipman, had come aboard with disturbing news: there had been an outbreak of plague in Smyrna. Whaley was badly shaken. When it came to fighting a duel or descending into the depths of the earth he had more guts than most, but his courage failed him 'at the very sound of the word plague'. (W, 71) Perhaps it was because he felt that dying in this way would be somehow inglorious. Yet he was right to fear disease. It would be the greatest peril he would face in the Ottoman Empire.

6

A SAVAGE AND REMOTE COUNTRY

After weeks at sea, the new arrivals must have found it strange to arrive on Smyrna's bustling quayside. They would have been impressed by the male Turks who passed them in brightly coloured turbans and clothes, with pistols and blades thrust inside their sashes. They would also have noticed veiled ladies, their eyebrows and nails painted with yellow-red henna.[1] They saw Europeans too, going here and there about their business. Many of them wore Turkish dress, but had hats rather than turbans to distinguish themselves as Christians. Whaley, Willson and Moore must have been bewildered by the riot of human and animal noise that assailed them. As well as the babble of various different languages they would have heard 'jackals howling in the hills, barking dogs ... the cries of sherbet and fruit sellers mixed with British sailors' songs, Greeks singing ballads ... and the muezzin's call to prayer'.[2] The streets were badly paved, covered in dust and often 'so narrow that when a loaded camel passed through the pedestrians had to seek shelter in doorways and shops to avoid being knocked down'.[3]

Yet the impression of a cramped and grimy urban area was deceptive: Smyrna was one of the Mediterranean's oldest and greatest cities. Located at a crossroads of trade between Europe, Asia and Arabia, it was one of the Ottoman Empire's most prosperous ports and handled six times as much commercial traffic as Constantinople while offering much cheaper commodities. The city's resident Europeans – mostly French, Dutch and English – controlled most of this commerce.[4] They were known as Franks, a common name for westerners in the Levant since the time of the Crusades. Many of them lived and worked on Frank Street, a long and busy thoroughfare that ran roughly parallel to the quays. 'Franks were as much at home in Smyrna as in Marseille. With the confidence of wealth, they felt the city belonged to them.'[5] They were not afraid to flaunt their riches, building fine country houses outside Smyrna,[6] hunting bears and wild boar and living 'in a style of elegance little inferior to that of an English nobleman'. (W, 159)

There were also other foreigners, with distinct quarters for Greeks, Jews and Armenians. The various ethnic and religious groups lived in 'a most particular union undisturbed by any difference of Religion or nation … even in wartime'.[7] Whaley found that 'all religions are tolerated; and the different churches, mosques and temples which present themselves to the view make a very singular appearance'. (W, 159) With some 100,000 inhabitants speaking a dozen different languages, Smyrna was a vibrant and sophisticated melting pot. It was here that Whaley and his companions would begin their adventures in the Ottoman Empire – but only if they could survive the plague they had heard about. Fortunately the midshipman's intelligence proved to be exaggerated. While the plague had ravaged the city over the course of the summer, by the autumn it had 'entirely ceased'[8] apart from some minor aftershocks. Whaley was more at ease when he learned that 'the death of two or three persons in a day was thought of no consequence at Smyrna'. (W, 71)

He and companions received a surprisingly warm welcome from two young brothers, John and Peter Lee. Members of an English mercantile family, the Lees had befriended them when they went aboard the *London* to welcome its European occupants. They invited them to the home of their aunt, Mrs Marguerite Maltass, on Frank Street. She was daughter of a French merchant who had emigrated from La Ciotat near Marseilles,[9] and though she was a 'most amiable' (W, 71) lady, the new arrivals were more taken by her four young daughters. 'These fair sisters were the first Smyrneottes we had seen, and from their beauty we formed a most favourable opinion of the charms of their countrywomen.' (W, 72) Following the enforced abstinence of their voyage, Whaley, Moore and Willson showed more than a little interest in the ladies but it does not seem that they got to consummate their passions on this occasion.

The following morning Whaley and his companions busied themselves writing letters to their friends and family, having heard that a mail boat was due to leave for Marseilles that evening. They then went for a stroll around the town and 'walked for a considerable time through the narrow streets staring at the multiplicity of new objects by which we were surrounded'.

(M, 11) The following day they accompanied one of the Lees to the custom house to have their luggage assessed. The customs official, a 'long bearded former general' (M, 14), received them in a haughty manner: 'We found him seated … on cushions at one side of the room, he scarcely deigned to look at us, and did not alter a muscle of his countenance; we were told to sit down and pipes were immediately handed [out], which we were obliged to make use of.' (M, 14–15) At length the official gave them permission to proceed, accepting Whaley's present of a spyglass without a glance or any expression of gratitude.[10] The official's high-handed demeanour was not surprising: most Turks, even the well-educated, believed unwaveringly in the Ottoman Empire's superiority to the West. Without doubt the Empire had once been streets ahead of Europe both culturally and militarily, but since the late sixteenth century a succession of weak and ineffectual sultans had presided over an increasingly insular and technologically backward society. Meanwhile, new European nation states and empires, financed by gold and silver from the New World, emerged. Nevertheless Ottoman rulers and people alike continued to hold 'an unshakeable belief in the superiority of Ottoman ways', adhering to techniques and weapons that had long been obsolete in Europe.[11] A visit to a Smyrna munitions factory confirmed Whaley's opinion that 'in this, as in other arts, [they were] centuries behind European nations'. (W, 80–1)

Yet his view of the Turks was not uniformly negative. While wandering the streets the previous day he and Moore had happened upon an impressive-looking building they took for a banqueting hall. On approaching they had been warned off by a 'surly looking Turk' who met them with 'a long harangue which we supposed to be replete with abuse'. (M, 12) They were about to take their leave when another Turk appeared and invited them to enter, telling them to remove their shoes in the portico. By now it had dawned on the foreigners that this was no banqueting hall. Inside the mosque they saw a number of worshippers completely engrossed in their devotions. Whaley was impressed by their obvious piety: 'not one Turk out of twenty that were there even lifted up his eyes to regard us, so intent were they on their devotion, which they performed with a degree of propriety and respectful solemnity that we rarely see observed by the more enlightened congregations of European churches'. (W, 78) He believed that had the situation been reversed, with two Turks 'dressed in the habit of their country' making their appearance in a western church, they would have been the subject of laughter and ridicule. 'For my own part I should probably be among the most noisy [and] inquisitive … these reflexions led me to comparisons which were by no means in our favour.'[12] In at least one respect, Whaley was prepared to concede that Turks were superior to Europeans.

***

By the end of his second day in Smyrna, Whaley was growing restless. It was time to resume his expedition. Where to next? He was still finalising the details of his itinerary and he may have floated ambitious plans in his conversations with the Franks of Smyrna, one of whom afterwards wrote: 'They go from hence to Cyprus, thence to Jaffa, and from that to Jerusalem; and … return to this place by Aleppo. They intend afterwards going to Constantinople to take a trip to the Black Sea, visit the Archipelago, land at Messina, view Mount Etna, and other parts of Sicily, and return … through Italy, Switzerland, and France.'[13] Ultimately Whaley's itinerary would turn out to be less ambitious, but the correspondent was correct that he planned to travel to Constantinople. In fact he had decided to visit the Ottoman capital before resuming his voyage to the Holy Land, partly out of interest and partly because Willson had business there.[14]

However, the detour would add at least 500 miles to their journey and would be far from straightforward, requiring a tough overland trek to the port of Scala[15] on the Sea of Marmara to take ship for Constantinople. The road led through north-western Turkey. Even today this is well off the beaten path for tourists and in Whaley's time it was a terra incognita. In 1803 the Scottish merchant Thomas MacGill found it 'extremely disagreeable, the only method [of travel] being on horseback, and if you want any comforts you must carry them with you. The accommodations on the road are horribly nasty, and those who are not content to sleep upon a plank, must provide themselves with a bed.'[16] The only purpose-built lodgings were khans and caravansaries, merchants' inns with rooms ranged on two or three stories around a central courtyard, but these establishments were few and far between and in any case they were often dirty and extremely basic. Accommodation of any other kind was hard to come by, and other hindrances also lay in wait. The roads were rudimentary and liable to deteriorate to the point of uselessness in bad weather, and the weather was unlikely to be benign so late in the year. Basic necessities would be in short supply and Whaley and his companions knew they would have to carry the bulk of their food with them. Apart from that there was the possibility of attack by bandits or marauding soldiers. The fact that they were foreigners and clearly more affluent than the average Turk made them a tempting target. 'On account of the season, and more particularly on account of the war,' John Lee begged Whaley not to make the trip, 'dreading that we should meet with parties of the victorious Turks, returning from the camp, who are always insolent, and frequently rob and murder travellers'. (W, 82) But he would not be dissuaded and Lee reluctantly agreed to help him make the necessary arrangements. Despite the difficulties Whaley estimated that he could get to Constantinople and back within a month and Captain Neil agreed to wait for him at Smyrna until this time had elapsed.

It then transpired that Willson had been struck down by rheumatism and was unable to travel. Before even starting on the road Whaley had lost a companion, but he and the others were determined to continue regardless and they set about recruiting some men to accompany them. In an intelligent move Whaley hired an Armenian named Paulo to accompany him as servant, interpreter and guide. Although he claimed improbably that he had 'travelled over most of the globe', Paulo was capable and loyal and he 'swore by the holy Sepulchre that he would with much pleasure lose his life to serve me'. (W, 82) Whaley and Moore also secured the services of a janissary to act as a guard. Trained under strict discipline, the janissaries were an elite armed force of the Ottoman Empire. They wore blue uniforms 'and a pleated white head-dress like a giant sleeve, sometimes decorated with plumes and jewels'.[17] Janissaries were also proud and impetuous, not above rebelling against the Sultan himself if they believed they had good cause. Finally, they engaged a black slave to look after the baggage, which would be carried by a couple of horses. This did not trouble either Whaley or Moore: in the Ottoman Empire slavery was a fact of life, and even in their own homeland black servants could be bought and sold openly.[18]

The small party set out from Smyrna on the afternoon of 4 December. Fired by enthusiasm and the spirit of adventure, Whaley and Moore must have felt that only now were they embarking on their journey proper. That evening they found accommodation at a luxurious establishment in the village of Bornova. Here they had access to a billiard table, enough food to feed twenty people, and ready-made beds. (M, 20) The first day's travel could be accounted a success, but this was as good as it would get. Early the following day they were on the road again, ascending the foothills of the Manisa Dağı range. Some distance further on a caravan of around thirty camels overtook them. Whaley was impressed by the procession and the steady gait of the animals, who followed one another in single file. But before long the sight would become so familiar that they no longer remarked on it. Indeed, after a while Moore became irritated by the 'melancholy discordant din of the camels bells'. (M, 29) Further along the road they encountered something that gave Whaley pause for thought: a plot of ground surrounded by tall cypresses, in which groups of painted stones, each with a turban carved on the top, were set upright in the earth. It was a burial ground for the victims of a recent plague, a consideration that 'for some time damped our spirits, and inspired us with gloomy and dismal ideas'. (W, 89)

That day they reached Manisa, a large town inhabited by Turks, Greeks and Armenians. It had once been a place of some renown, known in ancient Roman times as Magnesia ad Sipylum. Manisa had even been the capital of the Byzantine Empire for a brief period following the sack of Constantinople in 1204. In 1788, however, it was but a shadow of its former self, with narrow and dirty streets and 'very bad' houses, 'some of wood, others of stone or mud, all intermixed, without neatness or uniformity … few remains of imperial grandeur are now to be traced here'.[19] (M, 22) But if the town held little appeal for the foreigners they found that they themselves, with their outlandish clothes and strange voices, were the subject of fascinated attention. As they waited in the courtyard of the caravansary to be lodged, a great crowd of Turks gathered to stare at them. Finally they were handed the key 'of a miserable appartment' (M, 22), but however dismal the lodgings the travellers were exhausted and slept as soundly on their mattresses 'as we should have done on beds of the finest down of Europe'. (M, 25) During their first two days on the road Whaley and Moore had been absorbed by the sheer novelty of what they saw, from the alluring landscape to the exotic-looking camel trains. Even the filthy streets of Manisa were probably fascinating in their unfamiliarity: Whaley was sufficiently interested to complete a sketch of the town, one of several drawings he executed during the expedition.[20] So far they had been blessed with favourable weather and their mood was optimistic. But it did not take long for the weather, and the mood, to deteriorate.

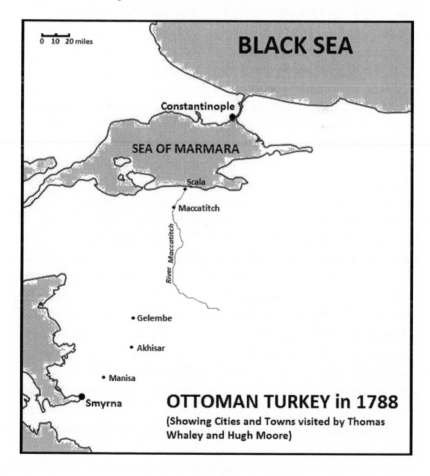

***

Early on the morning of 7 December the party left Manisa, heading for the town of Akhisar some thirty-two miles to the north-east. It would take them another five days to get to the Marmara coast: a tough, uncomfortable and tedious journey. Effectively Whaley and Moore were tourists, but they were in a land not set up for tourism or even travel and the inclement weather added greatly to their discomfort. On the road to Akhisar it began to rain heavily and by the time they reached their destination they were soaked to the skin. On 9 December they endured an eight-hour ride in the course of which 'it poured the whole day without intermission, all our coverings were insufficient to exclude the rain'. (M, 28) The next day their progress was slowed by deep furrows of mud in the road and swollen rivers that were difficult to ford. At one point the baggage horses ended up in a morass and only with difficulty did they recover their supplies.

Meanwhile the quality of the accommodation varied from bad to worse. As expected the options were severely limited, and every time they reached their halting place for the night they had to undertake a tiresome search for lodgings. If they were lucky they might find shelter in a caravansary or a house, but usually they had to be content with a stable or a shack. The provisions they had brought with them were soon gone and while they were sometimes able to procure boiled fowls, eggs or bread they often had to be content with less appetising rations. At Akhisar they lodged in 'a very bad room which indeed was little better than a ruin, and admitted cold and wet on every side'. (M, 27) Afraid of being robbed, they slept with their pistols and blunderbusses beside them. The following night, in Gelembe, they lay down in a mud-walled room while dogs 'of the wolf and mastiff kind' (W, 95) roamed the streets outside, howling incessantly. The night after that they stayed in 'a wretched hovel' at the side of the road. Drying their clothes as best they could over a charcoal fire, they dined on dried camel meat, 'salted and cut in thin slices which are well rubbed with garlic and dried in the sun'. (M, 29) While the Turks thought it 'a most delicate viand', Whaley was unimpressed with this 'stinking' fare. (W, 96)

Foul weather, bad lodgings and bad food were not the only things to trouble them. On 10 December they were still two days' ride from

Scala. Travelling through a wild and desolate stretch of country they encountered a party of foot-travellers who informed them that a band of deserters from the Ottoman Grand Vizier's army were in the vicinity, robbing and murdering everyone they encountered. The situation seemed desperate but, by Whaley's account, Paulo's ardent resolve to die by his master's side galvanised the whole group and they resolved to make 'a desperate resistance'. (W, 98) As evening drew in they discerned around twenty men approaching and prepared for battle. Whaley and Moore each had 'a double-barrelled gun and a case of double-barrelled pistols' (W, 99) and Paulo wanted to open fire as soon as the strangers were within range. Whaley managed to dissuade him, believing the men to be peaceful sailors, but Moore was not so sure: 'if they had at first entertained any evil designs, the display we made of our arms had the desired effect: they stopped to look at us as we passed, but did not attempt to molest us, though the formidable ruffians were all armed'. (M, 32) The next day they set off under another heavy downpour, punctuated by thunder and lightning. With no sign of a let up, tempers started to fray. On the banks of the River Maccatitch (Simav), which they were following to the town of Maccatitch (Karacabey),[21] they faced another dangerous encounter. This time the antagonist was from within their own party. When Moore criticised the janissary for allowing the slave to drive the baggage horses ahead of the party, the Turkish guard reacted fiercely:

> he got into a violent passion, and soon after, a miserable horse that carried our bedding having strayed a little out of the line, he ran at him with his drawn sabre, and attack[ed] him with it behind, till he forced him down the banks of a river, along the margin of which our road lay. The bedding which was trussed on each side prevented the horse being hurt by the fall, though the bank was very steep, but he rolled over into the water, and was rapidly carried down by the current for above half a mile. (M, 33)

Paulo hurled himself into the flood and rescued the animal and its burden, which was now thoroughly soaked. Infuriated, Moore confronted the janissary, who 'drew his sabre, and had not Mr. M[oore] levelled his gun at him he would most likely have been dreadfully wounded'. (W, 100) The guard threatened to abandon the party and return to Smyrna, something that filled Whaley with apprehension. What if the janissary, seeking revenge, decided to collude with the local peasants to rob and murder them? Whaley

> therefore used every means I could devise to pacify the scoundrel … at last Pauolo putting his arms round his neck kissed him several times in the most affectionate manner, which appeased him a little. He kneeled down, put his fingers in his mouth and made the most ridiculous grimaces, using at the same time the most impertinent language, such as 'Christian Dog,' 'Void of faith,' 'Unbeliever, etc.' Thus his rage exhausted itself, and Pauolo renewing his embraces, he at last consented to accompany us. (W, 101)

As a proud member of an elite Ottoman force, the janissary deeply resented the reproaches of his Christian employers. Moore, for his part, may have felt somewhat embarrassed at losing his temper and he glossed over the stand-off in his journal.

After this uncomfortable incident the companions endured a long ride through a stretch of deep and wet country. When night fell they were still miles from Maccatitch and twice they lost their way in the darkness, only to be set right by shepherds 'whose flocks the flashes of lightning enabled us to distinguish'. (M, 34) Finally, sodden and exhausted, they reached the town 'where we met our usual difficulties in procuring a lodging and supper'. (W, 101) After such a day the companions were keener than ever to reach the sea and be rid of the wilderness. Thankfully only a short distance remained to the coast.

The next day they reached the port of Scala, only to find that no ship would sail until the wind was favourable. This 'almost exhausted our patience'. (W, 102) It was eight days since the party had left Smyrna. The journey had been rain-soaked and uncomfortable and their food supplies had run dangerously low. As an experienced soldier Moore was used to hardship, but Whaley had led a more pampered life and in enduring the privations of the road he had begun to find out things about himself. 'When removed from all friends and relations, in a savage and remote country, your personal influence and property lose their weight and consequence and you are left to shift for yourself, with those advantages which nature and not any fortuitous circumstances may have bestowed on you.' (W, 96) Already, the expedition was making him aware that his life of privilege was but a façade, something he would not have learned had he remained at home frittering away his estates in the smoky, candlelit confines of a club or a gaming house.

Whaley and Moore had also had plenty of time to observe the country and its people and the conclusions they drew about Ottoman governance were not complimentary. They had been struck by the wretched condition of the inhabitants and their dwellings 'where the ragged ensigns of poverty were displayed' (M, 20), and dismayed to encounter places where atrocities had been perpetrated. Near Manisa they had come upon a ruined village that had been burned by one of the Sultan's ministers after the inhabitants failed to pay 'an immense sum which he came to levy from them'. (M, 21) 'Thus do these devoted people frequently fall victims to the rapacity and relentless cruelty of barbarous and despotic tyrants, who under the mask of duty to their sovereign veil the most atrocious acts of cruelty and oppression.' (W, 88) Disheartened by reports of Ottoman brutality, Moore wanted to know why 'Liberty' had 'confined thy animating beams to thy favored British shores'. (M, 29) Whaley, for his part, could not suppress 'a glow of exultation ... when I reflected on the preeminence of that most excellent constitution which we enjoy as British subjects, by which our lives and properties are so well secured'. (W, 97) Claims of Ottoman misrule and official brutality were nothing new in the accounts of European travellers, which for the most part described a society 'oppressed by rapine, murder and terror of its rulers'.[22] But if there was some foundation for this assertion, there was less for Whaley and Moore's unequivocal praise of British rule as enlightened, particularly as far as Ireland was concerned. They saw society from the perspective of the Anglo-Irish landed class and were blind to the injustice that had reduced most people in their homeland to destitution and subservience. A few years later the United Irishman Edward Sweetman described the lot of Irish Catholics, 'taxed without being represented, bound without their consent', as 'the very definition of slavery'.[23]

★★★

The next day the adverse wind persisted, blowing heavy gales and sleet, and the travellers were forced to endure a further wait. But by the evening it had abated and they persuaded their 'nokidah' or pilot, the boat operator who had agreed to take them to Constantinople, to bring them downriver so they could pass the time shooting ducks and hares. That evening they lay down to sleep in the open boat. In the night the wind became favourable, 'though the frost which accompanied it almost froze us' (M, 36), and at last, early in the morning, they prepared to leave. Whaley looked forward to finally reaching his destination after so many discomforts and dangers. But the Ottoman capital harboured dangers of its own, among them a peril far worse than anything he had encountered on the backroads of Anatolia.

7

SPLENDOUR AND POWER

Straddling the Bosporus, the narrow strait that separates Europe and Asia, Constantinople was the beating heart of the Ottoman world. Captured from the Byzantines by Mehmet the Conqueror in 1453, it was regarded as the gateway to all the exoticism and allure of the east. Visitors were beguiled by its superb setting, latticed palaces, lush gardens, luxurious bathhouses, elegant coffee houses and mysterious harems. 'Foreigners resident in Constantinople often wrote of Turkish "freedom and pleasure" … They referred not only to the lack of a rigid class structure, but also to the range of pleasures on offer.' The sensual pleasures that could be had included not only food, drink and music but also sex: in some respects, sexual attitudes and behaviour were much less restrained in the Ottoman capital than in Europe.[1]

A succession of eighteenth-century travellers had written descriptions of Constantinople, some of which Whaley had read in advance of his visit. Even so, when he and Moore embarked from Scala on 14 December 1788 they had only a vague notion of what to expect. With the wind driving the ship rapidly across the Sea of Marmara they reached the Princes' Islands near the Bosporus in a few hours. Suddenly Constantinople was within grasp and already there was a sense that they were transitioning from the backwaters of rural Turkey to a more urban and urbane environment. Their fellow passengers included the governor of Smyrna's secretary, 'a long meagre figure, whose skin appeared as dry and parched as old leather, and who really astonished us by the handfulls of opium which he swallowed every hour'. (M, 36) He seemed to presage the more sophisticated and streetwise characters they would meet in the city, as opposed to the bucolic Turks they had encountered on the road.

As the ship entered Constantinople's harbour, sublimely situated between three tongues of land and merging bodies of water, the view unfolded like a tapestry.[2] To their left they could see Seraglio Point, the peninsula where the Sultan's palace stood. First came the slender minarets and massive domes of Sultan Ahmet mosque (the Blue Mosque) and the mighty, Byzantine-era Hagia Sophia. Next came the Sultan's private gardens with their stately cypress trees, followed by the elegant domes and rooftops of the palace itself. Then Seraglio Point gave way to the Golden Horn, the inlet of water that spills into the Bosporus from the north-west. The harbour was full of craft, from tall sailing ships to small and shallow rowing boats conveying passengers across the strait. Ottoman flags fluttered in the breeze near the landing points where the inhabitants milled to and fro in bright clothing and colourful sashes. Moore was struck by 'the novelty of the objects by which a stranger is surrounded' and to him it seemed that 'all the effects of nature … have been exerted to contribute to [the view's] magnificence'. (M, 37)

The splendour masked a less glorious reality. Constantinople was the centre of the Ottoman slave trade, with supply lines stretching from as far afield as the Caucasus, Poland and the Sudan. In general, slavery was not as degrading in the Ottoman Empire as it was in the West and many of Constantinople's domestic slaves were treated better than European servants. At the same time, some twenty percent of the city's population were in bondage and could be bought and sold like livestock.[3] It was not long before the newcomers acquired first-hand knowledge of this. The *nokidah* stopped at Seraglio Point to report on his cargo, mooring alongside a Georgian ship. The occupants of this vessel included two young girls who rested their heads on the lap of an old woman 'to whom they appeared to be tenderly attached'. Nearby, a boy watched them 'with a dejected countenance'. (M, 37) Whaley and Moore learned that the three youngsters were siblings, Georgian slaves who were to be sold in Constantinople. The sisters' fate was all too easy to anticipate: Georgian women were much sought-after for the harems of Turkish nobles. Francois Poqueville, who saw three or four hundred females put up for sale at Constantinople's 'woman-market' around 1800, observed how buyers 'roamed about them from group to group, made them open their mouths, inspected their hands, and examined them as we do animals'.[4] Whaley and Moore would happily have given the Georgian girls their freedom, presumably by buying them from their present owner, but 'the ordinances for the regulation of the slave market rendered this impossible'. (M, 37–8) They had to be content with offering them money and their ardent wishes that they would not become the property of a cruel master.

***

The ship docked at the landing place of Tóp-Kháneh Scala on the western bank of the Bosporus, near the suburbs of Galata and Pera. As foreigners were not permitted to live in Constantinople's Turkish quarters, most European diplomats and grandees, along with their staff and servants, lived in Pera, the name meaning simply 'beyond'. After disembarking Whaley and Moore presented themselves at the English Palace, residence of the British ambassador Sir Robert Ainslie. They received a warm welcome from the ambassador, whose 'hospitality and convivial manners … made us soon forget all our sufferings from fatigue and hunger during our journey from Smyrna to this place'. (W, 103) Then in his late fifties, Ainslie had grown up in Bordeaux where his Scottish father was a merchant. He had been in his current position since 1775 and had won his hosts over by assuming 'the style and fashion of a Musselman [Muslim] of rank; in fine, he lived *en Turk*, and pleased the natives so much by this seeming policy … that he became more popular than any of the Christian ministers'.[5] Ainslie had good reason for currying favour with the Turks. The British saw the Ottomans as an important buffer between their colonial possessions in India and imperial rivals such as Russia and France, and Ainslie's job was to help prop up the rickety Ottoman Empire and cultivate friendly relations with its rulers. He enjoyed good relations with the Sultan, Abdülhamid I, and had encouraged him to declare war on Russia in 1787, an intervention that the French ambassador described as 'les perfides conseils du Chevalier Ainslie'. But Ainslie was widely respected for his 'ability, zeal and success'[6] and he would be a valuable friend to Whaley and Moore during their time in Constantinople. 'He is the pleasantest man I have ever met with,' Moore wrote, 'and treats us with so much attention that tho' so short a time here we feel quite at home.'[7] Also at the English palace the Irishmen met a number of officers from the *Pearl*, a British frigate then stationed in Constantinople. These men were old acquaintances of Moore, who had known them at Gibraltar.

Over the next few days Whaley and Moore immersed themselves in the sights, sounds and smells of the Ottoman capital. Mystified and disorientated by their surroundings, they found themselves in a state of culture shock. 'The scene is so totally different from any that other parts of Europe afford that we really at first conceive ourselves in a new world,' Moore wrote. 'The dresses manners and in short every action of the inhabitants bespeak them of almost a different order.'[8] Walking the streets they found the interior of the city as 'disagreeable and deformed, as the exterior ... is pleasing and magnificent'. They wandered around the suburb of Galata, a former Genoese colony overlooked by the steepled Tower of Galata, 'a Gothic monument strayed to the banks of the Bosphorus'.[9] They went with Captain Seymour Finch of the *Pearl* to shoot snipe on the Sultan's plantation. And they went to see the Sultan's barges sailing on the Bosporus: graceful, painted vessels with canopies supported on gilded, silver or ivory columns.

They also visited some of Galata's less reputable establishments, including a tavern where they saw 'the Dancing Boys, who are kept at those places for the most indecent purposes'. These boys were male prostitutes who dressed themselves in fine clothes and 'danced in a way which left nothing to the imagination'.[10] Whaley was revolted by what he saw:

> It would be very shocking to commit to the paper the disgusting attitudes and gestures into which they throw themselves. There were two Turks at breakfast in the gallery who were entertaining themselves in a manner that was horrid to the ideas of a rational being. These boys I just mentioned, have a method of cracking their fingers and fixing little bells to their wrists, with which they produce sounds and play tunes that are much admired. Being disgusted with this species of entertainment I hastened from a scene that made human nature shudder.[11]

In Smyrna Whaley had been disgusted to learn that the boys who worked in the city's bathhouse 'were often destined for other criminal purposes

... among those depraved votaries of sensual pleasures'.[12] His appalled reactions were to be expected. Western ideas of propriety required that one react to any suggestion of homosexuality with abhorrence. However, same-sex relations were openly countenanced in Ottoman Turkey.[13]

Their closeness to Ainslie allowed the Irishmen to mingle freely with the artists, bankers, diplomats and others who made up Constantinople's European elite. The arrival of two Irish adventurers en route to Jerusalem to win a wager caused something of a stir in the city's expatriate society. 'Nothing can equal the attention of every one of consequence to us here', Moore contended.[14] Those whose acquaintance they made included the Danish nobleman and banker the Baron Hübsch von Grossthal,[15] the French ambassador the Comte de Choiseul-Gouffier, the Neapolitan envoy the Comte de Ludolf, the latter's Spanish counterpart, Don Juan de Bouligny, the Dutch and Swedish ambassadors and the Italian painter Luigi Mayer. The Irishmen were also curious to know more of the city's Ottoman lords. No doubt they would have liked to have met the Sultan, but even the influential Ainslie could not obtain this honour for them. In any case Abdülhamid I was a retiring man who acted 'more as an advisor and arbitrator than as an absolutist sultan'.[16] The Grand Vizier, the de facto prime minister, and the Captain Pasha, the Grand Admiral of the Navy, were the real powers behind the throne. Of the two, the Captain Pasha, Hasan Pasha of Algiers, was probably the more renowned and formidable. The European diplomats respected him deeply, not least because he often went around with a tame lion by his side, and he was particularly close to Ainslie. Whaley and Moore were delighted to learn that the British ambassador had obtained an audience with this great Ottoman lord for them. The meeting was scheduled to take place at the Sultan's summer house on Seraglio Point, and would also be attended by Captain Finch and the officers of the *Pearl*.

Originally from Georgia, the Captain Pasha had risen to his exalted position from very humble origins indeed. Like many of his compatriots he was sold as a slave in Constantinople, eventually ending up in Algiers in the service of a Turk. When his master died, Hasan was sold again to pay off the deceased's debts. He managed to escape and made his way back to Constantinople, where he joined the Ottoman navy 'in the capacity of cagliongi, a post one step higher than a common sailor'. (W, 113) Intelligent and capable, he rose quickly through the ranks and was eventually given command of a vessel. He served in the Russo-Ottoman War of 1768–74 and was present when the Russians set the Ottoman fleet ablaze at Çeşme near Smyrna in 1770.[17] Although he was not in command of the fleet, Hasan proved to be 'a far more experienced and braver admiral' than the actual commander.[18] When his ship went on fire his crew jumped into the sea to save themselves but he stayed aboard 'exerting himself at the risk of his life for her preservation, till he found all his efforts were ineffectual in checking the progress of the fire, he then followed the example of his crew and swam to shore'. (M, 48) Hasan later made up for the disaster of Çeşme by driving the Russians out of the island of Lemnos, a strategic outpost from which they could have attacked Constantinople itself. In recognition of this he was appointed Grand Admiral, or Captain Pasha, of the Ottoman navy.[19] Since then he had 'filled this important station with much credit and honour to himself' (W, 113), overseeing the modernisation of the Ottoman navy and driving the Porte's belated efforts to catch up with the technologically more sophisticated European powers.

The Captain Pasha (see Plate 14) was the greatest Ottoman dignitary Whaley would meet and his consequence was matched by the ceremony of the occasion. On the morning of 22 December Whaley, Moore, Captain Finch and the officers of the *Pearl*, escorted by Ainslie's dragomen (interpreters) and janissaries, set off from Tóp-Kháneh Scala for Seraglio Point. When they arrived another dragoman met them and brought them to the reception room, 'a large appartment furnished *a' la Turc*, with cushions all around it'. (M, 52) The visitors saw the Captain Pasha seated at the upper end of the room, noting perhaps with relief that his lion was not present. He was splendidly attired in an expensive pelice and had put on his dress turban, 'an immense high cap with a cotton band'. (M, 52) Then in his mid-70s,[20] he was 'healthy and robust … [with] a fine open manly countenance but strongly expressive of that ungovernable ferocity which manifests itself on certain occasions'. (W, 113) For a man of his age, Hasan was extraordinarily energetic. Along with the Sultan and Grand Vizier, it was his duty to attend the scene of any accidental fire that occurred in the city, to boost the morale of those engaged in quenching the blaze. One such fire had actually broken out the night before, and though the Captain Pasha was then four miles away he had managed to reach the scene within twenty minutes. 'On these occasions no impediment lessens the quickness of his pace,' Moore noted admiringly. 'He rides at full gallop, on the bad pavement of Constantinople, over every thing that presents itself.' (M, 51)

Whaley claimed that the Pasha did them the honour of half-rising to greet them, much to the astonishment of the courtiers present: 'this was considered as the greatest condescension possible on his part; as a Turk is scarcely ever known to rise to salute a Christian'. (W, 116) Whaley was flattered to be thought worthy of such an honour, but Hasan had his own reasons for meeting the westerners. The war with the Russians was not going well. Earlier that year the Captain Pasha had engaged the Russian fleet at Ochakov on the north coast of the Black Sea and over the course of several battles the Ottoman navy had suffered a heavy defeat.[21] It had returned from the Black Sea in November having lost five large warships and two frigates and the Pasha was now in search of replacements.[22] He addressed himself first of all to Finch, questioning him about the British Navy. The Pasha had just bought a frigate, the *Sybelle*, from a company of London merchants (M, 44) and may have been sounding out Finch on whether the *Pearl* was also available for purchase. Only afterwards did he turn his attention to the men who had accompanied the officers of the *Pearl*. 'He took notice of Mr. Whaley's whiskers, and mine, as we had begun to let them grow previous to our assuming the Turkish habit.' (M, 52) The Pasha was amused to learn that they were wearing beards and planning to put on Middle Eastern dress in anticipation of a trip to Jerusalem.

A small army of slaves – by Moore's count there were around 150 – served the guests sweetmeats, coffee and sherbet. 'The dresses of the slaves … were magnificent, their robes were of sattin richly embroidered' (M, 53) and Whaley was surprised to see that each was armed 'with a fine case of pistols, and a sabre large and sharp enough to cut off the head of an ox'. (W, 117) Ottoman slaves, at least those in the service of a great dignitary like the Captain Pasha, could attain far greater status than their European or American counterparts. They also offered the visitors costly Ottoman luxuries: rose water, aloes wood and frankincense. Grateful for the courteous reception, Whaley and Finch each presented their host with a fine spyglass.[23] (W, 116–17) After chatting with the Europeans for an hour, the Captain Pasha got up to take his leave. Whaley was greatly impressed by this mighty lord and he refers warmly to his benevolence and generosity. (W, 112–14) He and Moore had been fortunate to meet one of the Ottoman Empire's most respected and forward-thinking leaders. The encounter also boded well for their onward journey, as the Captain Pasha had offered to furnish them with letters of recommendation to the Ottoman governors in the lands through which they were to pass. Significantly, he also promised to get them a firman, an official letter from the Sultan that would, in theory at least, guarantee them safe passage in the Holy Land. True to his word, he later issued these documents through Ainslie, and for the duration of their journey to and from Jerusalem the travellers guarded them closely, particularly the firman, which Moore carried in an inner pocket 'for greater security'. (M, 308)

★★★

It was now Christmas. Although the weather had turned cold Whaley gave little thought to the festive season, immersed as he was in the distractions of the Ottoman capital. At the same time he was particularly fond of a long-standing seasonal pastime – hunting – and he, Moore and two of the *Pearl*'s officers made plans for an excursion to the Forest of Belgrade (Belgrat Ormanlý), around twelve miles north of Constantinople near the Black Sea.[24] The forest was said to offer excellent hunting and Ainslie's offer to let them use a country house he had there seemed too good to pass up.

On 26 December the small party left Constantinople and sailed up the Bosporus to Büyükdere, intending to walk from there to the village of Belgrat a few miles distant. When they disembarked they found that it had snowed heavily. In places their way was impeded by snowdrifts so high 'as to render the walk very unpleasant, and some of the passes very difficult' (M, 59), and by the time they finally reached Ainslie's house they were cold and exhausted. Fortunately the ambassador had laid in a good stock of wine and sent his servants ahead to prepare dinner and the party passed

1. Nos. 85 (left) and 86 St Stephen's Green, Dublin. Richard Chapel Whaley was living in No. 85 (then No. 75) when he built No. 86 (then No. 76) in the 1760s. The buildings are now known as Newman House and are part of University College Dublin (UCD Newman House).

2. Richard Chapel Whaley, his wife Anne Whaley and their seven children, c.1768. The infant Thomas Whaley is fourth from the right, playing with a rattle – foreshadowing his addiction to 'play', or gambling, later in life. Wax bas-relief portrait by Patrick Cunningham (Mervyn Whaley).

3. Staircase of No. 86 St Stephen's Green, Dublin. The ornate stuccowork evokes the splendour and privilege into which Thomas Whaley was born in 1765 (UCD Newman House).

4. Portrait of Thomas Whaley as a youth, probably done in 1782 on the eve of his departure on his grand tour in France (Mervyn Whaley).

5. Whaley's stepfather John Richardson. In 1784 Richardson had to go to London to rescue Whaley from the clutches of a gang of sharpers. Late-eighteenth-century portrait by unidentified artist. Oil on canvas 75.88 × 63.18cm (Museum of Fine Arts, Boston: 55.1001).

6. Published in *Town and Country Magazine* in 1789, this double portrait depicts Whaley ('The Jerusalem Pilgrim') alongside a courtesan ('The Fille de Chambre') who may be his mistress Harriet Heydon (image courtesy of the National Library of Ireland).

7. Leinster House, Dublin. Whaley claimed that while attending a dinner here he decided on whim to travel to Jerusalem. View by James Malton, 1792 (Library of Congress).

8. Major-General Charles O'Hara, acting governor of Gibraltar at the time of Whaley's visit in 1788 (New York Public Library).

9. Captain Hugh Moore of the Eighteenth Foot, an Irish infantry regiment stationed in Gibraltar. Moore agreed to join Whaley on the expedition to Jerusalem and was integral to its success. From Sir Edward Sullivan (ed.), *Buck Whaley's Memoirs* (London: Moring, 1906).

10. St Michael's Cave, Gibraltar, *c*.1800. Lit by fire, the cave looks eerie and atmospheric, as it was when Whaley visited it in 1788. From Cooper Willyams, *A voyage up the Mediterranean in His Majesty's ship the Swiftsure...* (London: J. White, 1802) (image courtesy of the National Library of Ireland).

11. At the end of his voyage across the Mediterranean, Whaley reached the great Levantine port of Smyrna (now Izmir). Detail from a 1779 view by N. Knop (Rijksmuseum, Amsterdam: SK-A-3947).

12. Constantinople (Istanbul), *c.*1770–80. The suburb of Galata looks across the inlet known as the Golden Horn to the Sultan's Palace. Hagia Sophia and Sultan Ahmet Mosque (the Blue Mosque) are on the right. Detail from a view by Antoine van der Steen (Rijksmuseum, Amsterdam: SK-A-2056).

13. The Comte de Choiseul-Gouffier, French ambassador to Constantinople, 1784–91. After attending a New Year's ball at Choiseul-Gouffier's palace Whaley suffered a relapse of fever that nearly killed him (Heidelberg University Library: Choiseul Gouffier, *Voyage pittoresque de la Grèce* (Paris: Blaise, 1822), frontispiece – CC-BY-SA 3.0).

14. Hasan Pasha of Algiers, Grand Admiral of the Ottoman navy, 1770–90. His expression confirms Whaley's description: 'he has a fine open manly countenance but strongly expressive of that ungovernable ferocity which manifests itself on certain occasions'. Portrait *c.*1779 by Pierre Duflos (author's collection).

a cheerful evening. The forest was said to teem with wild boar, woodcock and pheasant[25] and they set out the next morning hoping for a good day's sport. But with the snow remaining deep, almost all the animals seemed to have taken refuge and they saw only a few roe deer that fled before they could be shot. (M, 60) Regretfully they called off the expedition and returned to Constantinople. The hunting trip had been a failure, but it would have a worse consequence than simple disappointment.

At eleven o'clock that night Moore awoke in their room at the English Palace to find that Whaley was running a fever. He sent for Mr Franklin, the surgeon's mate of the *Pearl*, who realised that the patient's condition was deteriorating: 'in the course of an hour he found the fever augment rapidly, and attended with a strong delirium'. (M, 61) But the surgeon had a remedy in mind: James's Powder, a fever medicine that had been developed in the 1740s by the English physician Robert James. Then in widespread use in Britain and Ireland, the powder was praised for its effectiveness. 'At the first stage of a fever, whether inflammatory or putrid, the Powder is the best medicine that can be exhibited and, if continued every six hours, [it] will generally cure in a short time', an advertisement proclaimed confidently.[26] Franklin was of the same mind and he gave the patient several large doses of the medicine. At first it seemed that the treatment was working, as Whaley's delirium seemed to abate. However, James's Powder was actually a highly dangerous substance. Although it was 'all the rage among the well-to-do, who alone could afford' it, in fact it was little more than a quack remedy containing mercury, lime and other toxic substances. The writer Oliver Goldsmith had died in 1774 after consuming large quantities of the powder, a fact of which neither Franklin nor Moore seems to have been aware.[27] For Whaley the powder brought only a brief respite and in the long run served to intensify and prolong his illness. Over the days that followed Moore was worried to see his friend's condition deteriorate, with the symptoms changing alarmingly. 'This dreadfull disorder ... assumed various appearances, sometimes having an inflammatory, at others a putrid tendency.' (M, 61–2)

Over the final days of December Whaley was bedridden and incapacitated, but on New Year's Day he felt better and was able to rise from his sickbed. Though still in a feeble condition, he decided to accept an invitation from the French ambassador Choiseul-Gouffier (see Plate 13) to attend a dinner and ball at his palace that evening. Then 36, Choiseul-Gouffier had been France's ambassador to the Porte since 1784 and was known for his cool-headedness. On one occasion, during a meeting with the Captain Pasha, he had received an unexpected and frightening visitor:

> At a time when he was talking animatedly, he suddenly felt something warm and heavy resting on his lap. Looking down, he saw the great head of a fearsome lion showing its teeth. Fortunately he realised that any sudden movement would be fatal to him and, concealing his emotions, he put his hand on the animal's mane and stroked it saying: He is beautiful, very beautiful. However, the Captain Pasha, divided between fear and anger, called his servants and swore to annihilate those who had let in the inconvenient third party. When the lion had been taken away, Hassan congratulated the ambassador for his intrepid presence of mind …[28]

Unflappable as he was, one man got under Choiseul-Gouffier's skin: Sir Robert Ainslie. There was little love lost between the French and British ambassadors, largely because their governments had conflicting priorities and ambitions in the Ottoman Empire. Hoping to undermine the close ties between France and the Empire, Ainslie tried to thwart the Frenchman when possible. When Choiseul-Gouffier described the Ottoman occupation of Greece as 'the stupid Muhammadan resting on the ruins of Sparta and Athens' Ainslie brought the comment to the Grand Vizier's attention. He also interfered with French efforts to end the war by encouraging the Sultan to insist that Russia return the Crimea and Oczahov as part of any peace settlement, an unrealistic demand that probably only served to prolong the conflict.[29]

Choiseul-Gouffier's aversion to his British counterpart did not stop him inviting Ainslie's guests to his soiree. He had already met Whaley and knew about his extraordinary wager and no doubt he felt the colourful Irishman would enliven the gathering. At the dinner Whaley found that 'my Jerusalem expedition was the general topic of conversation, as it was my intention to set off on the Monday following'. (W, 139) He and Moore had in any case made themselves conspicuous by turning up decked out in the Arab clothes they planned to wear in the Holy Land. While Moore felt they looked 'very awkward in our new dress ... [which] afforded no small entertainment to our English friends of the frigate' (M, 115), Whaley found it so comfortable that he could not be persuaded to take it off and he was happy to be the centre of attention at the ball that followed. (W, 138–9) Charmed by the attentions of the ladies, he was unable to resist the temptation to dance 'in spite of my Arabian dress ... I am convinced that my figure and movements were truly awkward and ridiculous.' (W, 139) But the dance did more than simply make him look silly. Still in a weakened condition, he was incapable of exertion. By nine o'clock he felt so bad that he had to leave and return home.

In the morning Moore found to his dismay that his friend's fever had returned, accompanied by 'the most alarming symptoms of a putrid nature'. (M, 114) Over the next few days Whaley's condition deteriorated rapidly. Moore maintained a constant vigil at his bedside. The danger and hardship the two men had faced together on sea and land had created a powerful bond between them. 'I dont know any considerations can ... change the friend I have been so happy to gain in Mr. Whaley'[30] the army officer had declared a couple of weeks earlier. Despite his care and attention, by 5 January death was at Whaley's elbow and Moore prepared 'to perform the most distressing and truly painful office of friendship, which was to assist in the final arrangement of his worldly affairs'. (M, 114) Since embarking on his expedition Whaley had been mortally afraid of falling victim to disease. His fears had proved justified and now it seemed that he and his great adventure would expire on a sickbed in Constantinople.

8

PLAGUE AND PIRATES

'The plague has made some progress in this city and neighbourhood, particularly in the canal, the harbour, and the Ottoman fleet ... all agree, that the contagion already rages with violence at Scio, Stunchio, Chesme, Ipsura, besides many other islands.'[1] So wrote Sir Robert Ainslie from Constantinople in May 1788, some seven months before Whaley arrived in Constantinople. As Ainslie and everyone else in the Near East knew all too well plague, or the 'angel of death' as it was called, was an inescapable reality of everyday life. Caused by the bacterium *Yersinia pestis* and transmitted by rat-borne fleas, the virus had killed many thousands in Constantinople over the course of the eighteenth century.[2] Europeans believed that the Turks' limited medical knowledge, combined with their failure to isolate plague sufferers and fumigate the clothes and cushions of deceased victims, allowed the plague to spread unchecked. By contrast, Ainslie informed Whaley, the Europeans of Constantinople rarely died of the disease owing to the superior cleanliness of their habits. (W, 147–9) Even so, western medical knowledge of the causes of plague remained limited. The role played by vermin was not appreciated and many believed that disease emanated from poisonous vapours carried on the air from the east.[3] For his own part Whaley was convinced that the 'pestilential air of Asia and Syrria' had given rise to his 'putrid fever', which he believed to be 'little less than the native disorder the plague'.[4]

But was it really the plague that laid him low? While it is possible that Whaley contracted the virus before he went hunting, it does not appear to have been active in Constantinople in December 1788. Also, Whaley would not have been invited to attend Choiseul-Gouffier's ball had anyone thought he was infected with plague. More likely his exertions during the hunting trip to Belgrat Ormanlý brought on the illness. During the trek to Belgrat village he had suffered badly from 'the intense cold of the morning and the heat of the meridian sun, together with the fatigue of walking' (W, 139) and eaten snow to quench his thirst. (M, 61) This had only made him more parched, as his body expended water and energy to melt the snow. It seems that severe dehydration and exhaustion, rather than plague virus, brought on his fever, and his condition was then exacerbated by the misguided administration of James's Powder.

Plague or not, Whaley's illness seemed terminal and in the early days of 1789 he hovered between life and death. What his thoughts were at this time is anyone's guess, but no doubt his desire to win his bet strengthened his will to live and somehow, in this dark hour, he pulled through. On 6 January his condition improved and soon afterwards Moore 'had the satisfaction to hear him pronounced out of danger'. (M, 114) Although the officer modestly credited Franklin for the patient's recovery, his own efforts had played a more important part. Whaley later acknowledged as much: 'but for the uncommon kind attention and care of Captn. Moore … I really sh[oul]d. have been the joke of many of my sporting Jerusalem bettors'.[5] Thus far on his journey he had faced storms, dead calms, foreign fleets, hostile janissaries and an uncomfortable slog through the Turkish wilderness. Now he had been brought close to death by a dangerous illness – but he had survived, and he made plans to resume his journey almost immediately. (M, 115) Only one thing mattered: reaching Jerusalem and returning home to win his wager.

***

A large proportion of Whaley's memoirs – in Sullivan's edition a total of two chapters, or fifty-two pages – are given over to his stay in Constantinople. Much of this narrative describes the sights he claimed to have seen, including the Sultan's Palace, the Hagia Sophia, Sultan Achmet mosque, the Basilica Cistern, the ruins of the Hippodrome, Theodosius's Gate (the Golden Gate, a triumphal gate of three arches in Yedikule Fortress), the city walls, a coffee factory, the slave market, the grand bazaar and a building which served as a *hamam* or bathhouse for Ottoman ladies.

In reality he visited few, if any, of these places. Moore's journal makes no reference to any of them apart from the bazaars, which the pair spent a day or two exploring (M, 59) and the Hagia Sophia, which Moore visited on his own.[6] From their arrival in the city on 14 December to their departure for Belgrat Ormanlý twelve days later most of their time was taken up with wandering the streets of Pera and Galata, attending social events, shooting snipe and admiring barges and warships on the Bosporus. After he fell ill on 27 December Whaley's movements were severely restricted. Moore makes clear that he relinquished the city's attractions (with the exception of Hagia Sophia) during this time in order to care for his stricken friend. (M, 62–3) When he wrote his memoirs some years later Whaley was no doubt conscious that his illness had stopped him seeing as much of Constantinople as he would have liked. He felt the need to embellish his account by passing off as his own the experiences of others, in particular a Monsieur Grand, 'a young French man of observation' he and Moore had met. (M, 62) Grand had written a description of the city and its places of interest, which Moore transcribed and pasted into his journal.[7] There is little doubt that Whaley drew heavily on this when he was compiling his memoirs.[8]

Monsieur Grand was not the only traveller whose material Whaley lifted. His description of the ladies' *hamam*, which he claims to have had from an acquaintance, 'a Grecian beauty of fashion', is one of the racier moments of his narrative. The scenes inside the bathhouse are described in detail: 200 females were in attendance, 'some in the bath, others negligently lying on couches, while their young and beautiful slaves, disencumbered like their mistresses of all artificial covering, perfume and plait their hair. The news of the town and the daily petty occurrences, as may easily be imagined, furnish ample materials for mirth and conjectures of various kinds.' Whaley saw this as a time of relaxation for Ottoman women who, he believed, were 'continually kept in a state of dependence and slavery'. (W, 137) However, he did not receive this account from a 'Grecian beauty' or indeed anyone of his acquaintance. It is taken almost verbatim from Lady Mary Wortley Montagu's description of her visit to a *hamam* in Sofia in 1717.[9] Whaley also claims to have seen dervishes whirling and inflicting mortifications on themselves. (W, 121–3) There is no mention of this in Moore's journal and again Whaley may simply have had the account from someone else. Generally speaking his memoirs reflect his actual experiences, but for his touristic descriptions he frequently used external material, especially in the case of Constantinople.

Overall Whaley and Moore took an ambivalent view of Constantinople and the Ottomans. They were impressed by the city's magnificence and the nobility of great dignitaries like the Captain Pasha and they could not deny that the empire was great, stretching from northern Africa to the Caucasus. But like other westerners they believed most Ottomans to be proud, barbaric, wasteful, libidinous and mired in archaic practices. Most British and Anglo-Irish travellers regarded their home islands as the pinnacle of civilization, the successor to the fallen grandeur of antiquity. Convinced of their moral superiority, they believed that 'Britain was now the home of those values once nurtured by Rome.'[10] Whether or not this was true one thing was certain: the Ottoman Empire had passed its zenith and was embarking on a slow, unmistakable decline. In many outlying provinces the Sultan's injunctions no longer carried weight. Whaley and Moore had been delighted to obtain the prized firman from the Captain Pasha, but how much use would it be when they reached the Holy Land?

★★★

On 18 January 1789 Whaley, though still in 'a very enfeebled state', decided to resume his expedition. Unwilling to face another uncomfortable land journey he and Moore hired a sloop, the *Constantinople Packet*, to return them by sea to Smyrna. However, calm weather had set in and for a few days it was all but impossible to get out of the Bosporus. The delay frustrated Whaley, who hoped to find letters from home awaiting him on his return to Smyrna. He had now been away for four months and in that time had had no word from family or friends. Adrift in the strangeness of the Ottoman world, he and Moore would have cherished any news from their loved ones. It is almost possible to sense homesickness in Moore's reference to the 'boisterous gales, or chilling breezes' of his homeland, so different from 'the glassy surface of the deep', undisturbed by a breath of wind, where he now was. (M, 117) Finally, on the evening of 21 January, a light breeze sprang up. With every sail hoisted aloft, the *Constantinople Packet* glided into the west.

Whaley's detour to the Ottoman capital had come at a cost. He was travelling against medical advice and would not fully recover from his illness for another few months. This was unfortunate, because one of the most dangerous parts of the journey now lay before him. The *Constantinople Packet* was to follow a straightforward route through the Dardanelles and around the north-western tip of Turkey to the Gulf of Smyrna. However, the onward voyage to the Holy Land would bring them south into the Dodecanese before bearing east past Rhodes and Cyprus towards the Holy Land. Pirates had haunted these seas for centuries and Whaley knew that having reliable companions by his side could be the difference between success and failure, life and death. He had left Constantinople with four: Moore, Paulo, and a cousin of Paulo's who had joined them in order to make the pilgrimage to Jerusalem.

After three days at sea the *Constantinople Packet* entered the narrowest part of the Dardanelles, guarded by the fortresses of Kilitbahir and Çanakkale. Whaley and Moore studied the great strongholds dispassionately, considering their batteries to be too badly manned and situated to repel a naval assault. (W, 156; M, 123) They could not have anticipated that 126 years later, during the First World War, these fortresses would successfully defend the strait against an Anglo-French fleet, forcing the Allies to undertake the disastrous Gallipoli campaign. In January 1789 the guns were silent: the war between the Ottomans, the Russians and the Hapsburgs had not yet penetrated that region. All the same Moore was about to have a first-hand taste of its consequences. With the ship delayed at Çanakkale for a customs inspection he went ashore in search of supplies. As he wandered around the village he was surprised to come upon two despondent European men weighed down by heavy shackles. 'For the love of God milord,' one called out, 'relieve the miseries of two poor prisoners that the torture of war has cast into a barbarous country.' (M, 120) They were German soldiers from the Hapsburg army and had probably been captured some months before when the Ottomans routed the Hapsburgs at Slatina near Bucharest.[11] Initially they were imprisoned in Constantinople but when an outbreak of plague or fever killed most of the inmates they were relocated to the Dardanelles. Moore had the utmost sympathy for these prisoners of war, 'exposed in the streets to the insults of a cruel and barbarous people … weighed down by the galling shackles of bondage aggravated by the grievous indignities they are obliged unrevenged to submit to for having done their duty'. (M, 121–2) No doubt the fact that he himself was a soldier who might one day suffer such a fate intensified his feelings and his opprobrium towards the Turks. But he was unable to help the prisoners and their fate is lost to history.

On 27 January the *Constantinople Packet* reached the Gulf of Smyrna, where she was becalmed some nine miles from the city. Impatient to receive the letters they were sure awaited them in Smyrna, Whaley and Moore decided to row the remaining distance in a pilot boat. They were around halfway there when a familiar-looking merchant ship loomed ahead. It was the *London*, embarking for the coast of Syria, and it seemed they had caught her in the nick of time. Surely Captain Neil would tarry for a day or two until they had finished their business in Smyrna and take them with him? He would not. Almost two months had elapsed since they had left for Constantinople and Neil had grown tired of awaiting their return. He was keen to be on his way and not even Whaley's desperate offer of £500 could change his mind. They would have to find another vessel to bring them to the Holy Land.

Disappointed, they continued to Smyrna only to be met by another setback. The Lees informed them that although three English packet boats had landed at Smyrna since their departure, not one carried any letters for them. Whaley was devastated. He was still in a debilitated condition and during the passage through the Dardanelles he had unwisely treated a recurrence of his fever with another dose of James's Powder. Now the crushing disappointment of receiving no word from home caused him to relapse once again. Worried that this time the illness would prove fatal, Moore managed to get the surgeon of a British frigate, the *Andromache*, to treat him. Luckily this physician knew his business better than Mr Franklin and instead of resorting to the harmful James's Powder he treated Whaley using Peruvian bark. The remedy was effective and the patient began to recover.[12]

A day or two later Whaley was reunited with his original travelling companion. Having recovered from his rheumatism, James Willson had decided against accompanying his compatriots to Jerusalem as he was still keen to visit Constantinople. He remains an elusive character in the story of the expedition. Even if Willson had only thrown his lot in with Whaley in order to have a chance of going to the Ottoman capital, his business there remains a mystery. Now he was officially abandoning Whaley, but the younger man did not hold this against him and provided him with letters of introduction, presumably to Sir Robert Ainslie and other European dignitaries in Constantinople. We do not know how Willson fared there. He must eventually have made his way back to his family in Ireland, presumably before the death of his wife Sophia in 1791. Surviving her by over twenty years, he was well into his seventies when he died in 1812.[13]

Meanwhile Moore had found a ship to take them to the Holy Land: the *Heureuse Marie*, a sturdy, 300-ton French vessel with ample cabin space. (M, 127–8) She had been lying idle in the harbour for some time and her captain was keen to find some way of defraying the cost of a voyage back to Marseilles. With a minimum of fuss a deal was struck: in return for £160 the captain would bring the Irishmen to the Holy Land, wait until they had completed their business there, and then return with them to Marseilles. Whaley was now well enough to travel and at midnight on 2 February he and Moore bid farewell to their friends once more and boarded the *Heureuse Marie*.[14] They 'went immediately to bed hoping to find ourselves in the morning at a good distance from Smyrna'. (M, 131) But again the weather was unfavourable and three days later a storm forced the ship into the harbour of Fogia Nova (Yenifoca) north of the Gulf of Smyrna. The voyagers found themselves stranded there for five days until at last conditions improved. Eight days after embarking from Smyrna they had covered barely thirty miles. The experience brought home the absolute uncertainty of sea voyages in the Age of Sail: the dependence on the wind, the helplessness in the face of storms and calms, and the long, tedious days spent 'storm stayed' (M, 134) in ports one had had no desire to visit in the first place.

On 10 February they again commended themselves 'to the treacherous surface of the ocean'. (M, 134) Driven by a favourable wind the ship made good progress, passing the port of Çeşme where the Russians had destroyed the Ottoman fleet nineteen years before. Soon afterwards, off the island of Chios, Whaley and Moore noticed a number of small galleys, each crewed by around twenty men. Before they could give much thought to these strange vessels a powerful south-west wind sprang up, and the following morning they found themselves north of the Dodecanese. A gale was now blowing from the south and the captain had no option but to take refuge. He steered the *Heureuse Marie* towards the crescent-shaped island of Patmos and cast anchor in its deep, sheltered harbour. Whaley and Moore were marooned once again, but they would discover that this latest storm had been a blessing in disguise.

★★★

Inhabited mainly by Greek Orthodox Christians, Patmos was best known for its association with St John the Evangelist. The saint is said to have written the *Book of Revelation* in a cave on the island after he heard the voice of God coming from a fissure in the rock.[15] From the deck of the *Heureuse Marie* Whaley could see the walls of a great castle overlooking a town. This was the Monastery of St John, built 700 years earlier near the site of the cave and surrounded by powerful fortifications to protect its treasures, which included icons, silverware and jewels.[16] The following day he and Moore walked up the hill to see the place, passing along the way a seminary where Greek students were learning to read scriptures and write.[17] Unimpressed by this limited curriculum, Whaley again compared the eighteenth-century Greeks unfavourably with their ancient forebears. 'What a difference between this and the School of Athens! ... The present inhabitants are only distinguished for meanness, poverty and ignorance.' (W, 164) It was an uncharitable statement, but at least he was still capable of charitable acts. On seeing that one of the students, a young Cypriot, was trying to obtain food 'as the poor lad was nearly starving', he 'ordered him five hundred [ship's] biscuits'. (W, 164) It was simple fare but it would sustain the student for the duration of his stay on the island.

At the monastery a monk welcomed the travellers and brought them to a room where they saw a strange box 'covered with embroidered purple velvet, fastened on with many silver clasps'. (W, 165) Whaley was keen to have the box opened up, 'but my curiosity could not be gratified without a liberal donation on my part. I therefore opened my purse-strings, and a lusty friar opened the coffin; but not till after he had sprinkled a proper quantity of holy water, crossed himself several times, and prayed upwards of twenty minutes. He then presented to my view a most disgusting spectacle.' (W, 165) Inside the box or coffin there lay a skeleton, wisps of hair still clinging to its head. The people of the island venerated it as a great relic, the remains of one of the island's saints. Moore had nothing but disdain for this 'superstition': 'no sooner is the head of the corpse uncovered, than these ignorant wretches approach it in the most devout manner, and kissing it with a blind adoration, they suppose they are to receive from it the greatest benefits'. (M, 145) Whaley thought they revered the bones as those of the Evangelist himself, but in fact they are the relics of the monastery's founder, John Christodoulos.

With no change in the weather for several days, Whaley and Moore had to divert themselves as best they could on the barren island. On 15 February the wind turned fair, but the *Heureuse Marie*'s captain, 'instead of taking advantage of the first of the breeze', refused to sail '*jusqu'à ce que le vent seroit decidé*' ('until the wind be decided'). (M, 156) His Irish passengers were annoyed but the delay turned out to be auspicious. A local doctor, a Venetian named Giuseppe Gilly,[18] invited them to attend a ball at his house where he promised to introduce them to 'all the prettiest women of this island'. (W, 166) Whaley was not about to refuse the offer. He had already taken notice of the Patmian ladies, in particular a silversmith's wife whom he deemed 'the most beautiful woman I ever set my eyes on'. (W, 163) At Gilly's house he and Moore were happy to see her again and make the acquaintance of several other females. Moore admired the large tiffany turbans they wore, from which two large lapels 'reach down to the waist … and are really beautifull'. (M, 152) He was less taken with their trousers, 'which hang down about their ankles, and form, not only the most unbecoming, but the most *inconvenient part* of their dress'. (M, 153) But inconvenient in what way? Moore's use of italics is suggestive. He and Whaley decided to take some of the women aside for a purpose other than dancing:

> having recourse to our medical friend as interpreter, we retired from the noise of the crowd with a *chosen few*. We here amused ourselves for some time in a very satisfactory manner with the ladies whom,

on acc[oun]t of their beauty, we had invited to be of our party, and though they could not speak any language we understood, they found means to make us comprehend that the doctor was a faithful interpreter. (M, 151)

This passage in Moore's journal is followed by a few blank lines, as if to suggest that something else took place which was left unrecorded. At no point in either his narrative or Whaley's is there a direct reference to a sexual encounter.[19] But just because they did not write about sex does not mean they did not indulge in it. Although he was only 23, Whaley was already an accomplished seducer of women. Moore, too, was a hot-blooded young male and he was not hindered by the discretion that would have been necessary in other circumstances. Both he and Whaley knew they would not have many more chances to gratify their desires on the expedition and it seems they took full advantage of the opportunities that arose on Patmos.

The morning after the ball, with the wind holding fair, the *Heureuse Marie's* captain agreed to embark. Whaley regretted leaving the friendly island. He knew that inhabitants lived in daily fear of a threatening force, one he now risked meeting on the high seas. For centuries the pirates who roamed the Dodecanese and the eastern Mediterranean had targeted Patmos and its monastery,[20] and at the time of Whaley's visit a small pirate fleet was prowling the surrounding waters. The day before his arrival three boats, each crewed by around twenty 'desperate free booters', had landed on Patmos and robbed one of the inhabitants of 'the whole amount of the poor man's wealth'. (M, 147) The man had got off comparatively lightly, as the pirates were capable of much worse depredations. According to Moore,

These villains lurk under the shores of the different islands, and in the frequent calms which happen in these seas, they row out to vessels which have not then the power of escape. If the size [of] the ship they wish to capture is such as to make them suppose the enterprize dangerous, they mark the station she is in at sun set, and under cover of the night, they run along side her, and are actually on board before the unsuspecting crew are aware of their danger ... eager to ensure their prey, they slaughter without remorse every living object that presents itself. (M, 148)

These 'desperate, cruel, and unrelenting' pirates were said to torture and murder their captives, a fate which Whaley and Moore may have only narrowly avoided. (M, 148) They now realised that the galleys they had sighted off Chios had been pirate boats, and only for the powerful wind that had sprung up they would have been attacked. 'Had we been proceeding with the light breezes that generally blow here, we should in all probability have had a visit from them. Their efforts to capture so large a ship would doubtless have been desperate, their number would have inspired them with confidence, and the consequences might have been fatal.' (M, 149) The close shave gave the voyagers pause for thought. Before weighing anchor they readied their firearms and mounted four iron cannon on the deck.

As the *Heureuse Marie* got underway there was no sign of the pirates, and even the captain realised that it was time to make as much distance as possible. Sailing swiftly, the French ship had by evening almost cleared the Dodecanese. The following morning brought a squall that carried away the fore topsail and by the afternoon a south-wester was blowing. All that night they 'scudded before the wind' (M, 158) in the grip of thunder, lightning and heavy rain. On 19 February they saw the coast of Cyprus away to the east, but with the wind still blowing hard the captain was afraid to approach land. For two more days the ship floundered on the sea until at last the wind veered westerly and it was possible to try for the Holy Land.

Initially it had been Whaley's intention to make for Jaffa, as it was located only forty miles from Jerusalem, but now the captain preferred to head for Acre, which was closer and had better anchorage. This decision was not to be made lightly: Acre was the domain of the powerful Ottoman governor of Sidon, Ahmad Pasha, known as al-Jazzar ('the Butcher'). Whaley knew him well by reputation from the writings of Constantin de Volney and Francois Baron de Tott, who described him as a 'monster'.[21] Also, landing at Acre meant the travellers would have to undertake a longer and more dangerous overland trip to Jerusalem. Yet the turbulent sea that beset them on all sides made these considerations seem somehow less relevant and they agreed to head for Acre rather than remain 'tossed about ... at the mercy of the waves'. (M, 159)

Just after sunset on 22 February they cast anchor in the Bay of Caiffa a few miles south of Acre. Whaley must have sensed that he had reached a decisive moment in his story. Hitherto, the sacred city he was bound for had seemed almost like a concept, a fanciful notion that might not translate into reality. Some of his acquaintances had even joked that the place did not exist. Now, from the bay, he could see the lights of Caiffa and the hallowed slopes of Mount Carmel, said to have been the home of the prophet Elijah, just visible in the waning light. Somewhere out in the darkness, beyond miles of wild, barren and dangerous country, lay Jerusalem.

9

THE HOLY LAND

The Holy Land had long been one of the most turbulent regions in the Middle East. For millennia emperors, kings and sultans had fought over the small strip of land on the Mediterranean's south-eastern shores. More often than not Jerusalem, a city sacred to Jews, Christians and Muslims alike, had been at the epicentre of the conflict. When the Muslim warlord Khalid ibn al-Walid captured the city in AD 637 he converted the Church of the Holy Sepulchre, believed to be site of Christ's tomb, into a mosque. In 1095 Pope Urban II called for a holy war to win it back and for nearly two centuries the Crusaders battled the Muslims for control of the city, before finally conceding defeat at the end of the thirteenth century. In 1516 the Turks had conquered the Holy Land and since then Jerusalem had been part of the Ottoman Empire. At the end of the eighteenth century the population of the Holy Land stood somewhere between 200,000 and 300,000, most of whom were Sunni Muslims, though there were substantial Christian and Jewish minorities.[1] It was encompassed by the Ottoman provinces of Sidon and Damascus, which were divided into smaller administrative districts known as *sanjaq*s. Each *sanjaq* had a district-governor, who was represented in each large town by a *mutasallim*, or deputy-governor.[2] As he passed through the different territories Whaley would encounter not only with these administrators, but also various local clans such as the Jarrars, based around Jenin, and the Tuqans, who controlled the Nablus area.[3] The countryside was also populated by other volatile factions, in particular many Bedouin tribes. Although these desert nomads were renowned for their hospitality, some were known to waylay and rob travellers. Whaley hoped that the firman he had obtained from the Captain Pasha would ensure a smooth passage as far as the Ottoman officials were concerned. But many of the other groups were antagonistic to rule from Constantinople, and would have scant regard for the Sultan's missives.

Whether or not Whaley was aware of this, he and companions must have sensed that they were embarking on the most hazardous part of the entire expedition. Over a hundred miles of unpredictable and potentially hostile territory lay between them and Jerusalem. Whaley had been advised that to minimise the risk of being attacked he should proceed with as few attendants and as little baggage as possible and try to give the impression that he had no valuables. Under no circumstances was he to wear European dress. (W, 75) He had taken this counsel on board and by now he and Moore were reasonably confident they could pass for Arabs. Both of them had full beards and since the start of the year they had habitually worn Arab or Turkish clothes,[4] anticipating later travellers such as Johann Ludwig Burckhardt and T.E. Lawrence, both of whom roamed the Middle East in Arab dress. This attire was well suited for desert travel, consisting of a keffiyeh, a headscarf either wrapped into a turban or worn loose on the shoulders; a thwab, an ankle-length tunic with long sleeves; and a sleeveless cloak. Even still, Whaley must have known that he could not blend in completely. He was blue-eyed and fair skinned and any Arab who saw him up close would know at once that he was a westerner.[5]

Despite the dangers, Christian pilgrims continued to trickle into the Holy Land. In the sixteenth century Sultan Suleyman I (Suleyman the Magnificent) had officially recognised the Franciscan Order as the custodians of the Christian shrines of Nazareth, Jerusalem and Bethlehem and the Franciscans had established convents beside many of them.[6] The convents acted as hostelries for pilgrims and Whaley and Moore hoped to make use of them whenever possible. Just after midday on 23 February they disembarked from the *Heureuse Marie* and set out on the decisive leg of their expedition, but not before hearing a final word from the truculent captain. He would, he declared, wait only twelve days for them to complete their business in the Holy Land. If they were not back within that time he would immediately embark for Marseilles. At a stroke this ultimatum limited the time they had to get to Jerusalem and back, adding to the pressures of a journey they already anticipated would be difficult and dangerous. Angry as they must have been, the Irishmen gritted their teeth and consented: acquiescence was preferable to the effort and expense that finding another vessel would entail.

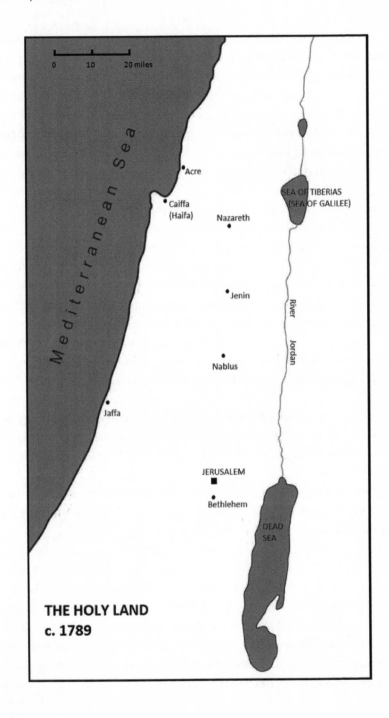

THE HOLY LAND
c. 1789

As they crossed the bay in a pilot boat they got a striking widescreen view of Acre. In the early eighteenth century the city had been 'mainly a pile of rubble and ruins' but construction programmes by Ahmad Pasha al-Jazzar and his predecessor Zahir al-Umar had transformed the place.[7] They could see the distinctive flat roof of al-Jazzar's palace and the striking dome and minaret of the great mosque he had erected a few years before.[8] They could also see the city walls, built from the remains of the Crusader fortifications that once stood there. After the Crusades Acre had stagnated for centuries, but in the 1700s the surging demand for cotton in Europe stimulated a dramatic revival in its fortunes. Highly profitable cotton exports had turned Acre, with a population of around 25,000, into one of the Levant's largest ports and, as at Smyrna, European merchants were heavily involved in the trade.[9] In theory Acre was subject to Ottoman rule, but its prosperity and the Porte's weakening authority meant that by 1789 the city was largely autonomous, with al-Jazzar conducting himself almost like an independent monarch.

On reaching the city the Irishmen and their companions found rudimentary accommodation at a khan that catered for European (mostly French) merchants and their families.[10] Mindful that their time was limited, they decided to leave for Nazareth in the morning and hired guards and mules (it seems that horses were unavailable) for the journey. They returned early to their room but sleep proved impossible as swarms of fleas descended and 'did not cease during the night to attack us on every side'.[11] (M, 171) After such an experience Whaley and Moore were glad the next morning to see the back of the place. They rendezvoused with their guards and muleteers, one of whom had agreed to act as a guide, and set out from Acre.

★★★

During their short time in Acre the Irishmen and their companions had managed to steer clear of al-Jazzar, but unbeknown to them he had heard of their arrival. Not long after they had left for Nazareth a message arrived at the khan to say that he wished to meet them. On learning that the Irishmen had already left the Pasha was disappointed but he expressed a desire to see them on their return. (M, 325) As they would discover, al-Jazzar's influence extended far beyond Acre and even to invoke his name was potentially dangerous. And yet something else had transpired that was more alarming than the inquiry from the notorious Butcher. Whaley and Moore did not know it, but despite their efforts to avoid attention someone in Acre had noted their passing and the fact that they were carrying no small amount of money.

The way to Nazareth led across the Plain of Acre, a stretch of rough lowland country. They had halted at a roadside fountain to eat breakfast when they noticed a group of men approaching. They were twelve in number and had dark wiry beards, bright eyes and strong, fine-boned faces. The travellers looked to their weapons but there was no need: the Bedouin tribesmen were only interested in their food. 'They did not wait for the ceremony of an invitation, but seated themselves along with us, and with great ease and familiarity began to help themselves to our fowls and mutton.' (M, 175) Whaley and Moore were afraid the unwelcome guests would consume all their provisions, if they did not plunder them outright. But as it turned out, the encounter was to their advantage. The Bedouin told them the road they were following led into a morass in which many travellers had perished. Their 'guide', it seemed, was worse than useless: 'on enquiring further into our conductor's knowledge of the road, we discovered that he had never been [to Nazareth] but once before and that he had almost entirely forgotten [the way]'. (M, 177) One of the Arabs offered to set them on the right road in exchange for a small sum. Whaley feared the man would lead them into a trap but Paulo, perhaps a better judge of Bedouin demeanour, assured him he would not be betrayed. With the new guide's help they corrected themselves, but then had to endure a gruelling ride through deep mud to get to the next village, Shefa-'Amr.[12]

The next day they reached Nazareth, believed by Christians to be where the archangel Gabriel announced the birth of Christ to the Virgin Mary. Since the Emperor Constantine's time there had been a church over the reputed site of the Annunciation.[13] It was now in the custody of the Franciscans,[14] and Whaley and his party hoped to be lodged in their convent as ordinary pilgrims. In fact none of them, bar Paulo's cousin, were pilgrims in the traditional sense but there seemed little point in letting the Franciscans know this. It was Lent and the friars were fasting, but they welcomed the travellers warmly and fed them an excellent meal in the convent's great hall.

Afterwards Whaley and Moore went to visit Ibrahim Abu Qalush, the deputy-governor or *mutasallim* who administered Nazareth on behalf of al-Jazzar. A Greek Orthodox Christian originally from Damascus, Ibrahim was a skilled military commander and could muster as many as 400 cavalrymen.[15] Whaley and Moore were surprised to find that he resided not in an impressive palace, but an old house that was falling into ruin. After greeting his visitors cordially, the *mutasallim* explained the reason for their dilapidated surroundings: his master al-Jazzar was an envious man and he wished to save 'both his head and wealth from the cruelty and avarice of his prince'. (W, 178) Nevertheless, Ibrahim was widely respected for his bravery and generosity[16] and he soon gave proof of this. As the Irishmen were about to take their leave the *mutasallim* offered to send one of his soldiers, a man named Mustafa, to escort them as far as Nablus, some forty miles distant. They accepted the offer gratefully: the muleteers and guards they had hired at Acre had no notion of the road. Ibrahim's soldier, on the other hand, was sharp-witted and knowledgeable and would prove an invaluable addition to the party.

★★★

They set off at five o'clock the next morning, accompanied by Mustafa and the prayers and good wishes of the monks. The next sizeable town on the road was Jenin, the hinterland of which was dominated by the powerful al-Jarrar clan. Backed by a peasant militia, the Jarrars possessed a formidable castle at Sanur a few miles south of Jenin.[17] They levied a tax on all pilgrims who passed through their lands and Whaley and the other non-Arabs would all be liable for this. However, Mustafa carried with him a letter from his master that he hoped would exempt them from payment. When they reached the town Mustafa went to negotiate with the Jarrar leader only to find that he completely dismissed Ibrahim Abu Qalush's letter. Soon they found themselves surrounded by several hundred irate townspeople loudly demanding payment. Only after a protracted negotiation did the Jarrars eventually reduce the amount of their demand and when the visitors had paid the sum they allowed them to proceed.[18] On the face of it, their disregard for Ibrahim's letter seemed strange. After all, the *mutasallim* of Nazareth was a subordinate of the terrible Ahmad Pasha al-Jazzar: surely they did not want to call the Butcher's wrath down upon themselves? But the Jarrars had little regard for al-Jazzar. Fiercely independent, they vigorously resisted any attempt to impose authority from outside. A year later al-Jazzar attacked them in Sanur Castle but despite a fifty-day siege and a heavy bombardment he was unable to make them submit.[19] The Jarrars also disregarded the Sultan's firman, which was logical enough: if they were prepared to defy al-Jazzar they were hardly going to acknowledge missives from far-off Constantinople.

The *mutasallim* of Jenin, Yusuf al-Jarrar, warned the travellers not to proceed further that evening as the country ahead was 'very dangerous, being in every part infested by robbers'. (M, 204) Whaley and Moore would have preferred to press on, but faced with this alarming intelligence they agreed to stay for the night and took a room at the local khan. They were surprised and somewhat put out to find that the *mutasallim* wished to join them for supper: they did not have much food and had been unable to get hold of any locally. After the meal they offered their guest wine, and finding that he liked it they 'took pleasure in filling him one tumbler after an other, which he emptied with the greatest avidity'.[20] After Yusuf had knocked back two quarts of wine it occurred to him that he had broken a strict law of Islam and might be caught in the act. 'Finding that these successive bumper's [i.e. tumblers] began to operate, and fearing a detection of this breach of his prophets precept, he at length thought it necessary to retire, and with some difficulty he attained the door, but not without many staggers'. (M, 208) In fact this was the second time that Whaley and Moore had plied an uninvited Muslim guest with alcohol. When they had been marooned in Yenifoca near Smyrna over two weeks before, a Turkish customs official had invited himself aboard the *Heureuse Marie* and sat down to dinner. They had given him strong ale, port, rum and lavender water (a perfume made from lavender, alcohol and ambergris) and returned him to the shore in a severely intoxicated state. On both occasions Whaley and Moore had been imposed on, and both times they decided it would be amusing to get their Muslim visitor drunk. But in Jenin, the prank had unfortunate consequences. Yusuf al-Jarrar retired to his seraglio, which was nearby, and soon afterwards they heard the sound of screaming. It seemed the drunken *mutasallim* had become violent and was beating his wives. (W, 187; M, 208) Perhaps somewhat guiltily, Whaley and Moore barricaded the door and went to sleep.

Early the next day the travellers were on horseback again. At one o'clock in the afternoon they reached Nablus. An attractive town situated in a narrow valley, it was mainly inhabited by Sunni Muslims, apart from a few hundred Greek Orthodox Christians and Samaritans.[21] Nablus was also an important centre of manufacture renowned for its olive oil soap, but these qualities were lost on the road-weary new arrivals, who regarded the place with indifference. To them it was like all other Ottoman towns: 'narrow, irregular, and dirty'. (M, 213) Their minds were on the forty miles of mountainous country that still lay between them and Jerusalem. This was shaping up to be the most dangerous part of the journey, as the road led through a wood where a hostile Arab tribe had recently taken up residence. (M, 219) Ibrahim's soldier Mustafa, who had proved to be a brave and valuable guide, was now due to leave them and return to Nazareth. Feeling it necessary to add a few more men to their party, they decided to approach the local *mutasallim* for assistance.

It turned out to be a wise decision: the *mutasallim* was a member of the powerful Tuqan clan, who enjoyed a good relationship with Ahmad Pasha al-Jazzar.[22] Happy to assist travellers bearing a letter from Ibrahim Abu Qalush, he promised to provide them with any guards they required. They also met an old sheikh who seemed to command great respect and authority. Probably a senior Tuqan, 'he was a man of great stature, and a venerable aspect, with a silver beard which descended on his breast'. (M, 216) Between them, the *mutasallim* and the old sheikh supplied four men to accompany the travellers, including two younger sheikhs. Seeing that the Europeans were still anxious about the size of their party, the old man laid his hand on his beard. 'If you fear any thing now,' he said, 'I will go with *this* to protect you, and with *it* I will answer for your safety.' (M,

217) This was a sacred oath indeed: to swear by one's beard amounted to swearing by one's manhood.[23]

The powerful statement greatly reassured the Irishmen. It remained now only to decide when they should leave Nablus. The dangerous wood lay several miles to the south. Judging it best to pass through it under cover of night, they spent a restless few hours at their lodgings before setting off at two o'clock in the morning. The party now numbered thirteen or fourteen, which Whaley considered to be 'equal to double that number of Arabs, as we were all well armed with guns, blunderbusses, and pistols'. (W, 189–90) The guards and guides rode at the front, followed by Whaley and Moore in the middle, with the servants and baggage bringing up the rear. Nervous and sleep-deprived, they rode more quickly than usual, keen to get through the wood before daybreak. By the time they reached it the first grey streaks of dawn were visible in the sky. The road led into a defile, enclosed on either side by 'a towering hill, cloathed with overhanging wood'. (M, 219) On the distant summits of the hills they could see the tents of the Bedouin, just about discernible in the gloaming. An ambush seemed possible at any minute. The path through the defile became narrower and the riders were obliged to go in single file, proceeding 'with as much expedition as the road would admit of, in profound silence'. (M, 219) Around half an hour later they emerged from the perilous wood and the guides pronounced them almost out of danger. Looking back, Whaley could still see the tents on the distant hilltops and knew how easy it would have been for the hostile Arabs to have attacked them.

The companions rode on through a barren and rocky country. There was hardly a blade of grass to be seen and soon the land became even more desolate. Composed of stacked layers of rock, the surrounding mountains looked strange and otherworldly:

> They seemed to be formed of regular strata of rocks, which were as exactly disposed as if they had been the work of art. In many places were small valley's, [sic] and the hills which encompassed them were composed of rocks thus arranged, which in many parts resembled a flight of stairs, and offered an easy ascent, and some of

the strata might be traced for the extent of a mile, stretching without interruption in regular courses along the face of the hills. (M, 221)

Cresting a hilltop they could see the distant blue of the Mediterranean away to the west. Some passing Arabs told them they were not far from Jerusalem and they sped on their weary mounts. Then, almost abruptly, the city appeared in the distance. A sketch done fifty years later by the Scottish artist David Roberts gives a sense of what they beheld: mighty walls enclosing buildings, domes and minarets that rose shimmering in the afternoon light (see Plate 15). The sight 'excited in our breasts emotions not to be described'. (W, 190)

It was the last day of February, over five months since Whaley had embarked from Dublin to begin his odyssey, and almost four since he and Moore had left Gibraltar. In that time he had sailed the length and breadth of the Mediterranean, surviving devastating storms and the hostile attentions of foreign fleets and bloodthirsty pirates. He had navigated the rain-soaked roads and swollen rivers of Turkey and nearly died of fever in Constantinople. Still weak from his ordeal, he had landed in Acre and covered over a hundred miles of harsh and intimidating territory. Now, at last, he had reached his goal, and he felt an extraordinary sense of achievement. Hitherto his life had been characterised by persistent misadventure, unbridled extravagance, calamitous losses and prodigious debt. Most of his schemes had come to nothing, and those who had bet against him getting to Jerusalem had been confident that a man such as he could never accomplish the long and difficult journey. He was about to prove them wrong, while also proving to himself that not every project he embarked on was doomed to failure. Yes, he could attain his objectives; yes, he could realise the grand plans of exploration and adventure he had nurtured since boyhood; and yes, he could become one of only a few of his generation to visit the sacred city. Though his loved ones were separated from him by interminable leagues of land and sea, he 'would that moment [have] give[n] half the world to have been able to communicate to them a knowledge of our situation'.[24] (W, 191) Whaley felt the anxiety and fatigue of the long night give way to feelings of triumph and gratitude:

the emotions that took possession of my heart beggar all the eloquence of language. I immediately alighted from my mule and after my transports had a little subsided, returned sincere thanks to providence, for our late arrival. I had not one friend in Ireland, the recollection of whom did not come in aid at this happy moment, to compleat the fulness of an overflowing heart. my inward exultation indeed was far superior to the proud feelings of the most renowned conqueror.[25]

His companions shared his jubilation. The four guards who had accompanied him from Nablus broke ranks suddenly and galloped ahead. 'Returning at full speed, they gave a war [w]hoop and as they passed, saluted us with their lances.' (M, 223) Moore, likewise, applauded his companion's success. He had not been present when the great wager was laid and it seems he had no money riding on it, but he 'could not, after having so long shared with him the fatigues and dangers of such an expedition, but feel on this occasion a sympathetic glow of satisfaction'. (M, 222)

Soon Whaley would be in Jerusalem, which countless pilgrims had visited before him. His 'pilgrimage' was different, though: he had only travelled there to win a bet, and to be able to say he had done so. As far as the spiritual side of things was concerned he was, ostensibly at least, indifferent. What he did not realise was that Jerusalem would affect him profoundly, awakening feelings and emotions that had long lain dormant.

10

JERUSALEM

'When we behold its walls levelled, its ditches filled up, and all its buildings embarrassed with ruins, we scarcely can believe we view that celebrated metropolis, which … for a time, resisted the arms of Rome herself; though, by a whimsical change of fortune, its ruins now receive her homage and reverence.'[1] Constantin de Volney's description of Jerusalem as it was in 1784 evokes the state of the city after many centuries of conflict and upheaval. Now into a third century of Ottoman rule, it was a mishmash of old crumbled remains, walls, towers, churches, convents, synagogues and mosques, all seemingly piled on top of one another. Whaley and Moore nevertheless discerned a latent splendour there: 'we arrived at Jerusalem, and were much surprized to find that ancient city, which had braved so many revolutions and been so often reduced to ruins by its barbarous conquerors, still retain the appearance of a place of importance, more than any other town we had seen in Asia'. (M, 223) History itself seeped from beneath the battered facades: Jerusalem had seen over four millennia of continuous occupation.

In that time it had become the holiest city on earth. Its walls enclose some of the world's most revered shrines, centres of pilgrimage for Christians, Jews and Muslims. To the east the skyline is dominated by the Temple Mount and the Dome of the Rock, sacred to Jews as the site of Solomon's Temple and to Muslims as the place where the Prophet Muhammad ascended to heaven. To the west stand the great bell tower and domes of the Church of the Holy Sepulchre, venerated by Christians as the site of Christ's tomb. Since early medieval times pilgrims had travelled from all over Christendom to worship there. In the eighteenth century the flow of Greek and Eastern Orthodox pilgrims was still steady but the number of Europeans making the trip had fallen dramatically.[2] But some westerners continued to visit Jerusalem, and the clergyman Richard Pococke (1738),[3] the Biblical scholar Charles Thompson (c.1740), the Swedish naturalist Fredrik Hasselquist (*c.*1750), the merchant Richard Tyron (1776) and Volney (1784) were among those who left accounts of their experiences.[4] They were not all motivated by religious conviction. When asked if his interest in the sacred places was inspired by devotion, Hasselquist 'answered without ambiguity, No'.[5]

Jerusalem's main Franciscan convent is the Convent of the Holy Land, also known as St Saviour's, sited in the Christian quarter near the Church of the Holy Sepulchre. Since its foundation in 1558 St Saviour's had grown into an extensive complex dominated by a large central building with huge doors.[6] While the friars always told the pilgrims who stayed with them that their lodgings were gratis, Volney believed 'it would be neither civil, nor very safe to depart without making an offering greatly exceeding the usual price of apartments'. On top of this the Franciscans earned 50,000 piastres (£5,000) annually from making and selling beads, crosses, scapulars and other religious items.[7] With this kind of income they did not lack for much and kept a plentiful table. Edward Daniel Clarke, who visited the convent in 1800, described them as 'the most corpulent friars we had ever seen'.[8] Whaley and his companions found little to complain about in the four nights they spent there. The friars served them tasty dishes including fricassée, roasted goat, boiled fowls, hashes, rice and wine. They warmed to the procurer, the monk in charge of provisioning, not least because of his generous sharing of 'a bottle of excellent old rum'. (M, 226a) As for the quality of the accommodation, the convent seemed luxurious and well furnished in comparison to the sort of lodgings normally found in the Ottoman provinces.[9]

After a short rest Whaley and Moore went to pay their respects to Jerusalem's *mutasallim* and present him with the Sultan's firman and the Captain Pasha's letter of recommendation.[10] The *mutasallim*, it turned out, was a close friend of the Captain Pasha and he assured the Europeans of his protection, even offering them the use of his horses and a guard of janissaries.[11] Eager for news of the war, he was pleased to hear of the Ottoman success against the Hapsburgs in the autumn of 1788. (M, 225) This was the first he had heard of events that had occurred some five months earlier: it could take a long time for news to penetrate the far reaches of the Ottoman Empire. From the window of the *mutasallim*'s reception room, the Irishmen had an excellent view of Jerusalem's grandest site: the Temple Mount. This great platform, surmounted by the Dome of the Rock and al-Aqsa Mosque, is the supposed site of the mysterious Temple of Solomon, said to have been built in the tenth century BC to house the Ark of the Covenant.[12] They knew this was the closest they would get to the reputed resting place of the fabled Ark, as any Christian who set foot on the Temple Mount had to convert to Islam under pain of death. The Sultan did occasionally grant firmans to travellers permitting them to walk on the Temple Mount, but on their arrival in Jerusalem they invariably declined to do so, realising that any trespass would 'excite the rage and indignation of the populace'. (M, 226a) It was a sign not only of how out of touch the Porte was with the Ottoman provinces, but also of how meaningless its decrees sometimes were there. Whaley, for his part, had no desire to enter the Temple Mount and risk 'the necessity of abjuring our Faith and of being banished for ever from our dear land of saints. An attempt to gratify our curiosity, under such a cruel alternative would have been the greatest madness.'[13] He and Moore took their leave. The next day they would visit the most sacred of all Christian shrines, the Holy Sepulchre itself.

★★★

The Church of the Holy Sepulchre, also known as the Temple of the Resurrection, is believed to be built over the hill where Jesus was crucified and the tomb in which he was laid. In the fourth century AD Helena, mother of the Roman Emperor Constantine I, discovered the site and had a martyrium built there. Around 1048 a great rotunda was erected around the tomb and when the Crusaders captured the Holy Sepulchre fifty-one years later, they extended the building to also take in the reputed site of the crucifixion. Accompanied by a guide and a janissary from St Saviour's, Whaley and Moore entered the church on the morning of 1 March. Whaley was awestruck by its size and magnificence and surprised to find it inhabited by many different Christian sects. Scores of Roman Catholic, Greek Orthodox and Armenian Christians lived within its walls, along with Copts, Ethiopians and Syriacs, and no love was lost between them. But Whaley and Moore were too preoccupied by their surroundings to pay much attention to this. They explored the church's many chapels and shrines by the flickering light of vast numbers of tapers and lamps. Bearded men and veiled women could be seen wandering through the great edifice, kneeling in chapels and standing rapt in adoration of shrines and monuments. In the south transept, near the Chapel of Adam, Whaley and Moore came upon two old tombs of white limestone, each with a marble slab and a gabled canopy. Latin inscriptions proclaimed them to be the mausoleums of Jerusalem's first Crusader rulers, Godfrey of Bouillon and his brother Baldwin I. Though the tombs had 'been long since violated, and the bodies carried away' (M, 230) the inscriptions remained to commemorate the deeds of the powerful Crusader warlords.[14] It is not clear whether Whaley knew what the words meant but he and Moore copied them down in full.[15] They were among the last visitors to do so, because twenty years later the tombs and inscriptions were gone. When the Church of the Holy Sepulchre was damaged by a fire in 1808 members of the Greek Orthodox community, keen to erase any evidence that the Latin Christians had once possessed the Holy Sepulchre, destroyed them.[16]

Leaving the tombs of the Crusader kings they went on to explore the rest of the church. Moore drew up a list of the shrines they visited, which Whaley later used in preparing his own account. (M, 233–53; W, 201–7) Those they saw included the Chapel of the Division of Robes, 'supposed by the superstitious to be … built on the spot where that division was made' (M, 234); the Altar of the Flagellation, thought to hold a piece of the pillar where Christ was scourged; the Chapel of the Cross, said to contain a fragment of the True Cross; and the Chapel of the Crucifixion. Finally they entered the massive domed rotunda, encircled by finely-wrought golden lamps, the gifts of Europe's Catholic monarchs. (M, 255) At its centre stood a small aedicule, a freestanding chapel within the church. Drawings by the artist Luigi Mayer, whom Whaley had met in Constantinople, depict the scenes around the aedicule: believers were on their knees everywhere, venerating the chapel with awestruck reverence (see Plates 16 and 17). This, they believed, was where Christ's body had been laid.[17] Whaley and Moore entered, descended some steps and found themselves in a cavern that had been hollowed out of the rock. Behind a small door lay two slabs of white marble, one on its side and the other placed over it as a lid. It was intensely hot: fifty silver lamps burned day and night in the small, confined space. (M, 253) As Whaley stood before the sacred tomb, he felt a strange thrill of emotion course through his body:

> I was struck with a kind of awe, on entering this holy shrine, and felt what I never had experienced before. nor could the most intrepid free thinker, have wholly divested himself of such sensations. I had been taught from my infancy, to believe [in] scriptures and was glad to find that at 23, I was not so abandoned as to have entirely forgotten these precepts of religion which my kind parents had so carefully instilled in my heart. I bowed with awful submission at the sacred monument of our blessed saviour, and felt an [sic] spirit of penitence and contrition more sincere than I had ever done before during my whole life.[18]

It is not, of course, uncommon for pilgrims visiting the Holy Sepulchre to feel this way.[19] What made Whaley's reaction so striking was that it was so unexpected. Throughout his life thus far, he had not shown much in the way of religious conviction and it was common knowledge that he had only set out for Jerusalem in order to win a bet.[20] His 'pilgrimage' had been inspired by devotion not to Christ but to 'the fickle goddess', Fortuna. But in the Holy Land he had felt a reawakening of religious conviction. In Nazareth he had been fascinated to visit the Church of the Annunciation, built on 'the very spot where the house of the Holy Virgin stood, and where she was visited by the angel' (W, 175), and as his journey continued he came to believe that a higher power was watching over him. On first sighting Jerusalem he had been overwhelmed with 'gratitude to that Providence which had protected us'. (W, 190–1) Now, at the Holy Sepulchre, he found himself 'so wrapt up in meditation that not a word was uttered'. (W, 201) Previously called a 'Jerusalem Pilgrim' in jest, he had become one in earnest.

Hugh Moore was also a Christian believer, though his faith was of a different character to Whaley's. While he consistently referred to

Jesus Christ as 'our Saviour', unlike Whaley he does not seem to have experienced any particular religious feelings at the Holy Sepulchre. If anything he maintained a healthy scepticism. When told that 'linen which had been stained with the blood of our Saviour' was found when the tomb was opened in 1555, he dismissed the informants as 'ridiculous and ignorant', which Whaley did not do. (M, 253) Moore was a practical, no-nonsense Presbyterian, deeply adverse to anything that smacked of religious 'superstition', and he disdained many of the devotional practices he saw going on around him. Some pilgrims were making hurried circuits of the Church, kneeling at each altar to pray and then kissing the stones: for Moore such behaviour was 'improper to the last degree'. (M, 256) He dismissed the traditions that were associated with the different shrines and chapels. Whaley, meanwhile, was inclined to take the same beliefs and traditions at face value. (M, 257)

Their contrasting dispositions were also evident over the following two days, which they spent wandering around Jerusalem and its environs 'in search of any thing that might be curious or interesting'. (M, 260) On 2 March they followed the Via Dolorosa, the supposed route Jesus took on his way to his crucifixion. Moore noted that the different sites along the route were connected with Christ's Passion only by reputation but Whaley had no such equivocation. At the Armenian Convent they saw a skull in a glass case that was 'said to be *certainly* the head of St John the Baptist, and … held in the highest veneration by the Catholicks'. (M, 263) Moore was sceptical of the claim but Whaley again felt religious feelings stirring within him:

> it is not my province, to investigate whether or no it be possible to preserve a head for near 1800 years. Faith and religious faith in particular carries with itself such soothing ideas, it creates in your bosom such comfortable and innocent sensations as must find a much greater stock of happiness than all the knowledge and self sufficiency of a sceptic philosopher can bestow.[21]

Perhaps he and Moore had an exchange of views, as Whaley declared he would rather be accused of superstition 'than for a moment to lose sight of those exalted views, and pleasing hopes, with which … the revealed truths of religion, fill the mind of man'. (W, 210) If they did discuss the matter they seem to have agreed to disagree.

The next day they visited the Citadel, the great castle adjoining the Jaffa Gate. Though said to have been built by King David in fact it has nothing to do with the Biblical monarch. Dating from the second century BC, the Citadel had been extensively reconstructed during the Middle Ages and in 1789 it was Jerusalem's principal Ottoman fortress. Its governor, who seemed in somewhat reduced circumstances, received his guests in an upper chamber furnished with 'coarse and inferior' carpets. Serving them coffee, pipes and lemonade, he told them that King David had kept his women in two of the adjoining rooms but as he was using them 'for the same *pleasing purpose*, we could not ask permission to enter, though we wished exceedingly to see their present inhabitants'. (M, 272) Since leaving Patmos two weeks before, neither Moore nor Whaley had had much contact with females and now they took more than a passing interest in the governor's cloistered women. While annoyed to be denied an opportunity of 'beholding, and admiring the choice of their females' they also felt genuine sympathy 'for the sufferings and confinement to which they have been universally subjected, a mode of treatment, that must totally suppress [their] spirit and vivacity'. (M, 269–70) Women, Moore insisted, were better off in Christian countries, where 'instead of walls and iron grates, the impulses of nature, controuled by religion only, and moderated by sentiment well refined, point out the virtuous path which they ought to pursue, where the weight they hold in the social scale, ensures them our respect'. (M, 270)

Moore's claim that Christian women had a better lot than their Ottoman counterparts is not entirely convincing. It is true that Ottoman females had few rights and freedoms: their appearance and movements were severely curtailed, their clothing obscured their bodies and rendered them virtually invisible, and in the eighteenth century new legislation 'drastically restricted the few remaining opportunities women still had to go out on to the streets and squares'. At the same time, eighteenth-century Ottoman women had rights that were denied to European females. Legally, they were allowed to retain control of their property after marriage. They were also able to take court cases, and women with access to money could initiate divorce proceedings against their husbands. Most European women did not have these rights. And while it was true that wealthy Muslim men had multiple wives, among the middle and lower classes monogamy was the norm.[22]

***

It was now the evening of 3 March and almost time for Whaley and Moore to set out on their return journey to Acre. The *Heureuse Marie* was due to weigh anchor in four days, barely sufficient time to make the journey, but there was still one place Whaley wanted to visit. He knew this would be his only chance to see Bethlehem, which lay just eight miles to the south. He and Moore decided to do the round trip the next day and then leave immediately for Acre, journeying through the night to make up the lost time.

They set out early in the morning, riding through a barren and hilly country, and reached Bethlehem at eleven o'clock. The town had been in decline for centuries and while it still had several thousand Christian inhabitants[23] most of them were destitute. Looking around them, Whaley and Moore saw scenes of poverty and 'ruinous huts, inhabited by wretches, who have scarcely rags sufficient to cover their nakedness'. (M, 281) The travellers made their way to Bethlehem's Franciscan Convent and the Church of the Nativity, which had undergone many alterations since it was first constructed in the fourth century.[24] Although centuries of dust, soot and rainwater had obscured the superb mosaics, and most of the marble that had covered the interior had been removed, the church still retained vestiges of its ancient splendour.[25] A small flight of steps led to the Grotto of the Nativity and there, beneath an altar, was the spot where the infant Jesus is believed to have lain. On viewing it Whaley must have felt his mission was at last accomplished. From a terrace on the roof of the convent he could see surrounding countryside stretching into the distance. In a straight line, Dublin was over 2,500 miles away. He was the furthest from home he had ever been, or ever would be, and he had tarried too long. With only three days left to cover the 120 miles that separated him from Acre he could delay no longer. Two hours later he and his party again reached Jerusalem and St Saviour's. Road-weary and dishevelled, they now faced an even longer journey, with scant time for rest.

Before Whaley and Moore left the convent they went to see the superior, whom they had not yet met.

> We found him leaning on a couch in his appartment, and he appeared to be a good deal oppressed by a feverish cold. He raised himself and received us politely. He was a man far advanced in years, yet he possessed a natural vivacity in his countenance, which a life of retirement had not entirely deprived him of, and which a long beard, with the cowl, and dismal Cordelier habit, could not altogether disguise. (M, 298–9)

The old monk questioned them 'particularly concerning the motives of our journey'. (M, 299) He may have realised that the two men were on no ordinary pilgrimage: possibly they had inadvertently dropped hints around the convent that the whole thing had been undertaken for a wager. Indeed, this was why they had visited him: Whaley needed proof that he had visited Jerusalem, 'a certificate, properly drawn up, signed and witnessed, stating the time of our arrival at Jerusalem ... to be produced to my friends in Ireland'. (W, 223) Whether or not the superior suspected the motive behind the request he made no further inquiry and issued the document.

Now they could take their leave. They gathered their companions – Paulo, the two Nablus sheikhs, and five guards and servants – and mounted on horses borrowed from the procurer they left Jerusalem for the last time. It was almost midnight on 4 March. Although they had had almost no sleep and were facing a long ride in the darkness, Whaley and Moore were in cheerful mood. The night was fine with a bright moon and they had each drunk half a bottle of wine, stowing another in their baggage for the road. But it was not the weather or the alcohol that lifted their spirits. Whaley knew he had 'accomplished what appeared to most of my friends insuperable'. (W, 225) He and Moore looked forward to a triumphant return home, 'having accomplished an enterprise which they supposed to be replete with a thousand dangers, the greater part of which existed only in their own imaginations'. (M, 301) But very real dangers still lay ahead of them, as they would discover on the road to Nablus.

11

FLIGHT

The country ahead was dark and desolate. The road led into the barren mountains, the land strewn everywhere with loose stones and devoid of vegetation other than the black patch of a fig tree plantation here and there. Despite the rough terrain they were able to ride at a relatively quick pace and by daybreak they had covered the most difficult section of country. After halting at a roadside spring to wash away the dust of the road and eat a breakfast of cold goat's meat they pressed on and by midday they were only three miles from Nablus. The country had become less mountainous, and instead of threatening rocky heights they now found themselves riding through open countryside and tracts of tilled land. In these settled surroundings, their judgement clouded perhaps by sleep deprivation, Whaley and Moore allowed their habitual vigilance to lapse. Ordinarily they would have zealously observed safety in numbers, but now they allowed the small party to fragment. Chatting idly, the two Irishmen drifted ahead with one of the Arab sheikhs, while the other sheikh, the servants, the guides and the baggage horses lagged somewhere between 200 yards and half a mile behind. There seemed to be no cause for alarm: they were now in the cultivated hinterland of Nablus, the town itself was only a short distance away and, in Moore's words, they were 'proceeding, as we imagined, in perfect security'. (M, 303)

There was movement on the road ahead. A group of men was approaching. They were Arabs, some twenty in number, with muskets slung on their backs and different kinds of pistols, sabres and short swords thrust inside their girdles. Even so, they did not seem hostile and even gave the Irishmen a friendly salute as they passed. Moore remarked that the country was so dangerous that even the peasants had to travel fully armed, but scarcely had the words left his mouth when an uproar from behind made him realise that these men were not peasants. They turned and saw with horror that the men were attacking their servants and guides while Paulo, standing at bay with a blunderbuss and pistol, shouted for them to return. Whaley and Moore readied their guns, galloped back down the road and would have opened fire on the assailants had the Arab sheikh not persuaded them 'to lay down our arms on our saddles, and to allow him to advance to settle the dispute'. (M, 304) The Irishmen acceded reluctantly and reined in their steeds, but if they expected the sheikh to mediate a peaceful resolution they were mistaken. 'When we came within about twelve paces of the *scene of action*, he made a signal that we should remain there, and he advanced, apparently in a violent passion, with his lance poised, and at full gallop, as if he meant to perforate and ride over every one who opposed him.' (M, 304)

The encounter had been going badly for Paulo's group. One of the attackers had shattered a baggage conductor's lance with a swing of his sabre and he and some of the others were beating the man severely. Whaley's sheikh galloped into the fray, leapt from his horse and drew his sword, but this ostentatious display seemed ineffectual. One of the robbers seized a baggage horse and began to drive it away. Six others approached the two Irishmen, levelled their muskets at them and ordered them to throw their guns to the ground. Shocked and incensed though they were, Whaley and Moore had already lowered their weapons and had little option but to comply. They railed at the sheikh for stopping them from firing when they had the chance but, as they would later find, this advice had saved their lives. Meanwhile the struggle between the other assailants and Whaley's servants continued to rage. Several blows were struck and swords were drawn on both sides. But even as the dispute threatened to escalate the robbers began to have second thoughts about the wisdom of their actions: perhaps they realised, or were told by their adversaries, that the foreigners were under the protection of Nablus's *mutasallim*. The swords were sheathed and the confrontation simmered down.[1] Whaley's guards pleaded that they be allowed to keep their remaining possessions and continue on their way. Surprisingly, the robbers agreed, so long as they could retain the baggage horse they had already taken. Whaley and Moore agreed readily to these relatively favourable terms. The baggage contained only their utensils and provisions, and in any event the captured horse and its burden were already half a mile away, being driven towards the mountains by the Arab who had seized it. Disengaging themselves, the Irishmen resumed the journey to Nablus with only their pride wounded.

Whaley had long feared that he would be waylaid on the roads of the Holy Land. Now that it had finally happened he was 'burning with stifled indignation'. (W, 226) He had not relished being held at gunpoint while the robbers beat his servants and made off with his horse and baggage. As they proceeded towards Nablus, the guards assured him that the *mutasallim* would soon arrange for the return of the stolen items. But this would prove more difficult than expected.

★★★

The view of Nablus in David Roberts's 1839 sketch (see Plate 18) is probably not much different from how the town appeared at the time of Whaley's visit, even allowing for the passage of fifty years. Sheltered in a narrow, fertile valley it was an idyllic-looking place, with white houses, domes and minarets nestled amid groves of trees and rich foliage. Water flowed everywhere in Nablus, with twenty-two springs feeding public fountains, mosques and commercial establishments as well as private homes and gardens. From medieval times to the nineteenth century, travellers were entranced by the place. 'Its beauty can hardly be exaggerated,' wrote one visitor in 1882. 'Clusters of white-roofed houses nestling in the bosom of a mass of trees, olive, palm, orange, apricot, and many another varying the carpet with every shade of green ... There is a softness in the colouring, a rich blue haze from the many springs and streamlets, which mellows every hard outline.'[2] But the picturesque setting was far from Whaley's mind as he covered the final dusty stretch of road. Ahead he could see the two great peaks that overlooked the town on either side: Mount Ebal, the mountain of curses, and Mount Gerizim, the mountain of blessings. Which would bestow its influence on him?

They found the *mutasallim* of Nablus sitting on his terrace. As a member of the powerful Tuqan clan that controlled the town and its hinterland, he commanded considerable respect and influence and during the Irishmen's previous visit to Nablus he had shown that he was disposed to assist them by sending four men to escort them to Jerusalem. The news that they had been attacked in his jurisdiction caused him considerable alarm: 'he seemed struck with astonishment [and] changed colour several times'.[3] (W, 228) The *mutasallim* was answerable to Ahmad Pasha al-Jazzar, and if his master learned that men travelling under the Sultan's protection had been robbed the consequences would be grave indeed, and not just for the robbers. To underline the point Moore produced the firman, the official Ottoman letter that guaranteed them safe passage in the Holy Land. The *mutasallim* examined the document carefully. He knew that the Arabs who had attacked Whaley's party were Bedouin. Although these desert nomads lived in largely independent tribal groups, the *mutasallim* had a sort of loose authority over the local Bedouin sheikhs and he ordered that these men assemble immediately at his palace.

The *mutasallim* told Whaley and Moore they had been right not to use their guns during the encounter. 'I thanck [*sic*] my prophet,' he said, 'and so you should yours, for having inspired you to act so wisely.'[4] Had they shot any of the robbers 'our lives were the only attonement that would have been accepted by the friends of our opponents, for having drawn the blood of their relations' (M, 309) and the *mutasallim* would have been unable to protect them. In answer to his summons, thirteen of the local sheikhs presented themselves at his palace. The *mutasallim* informed them that this ambush had been particularly ill-advised, for these foreigners were friends of the Sultan himself. 'He concluded by assuring the Shaiks that total destruction awaited their town if our goods were [not] found and restored before sunset ... [al-Jazzar] would be glad of this pretext to send an army of twenty thousand men to pillage and lay waste the town and neighbourhood.' (W, 228) This persuasive speech had the desired effect. The mere mention of the Butcher's name was enough to send the sheikhs hurrying into the wilderness in search of the robbers and their plunder.

It seemed that things were looking up for the Irishmen. Conscious that they had just two days to get to Acre they proposed to press on immediately, leaving their servants behind to wait for the return of the baggage. But the *mutasallim* insisted that if they left before the sheikhs returned the robbers would undoubtedly try to kill them to stop them reporting the incident to al-Jazzar. Whaley and Moore realised that the threat of the Butcher's vengeance was a poisoned chalice that served only to delay and endanger them. With no option but to stay in Nablus for the night they returned to the house of the Greek with whom they had previously lodged and went to sleep.

The next morning they found themselves under virtual house arrest. The *mutasallim*, afraid that al-Jazzar 'would punish him, or perhaps lay the entire district under contribution' (M, 311), refused to allow them to leave until the sheikhs returned. They waited impatiently, hoping to get shut of Nablus that morning, but it was not until two o'clock in the afternoon that the sheikhs arrived back. They had found the bandits in the mountains and persuaded them to hand over the horse and baggage. The robbers had admitted that they had been tracking Whaley's party for days, having 'received the most correct information concerning us, from Acre, the day after our landing there … they said they were not ready to intercept us as we were going to Jerusalem, but they acknowledged that they had been three days in expectation of our return; and determined to stop us, as they heard we were rich'. (M, 312) And yet, Whaley and Moore were surprised to discover, the baggage was more or less intact: even their silver knives and forks had been left undisturbed. They soon realised why: their Muslim attackers had developed an aversion to the booty after finding a cold ham among the provisions.[5] Whaley was amazed that they were so scrupulous about a matter of religion when they 'deemed it no crime to plunder us, or even to take away our lives, if they could have done it with impunity'. (W, 230) Moore believed the entire country to be 'peopled by villains who have reduced depredation to a system, and who exist on the spoils of strangers, whose bad fortune leads them within their grasp'. (M, 315) Such an assessment, while understandable in the circumstances, was neither fair nor accurate. While some Bedouin, 'with limited resources and struggling to survive in a harsh environment', did have a reputation for ambush and robbery, they were in a minority.[6] Most Bedouin were peaceful and generous. Whaley and his companions had encountered groups of armed nomads on several occasions and only once had they proved to be hostile. Whaley himself later acknowledged that they were 'neither cruel or wicked: on the contrary they are known to exercise the most generous acts of hospitality and benevolence to those who fall in their way, and whose distress seems to claim their protection'. (W, 235) Nor did they live completely outside of settled society, as many intermingled with peasants and traded with the towns. 'If one puts aside spectacular accounts of a few bedouin raids and focuses on the routines of everyday life, mutual dependency and cooperation become clear.'[7]

Tense from the ambush and forced detention they had undergone, and unnerved to discover that they had been shadowed since their arrival in Acre, Whaley and Moore were less inclined to take a balanced view of affairs. They were determined to plan 'the best mode of making our escape from this diabolical country' (W, 230). But to do so seemed far from straightforward.

> Many, and widely differing from each other, were the plans suggested to us by the people we consulted, and we at length found their counsel by far more perplexing than satisfactory … we saw it could only serve to magnify our apprehensions … We also saw that if any design had been favoured of attacking us a second time, from the supposition of our having money, every moment of delay here, afforded time for the proper arrangement of their plan, and for strengthening their party … (M, 312–13)

Believing that any plan they divulged would be communicated to the hostile parties that lay in wait, Whaley and Moore let it be known that they intended to leave Nablus at dawn the next day. Having hired a few more guards and guides to accompany them they went to their lodgings and slept. At ten o'clock that night Paulo woke them. 'Finding that the town was quiet and the people had all retired for the night, we immediately got up, went out with two of our people to the stable, got out our horses, awoke the remainder of our escort, and making them mount instantly, we resolved on a precipitate retreat.' (M, 313–14) For a second time they left Nablus under cover of night and as silently as possible. They now had nine guards and guides with them, but they did not trust the men they had hired. Would they lead them into a trap?

★★★

As midnight approached clouds massed overhead and pitch darkness descended. At the head of the small troop was a grey mule belonging to one of the guides and Whaley and Moore followed it doggedly, but when it started to rain heavily all chance of keeping to the path was lost. They found themselves straying hopelessly in the trackless wild: 'we wandered about for a length of time, sometimes among corn, and sometimes among stones and brushwood, where our horses could with difficulty keep their feet'. (M, 314) With a sense of mounting crisis, the Irishmen began to worry that they would stumble into an Arab encampment and have 'the entire horde to combat'. (M, 314) When one of the guides went missing Whaley feared the worst. His frayed temper snapped and he threatened to blow another guide's brains out. The man protested his innocence and 'swore that he would sooner lose his head than betray us', but 'the darkness seemed still to increase, and for some time we remained in a dreadful sort of suspense'. (W, 232)

The night wore on, with the pitch black and rain-sodden march threatening every moment to terminate in disaster. Then they heard the barking of dogs. They had arrived at a village, where the guides proposed they take shelter for a couple of hours. Whaley and Moore were unwilling to tarry in what they believed to be a hostile area but the return of the missing guide, who had lost his way after falling into a pool of water, reassured them somewhat. They took shelter in a rudimentary shack and though now completely soaked, sheer fatigue overcame their discomfort and they flung themselves on the floor to sleep. When they awoke some hours later they realised that somehow they had proceeded more or less in the right direction and were now within three miles of Jenin. Anxious to avoid another meeting with the troublesome Jarrars they pushed on through the town while its inhabitants were still asleep. By nine in the morning they had reached the vicinity of Nazareth. Within the jurisdiction of the friendly *mutasallim* Ibrahim Abu Qalush the Irishmen felt safer. They dismissed the men they had hired at Nablus and continued accompanied only by Paulo and one or two guides.

As they approached Nazareth an extraordinary cavalcade appeared on the road ahead. It consisted of around two hundred men and women, many mounted on asses, making in Moore's view 'the most ludicrous exhibition that can be conceived'. (M, 316) They were Christian pilgrims on their way from Constantinople to Jerusalem and were distressed to learn that Whaley's party had been attacked near Nablus. 'The poor wretches appeared absolutely terrified at the idea of what they were to encounter.' (M, 316) Hardened by their experiences, Moore and Whaley viewed the new arrivals with some disdain, having forgotten their own blunderings when they arrived in Smyrna some three months before. Leaving the ragtag pilgrimage behind they rode on into Nazareth. It was 7 March, the day on which the *Heureuse Marie* was due to sail, but the Irishmen had now all but abandoned their efforts to get to Acre in time. The port was still over twenty miles distant and after two and a half days of gruelling travel and intermittent sleep they were utterly exhausted. Returning to the Convent of the Annunciation, where the monks again received them with kindness, they retired to their chamber and went to sleep.

The two days since their departure from Jerusalem had probably been the most dangerous of the entire expedition. Whaley and Moore could easily have been shot during the battle with the robbers or, had they themselves injured anyone, ruthlessly hunted down by their assailants' relatives. On reaching Nablus they had suffered the ordeal of forced detention and the anxiety of fearing they would be attacked as soon as they resumed their journey. Their nocturnal flight through the rain-sodden wilderness had been an arduous, intimidating and nerve-wracking experience. The shadow of one man had lain over the entire episode. Neither Whaley nor Moore had met or even seen Ahmad Pasha al-Jazzar, but since arriving in the Holy Land they had heard his name time and again. The threat of his awful vengeance had ensured the recovery of the stolen baggage, but it had also put Whaley and Moore in danger: some would have seen them dead rather than have them report the incident to the dreaded governor of Sidon. The Irishmen did not yet know it, but al-Jazzar himself was already well aware that they were in the Holy Land. When they returned to Acre they would be taken to his palace, and there they would come face to face with the Butcher himself.

12

THE BUTCHER

After they had rested Whaley and Moore received a visit from Ibrahim Abu Qalush. Over the course of a two-hour chat on different topics the Irishmen were again impressed by the *mutasallim*'s judgement and insight. Horses were one of the points of discussion. As a cavalry commander Qalush knew a fair bit about this subject. He would have been aware that for many years Ottoman concepts concerning horses and their relationship with humans had influenced equestrian culture in Britain and Ireland, where a horse could only be considered a thoroughbred if its bloodline was traceable to a select number of Arabian specimens.[1] When Whaley mentioned that he would like to bring a stallion back to Europe, Qalush suggested he approach Ahmad Pasha al-Jazzar. His master, he believed, would probably be pleased to receive the foreigners and might even present Whaley with a horse from his stud, were he made aware that he was seeking one. But, the *mutasallim* warned, the Butcher was not to be dealt with lightly. He was avaricious, cruel and despotic and only by raising and contributing huge taxes had Ibrahim Abu Qalush managed thus far to evade his wrath.

Though they had missed their deadline Whaley and Moore still hoped to rejoin the *Heureuse Marie*. Optimistic that the captain would give them one or two days' grace before he weighed anchor, they set out for Acre early the next morning. Before they departed the Guardian of the Convent, Brother Archangel, presented them with a certificate confirming they had visited Nazareth, another valuable proof that Whaley had been to the Holy Land (see Plate 19).[2] Guided by the convent's procurer, they returned by a shorter, more efficient route than the one followed on the outward journey. As they crossed the Plain of Acre they noticed a long line of horses accompanied by their Arab handlers. They turned out to be steeds from al-Jazzar's stud and Moore declared them to be 'the most beautiful animals I had ever beheld'. (M, 324) The Pasha was said to possess as many as 500 horses from various parts of Asia and Africa. Whether he would allow Whaley to have one was another matter.

They rode on into Acre, and though a day late for their rendezvous with the *Heureuse Marie* they were pleased to find that the French ship had not yet departed. The captain's mood may have softened during their absence as he evidently permitted them to finish their business in the town before setting sail. It now remained to be seen if al-Jazzar would grant them an audience. The signs were that he would. On returning to the European khan they learned from a French merchant named Megatt about al-Jazzar's inquiry following their departure from Acre twelve days previously. He had wanted to know if they had any western firearms they were prepared to part with. Whaley had with him a sort of early revolver that could fire eight balls one after the other[3] and Megatt believed that al-Jazzar might well part with a horse if presented with this unusual weapon. In the morning they sent to the Pasha requesting a meeting but a reply came that he would be unable to see them until the following day. The delay was unwelcome: at the khan they had been allocated the same room they previously occupied and 'soon perceived that the stock of fleas had not diminished, as we could discern millions of them performing their gambols on every part of our beds'. (M, 326) After spending another night at the insects' mercy they rose from what Moore called 'the worst beds we had ever lain in' (M, 328) and sent again to al-Jazzar, who agreed to receive them at two o'clock. Accompanied by Megatt, Whaley and Moore went to the palace entrance at the appointed hour only to find themselves kept waiting indefinitely, so much so that they began to suspect that the Butcher was insulting them. They considered leaving 'without being gratified by a sight of the tyrant' (M, 329) but Megatt, conscious that al-Jazzar would not be impressed by this, convinced them to stay put.

★★★

Ahmad Pasha al-Jazzar had had an extraordinary career, having risen from poverty to become the most feared ruler in all of Syria and the Holy Land.[4] Born in Bosnia in the late 1730s he had left his homeland aged 16 or 17, never to return. According to some sources he fled after attempting to rape his sister-in-law or 'stabbing a woman who did not submit to his wishes'.[5] Somehow, maybe by selling himself into slavery, he entered the service of Ali Pasha, the Ottoman governor of Egypt. In Egypt Ahmad served several Mamluk[6] masters and soon got a reputation for ferocity. When the local Bedouin killed one of his masters he avenged him by ambushing and killing some seventy Bedouin, after which the Mamluks dubbed him al-Jazzar, 'the Butcher'. However, after coming under suspicion of disloyalty to the Mamluk leader Ali Bey al-Kabir, he had to flee Egypt. In 1770 he was in Lebanon in such poverty that he had to sell the clothes off his back to get food, but from this nadir began a meteoric rise. Al-Jazzar made his way to Damascus, where he entered the service of the local Ottoman governor, Uthman Bey. With the Russo-Ottoman War of 1768–74 underway, al-Jazzar was given the task of defending Beirut against the Russian fleet.[7] He took the opportunity to establish a personal power base at Beirut, showing himself to be an efficient and ambitious Ottoman administrator. He rose steadily in the ranks until in 1776 he became governor of the province of Sidon, which included Acre and much of the Holy Land.

As governor of Sidon he acquired a reputation for ruthlessness and brutality. In the opinion of one historian 'just about anyone who succeeded al-Jazzar was bound to look good in comparison ... not a single contemporary chronicler had a kind remark to make about this Bosnian mercenary turned pasha'.[8] Certainly, al-Jazzar had a strong capacity for savagery and European travellers criticised him harshly.[9] Constantin de Volney described him as ruthless, vain and avaricious, but his sketch was mild compared to that of the Baron de Tott, who claimed that when defending Beirut from the Russians he had 'immured alive a great number of Greeks, when he rebuilt the walls of Barut [Beirut] ... The heads of these miserable victims, which the Butcher had left out, in order to enjoy their tortures, are still to be seen.'[10] Whaley had read both Volney and de Tott and their narratives would have coloured his opinion of al-Jazzar before he even set foot in the Holy Land. Ibrahim Abu Qalush and the European merchants of Acre had told him more tales of al-Jazzar's brutality. The merchants had related in graphic detail an atrocity they claimed the Pasha had committed some years earlier. Al-Jazzar had long been involved in intermittent hostilities with the Druze factions of Mount Lebanon, and the merchants claimed that when suppressing one of their rebellions he had persuaded over 1,000 men, women and children to surrender on a promise of mercy. Then he had them brought to Acre and, 'without distinction of age or sex, butchered in cold blood'. (W, 170) The merchants, who had been forced to watch, were dismayed to see a beautiful young girl brought forward to be executed. Ignoring their pleas for mercy, al-Jazzar had her beheaded, showing 'particular signs of satisfaction when she suffered'. (M, 336) He then packed the victims' heads in boxes and sent them to Constantinople as a present for the Sultan.[11]

Despite these tales of brutality and massacre, the governor of Sidon may not have been quite as bad as described. Europeans were fond of portraying al-Jazzar as the incarnation of the 'despotic' Ottoman Empire and for them 'his picture, as the tyrant par excellence, could not be drawn in colors too dark or bloody'.[12] There do not seem to be any independent accounts to verify the story of the mass execution of the prisoners from Mount Lebanon and it may be an invention. Meanwhile, some Arab chroniclers offered a more balanced and sympathetic account of al-Jazzar, highlighting his capacity for loyalty and charity. Although Europeans believed that the title of 'Butcher' denoted savagery and malice, in fact it was 'meant as a term of respect and did not reflect a perception of general cruelty of character'.[13] Also, those who had the opportunity to observe al-Jazzar over a sustained period understood that he had good points as well as bad. Jean-Pierre Renaudot, who served as French vice-consul at Acre in the 1780s, saw him as 'a mixture of vice and virtue … He wants to lord it over all, to judge everything, and his judgements always reflect the state of his soul. He is sometimes just, great and generous, at other times furious and bloody. He stabs with one hand and gives his own blood with the other.'[14] But would Whaley find the Pasha in a generous or a furious mood?

★★★

A dragoman or interpreter came with the news that the Pasha was at last ready to receive them. The visitors were brought through a narrow passage into a sort of courtyard. The area was being turned into a garden and they could see many slaves cultivating the earth: 'all appeared very attentive to what they were doing, and seldom ventured to raise their eyes from the ground'. (W, 170–1) Nearby, under the shade of an orange tree, sat the man they had come to see: the Butcher himself. As they approached 'he raised his eyes and saluted us with his hand. We returned his compliment, and he desired we should sit down beside him.'[15] (M, 330)

Al-Jazzar was clothed in two magnificent black pelices (furred outer garments), an embroidered undergarment and a turban. In his girdle he carried pistols and a short sword, the handle of which was studded with large diamonds. He was known to apologise for this ostentatious weapon, 'saying it was a badge of office ... and therefore could not be laid aside'.[16] Then around 50 years old, he was 5 feet 10 inches in height and built 'like an Hercules'. To his visitors he seemed to have the face 'of an assassin, his neck short, his eyes black, small, and sunk in his head ... his features most strongly expressive of the barbarous ferocity of his mind'. (M, 334) Certainly, the Pasha had a steely and threatening countenance. In a 1775 portrait by Thomas Aldridge he stares balefully from the canvas with heavy-lidded eyes (see Plate 21). In another representation, dating from around 1800, al-Jazzar looks fierce and implacable as a condemned criminal kneels before him (see Plate 22).

Al-Jazzar called for coffee and sweetmeats to be served and then dismissed all his slaves with a perfunctory 'begone'. As they departed Whaley and Moore may have noticed that some were missing an eye, an ear or a nose: the Pasha was fond of punishing his underlings by disfiguring them in this way. With Megatt taking the role of interpreter, al-Jazzar turned to his visitors and commenced an extraordinary address. 'You are Englishmen,' he began, unconcerned by the technicality of whether they were Irish, English or Anglo-Irish. Probably Whaley and Moore had announced themselves as Englishmen and their host took this at face value. 'The English are a brave people,' he went on, 'and never lie, I therefore love them; as a proof of which I have done you the honour to make you seat yourselves beside me.' He said he had dismissed his slaves so that he might be at liberty to converse freely with you, without the restraint I should feel before other witnesses. Know that you sit beside the greatest and bravest man in this world. All Europe will wonder at this mark of my regard, and will envy you the honour of this interview, all the world will be informed of the honour you have had to sit with me under this tree. (quoted, M, 330)

The stranger, al-Jazzar insisted, would always find a protector in him. (W, 169) The claim had a ring of truth: as Whaley and Moore were all too aware he was reputed to inflict terrible vengeance on any who attacked foreigners in his dominions. While he was speaking, the Pasha seemed to shake off his grim demeanour. He was strangely animated and 'even condescended to smile'. (M, 330)

The conversation turned to politics. Al-Jazzar complained that the Russo-Ottoman War was 'ruining' his country. It was also hindering the Porte's efforts to govern the Ottoman provinces,[17] and while al-Jazzar remained loyal he had grown so powerful that he did not mind openly criticising the Sultan and his ministers. In an extraordinary outburst he informed his guests that the Sultan was a 'fool', the Grand Vizier 'a great rogue' and the Captain Pasha 'an arrant coward'. 'I despise them all,' he declared. 'I am a greater man than any of them.'[18] (quoted, M, 331) Privately Moore was taken aback at 'the insolence of this ignorant barbarian'. (M, 331) But he and Whaley knew they might be able to turn his egotism to their advantage. Megatt had advised them to flatter the Pasha and give the impression that in their own country they were people of great consequence, friends of England's 'young king', the Prince of Wales. Then they could introduce the real business of their visit. They told al-Jazzar that they had heard of his renown and 'bent our course to the Syrian coast, more with a view of having the honour of beholding, and being known to so great a man than from any other inducement the country afforded'. (M, 331) They wanted to acquire an Arabian horse as a present for the Prince of Wales. Might al-Jazzar possibly grant them one from his stables?

Most of those who advised them on how to handle al-Jazzar believed he would react favourably to such a request. Whaley and Moore were therefore shocked when it elicited a blunt refusal. No, he would not give them a horse. He explained that as he had already turned down similar requests from both the Sultan and the Captain Pasha he could hardly oblige a Christian. For Moore this was an insincere and contradictory excuse: if al-Jazzar was prepared to insult the great lords by denying them a horse then he would not care about offending them further by giving one to a Christian. However, al-Jazzar may have had another reason for his refusal. Probably he realised that his guests were lying about the reason for their visit. He knew that they had already passed through Acre without making any effort to meet him and have 'the honour of beholding, and being known to so great a man'. It was obvious that he was not the main purpose of their trip.

At the same time al-Jazzar was not about to pass up the opportunity to boast and without further ado he turned the conversation back to his preferred subject: his own greatness and mighty deeds. He proceeded to give them an account of his life, his exploits in Egypt, his military prowess, and the number of men he had killed.[19] He then turned his attention to his guests' gifts. He was impressed with Whaley's gun and amazed to be told it could be fired several times with one loading. Moore was disappointed to see 'so beautiful and ingenious an instrument so very ill bestowed, without a prospect of any advantage accruing to my friend from his generosity'.[20] (M, 333) Whaley, for his part, was probably less concerned by the loss of the pistol. It had cost him fifty guineas, but this was no great sum to a man who regularly spent far greater amounts, and he could always purchase a replacement. It was not so easy, though, to come by an Arabian stallion, and while al-Jazzar's refusal was disappointing he had not given up hope of attaining one.

Meanwhile he and Moore trod carefully, wary of their host's reputation for cruel and unusual punishments. Both referred to a savage penalty al-Jazzar allegedly meted out to slaves who displeased him. The offending party was laid face down 'across a bar of wood, with his hands and feet held to the ground' (W, 171). Then, taking out a small silver hammer, al-Jazzar struck him between the shoulders, directly on the spine. 'Some of these unfortunate wretches have been known to languish for two years after this blow, in extreme misery.' (M, 334) Whaley claimed that they witnessed al-

Jazzar preparing to inflict this awful fate on an offending slave, and that he managed to intervene to save the man's life: 'I had the heartfelt satisfaction ... to have [the punishment] mitigated; and a severe bastinadoing expiated his fault.' (W, 171) Moore's journal makes no mention of this incident and in all likelihood it did not happen, at least not while Whaley was present. After all, al-Jazzar had dismissed all of his slaves and attendants so that he could speak freely with his visitors. Here the temptation to paint himself as the heroic saviour of the oppressed was too great for Whaley to resist.

Whaley also asserted that al-Jazzar paraded the women of his harem, 200 in number, veiled and dressed in white, before them, but that he was too 'taken up with gloomy reflections on the cruel hammer scene, and the wretched state of servility to which these unfortunate women were doomed' to enjoy the procession. (W, 172) Again, this must be dismissed as an invention. Al-Jazzar did maintain a large harem, which included eighteen white women, but he guarded these females jealously behind closed doors. 'They entered never to go out again.'[21] Whaley's suggestion that the Pasha paraded them before him in order to do him honour is not credible. Comparison with Moore's journal shows that in general Whaley's reporting of events is fairly accurate, but from time to time he felt the need to embellish his experiences.

Having spent around an hour in al-Jazzar's company and grown weary of his boasting, the visitors decided to take their leave. As they were about to depart, two servants came up with al-Jazzar's parting gift: two expensive pelices, which they tied around their shoulders and then withdrew, 'each of them making three reverences ... We then turned to the Pasha and saluted him in like manner, placing our right hand to our heart, and thus terminated the audience.' (M, 337) Though Whaley left without having got what he came for, he and Moore had been enthralled to meet the notorious Butcher. They looked on him with a sort of fascinated revulsion as a bloodthirsty and remorseless tyrant, the most detestable character they had yet encountered. 'Having attained the summit of human atrocity and villainy, [he] ignorantly conceived himself to be one of the greatest and most eminent of mankind', Moore sniffed. (M, 336) Whaley found himself reflecting 'with indignation on the savage cruelty of this monster'. (W, 171) They did not know that he was yet to perform his greatest deed, one that would make him famous throughout the Ottoman world and even in Europe. In the spring of 1799 al-Jazzar was besieged in Acre by a French army commanded by a brilliant young general. Assisted by British troops, the Butcher held out against the French for two months, killing over 1,000 of them. Eventually the young general was forced to abandon the siege and retreat ignominiously to Egypt. Thus did the ageing Ahmad Pasha al-Jazzar, ten years after Whaley's visit, become the first man to defeat Napoleon Bonaparte in battle.[22]

★★★

Moore's journal ends abruptly with him and Whaley taking their leave of al-Jazzar. His chronology of events indicates that on the same day, 10 March, they embarked for Europe. His timing may be out by a day or so, because before they left Whaley made a last-ditch effort to acquire a horse. Ibrahim Abu Qalush had told him that a fine specimen, a stallion, was up for sale in Caiffa twelve miles to the south and Whaley decided to try his luck there. On arrival he was 'conducted [to] the place where this rare animal stood; and truly nothing but the pencil of Apelles [an ancient Greek painter] could do him justice'. (W, 237) He willingly stumped up 10,000 piastres (£1,000) for the horse and had it sent to Acre to be put on board his ship.[23] And with that, their time in the Holy Land was at an end. They returned to Acre and informed the *Heureuse Marie*'s captain that they were ready to depart 'and accordingly … we set sail with a fair wind, and bid an eternal adieu to Palestine'.[24] (W, 238) Hundreds of miles of unpredictable sea swells lay ahead, and Whaley did not know if they would bring storms and pirates or fair weather and plain sailing. It would be many weeks yet before he again saw his homeland.

13

RETURN

The fair wind soon turned foul. For two days adverse gusts shunted the ship this way and that, and with another storm in the offing the captain decided to make for Larnaca on the coast of Cyprus. Like the rest of the Levant, Cyprus lay under Ottoman rule. Most of its inhabitants were Greeks, the descendants of Peloponnesian colonists who had arrived around 1200 BC. The Ottomans had seized the island in 1570 and since then it had suffered under the misadministration of a series of corrupt and inefficient governors. Though Whaley had not planned to include Cyprus in his itinerary he was not entirely disappointed at having to delay there. It was now 13 March 1789, and with at least six months left to complete the expedition he could afford to linger for some days. He and Moore decide to explore the island. Strangely, the captain of the *Heureuse Marie* does not seem to have objected. Perhaps now that he was away from al-Jazzar's domain he was prepared to allow his passengers more leeway.

The next day Whaley and Moore embarked on a ten-day tour of Cyprus, taking in Episkopi (west of Limassol), Nicosia and Famagusta.[1] The trip was mostly uneventful but they did have a couple of unexpected encounters. In a village on the road to Nicosia a local woman begged them to aid her 12-year-old daughter, who was lying ill with fever. Whaley, who 'had learned to think of infection with as much indifference as the best Mussulman' (W, 242), decided to treat the girl by administering James's Powder. His own experiences with the powder had left him no wiser as to its toxicity and it is not known what effect it had on the patient. Probably it only served to prolong her illness if it did not kill her outright, but to be fair Whaley's methods were no different from those of many trained physicians. As they left the village he realised 'that we had not only acquired the character of men skilled in physic but also that of magicians'. (W, 242)

When they arrived at Nicosia the travellers saw the effects of Cyprus's economic stagnation, with the city falling into ruin and its once-impressive walls crumbling. But something else about Nicosia made a bigger impression on Whaley: the attractiveness of the local women. He sent Paulo to enquire after Madam E—, a Nicosian lady to whom he had been given a letter of introduction in Larnaca. When the servant returned he had the lady in question and her entourage with him. Paulo's blithe assertion that his master was the son of 'the King of Ireland' cannot have failed to interest the Cypriot gentlewoman, and she and Whaley struck up a rapport. She invited the newcomers to spend the night at her brother's residence at the edge of town and over the next twenty-four hours she and Whaley got to know one another intimately. Early the next morning the two met for a tryst in the garden. First Patmos, now Cyprus: Whaley was finding the islands of the Mediterranean to be fertile ground for a spot of casual romance. But he was not inclined to tarry and that evening the travellers 'took leave of our hospitable and truly amiable friends with much regret'. (W, 248)

Madam E— was not the only Cypriot female to attract Whaley's attention. On another occasion he noticed a young girl sitting at the door of a humble residence. 'The beauty of her complexion, the regularity of her features, and above all, the innocent, modest and tender simplicity of her countenance made me gaze on her with wonder, delight and admiration.' The girl's parents soon took notice of the rich-looking stranger, but he could not have anticipated what happened next. Without hesitation they offered to sell their daughter, whose name was Theresina, to him. 'I was the only person that was astonished at so extraordinary a transaction', Whaley insisted, and though he privately condemned 'the selfish and interested character of her parents' he did not object to their proposal. 'Within a quarter of an hour, the bargain was struck, I paid about 130 £ and Theresina was mine.'[2] The idea of selling one's offspring into slavery seems shocking in the twenty-first century, but in the Ottoman Empire poverty often forced Christian and Muslim parents to this pass. They were not motivated simply by financial gain. Many believed, and not without reason, that slavery would improve a child's fortunes. Slave girls were often given a good education and could aspire to marry Ottoman dignitaries.[3]

By Whaley's account Theresina accepted the change in her circumstances without much fuss. She shed 'a few tears ... [but] they were soon dried up, when I had provided her with all the most costly dresses that Eastern magnificence could produce.'[4]

On 24 March Whaley and Moore completed their tour of the island and returned to Larnaca. They were now almost ready to leave for Europe, but first Whaley had a couple of things to attend to. Paulo was due to leave his service and return to Smyrna. Time and again the Armenian had proven himself a loyal and brave retainer, and Whaley was keen to reward him. Meanwhile he also needed to decide what to do with Theresina. It was easy to join the dots and Whaley claims that both acceded happily to his proposal that they get married. He gave them money and soon afterwards they took ship for Turkey. Whaley seems to have kept up a correspondence with them as he was able to report in later years that they were 'comfortably settled at Smyrna, where Paoulo carries on some trade, and they live in simple and happy mediocrity'.[5]

What he did not anticipate was that he too would receive a proposal. At the British vice-consul's house in Larnaca he received a letter from Madam E—, inviting him to stay in Cyprus, presumably in order to marry her. The letter 'breathed such warm professions of inviolable attachment, disinterested friendship and esteem, as would have induced any man but myself to settle for life in this paradisiacal island'. She was to be disappointed. Whaley was far from finished sowing his wild oats. 'To the mind of a man, such as I then was, the slave of passion and the votary of licentiousness, such an idea [i.e. marriage] would be no less horrible than that of self-destruction.' (W, 263) But as he would find in years to come, the path of 'passion' and 'licentiousness' carried many risks and self-destruction was not the least of them.

★★★

On 26 March the *Heureuse Marie* set sail from Larnaca for Marseilles. She was not a fast ship and the passengers faced a six-week voyage (by comparison the *London* had made it from Gibraltar to Smyrna, around the same distance, in three and a half weeks). For the most part it was a tedious journey. Moore seems to have whiled away the hours writing in his journal, which after all was its purpose: 'the undertaking I meant merely as a *passe tem[p]s* at sea, to dissipate the many heavy hours of ennui'. (M, preface) Doubtless Whaley also compiled his own notes on the expedition. Supplemented with extracts from Moore's journal, these later formed the basis of his memoirs. As monotonous as the voyage was, they would have preferred not to encounter two of the things most likely to break the tedium: a storm or a hostile incident. The seas stayed relatively calm, but nearing Malta around the middle of April they sighted a Tunisian ship. She had no visible guns but using his spyglass Whaley discovered that she 'was full of men armed with sabres and pistols'. (W, 267) When her captain hailed the *Heureuse Marie* and brusquely demanded brandy, a chart and a compass, they complied, more out of fear than a willingness to oblige. The Tunisians allowed them to proceed without further interference, which was just as well: the cumbersome *Heureuse Marie* was unlikely to outrun another vessel.[6]

At last, on 6 May, they came to anchor in Marseilles. Having reached Europe again the Irishmen felt they were almost home and certainly Whaley sensed a change in the air. Although he had suffered no further relapse since leaving Smyrna at the start of February, his illness had left him in a somewhat debilitated condition during the weeks that followed. Only in Marseilles did he find himself properly 'regaining my strenght [*sic*] ... the smell of Europe has again revived me, and I already find myself geting strong and fat ... no doubt by the time I get to Ireland I shall find myself in better health and spirits than I have had for some time past'.[7] But he and Moore would not be going anywhere just yet. The port authorities at Marseilles rightly feared the spread of plague and the occupants of all vessels, regardless of whether they were ill, were segregated for several weeks in a lazaretto or quarantine station. After the long voyage the delay must have been frustrating but Whaley had at least one consolation: after many months, he finally had news from home. Waiting for him at Marseilles was a sheaf of letters 'which are all I have got since I left England they have been following me over Europe and Asia'.[8] In all there were twenty missives, including one from Samuel Faulkner and no doubt others from his mother, stepfather, siblings and friends. All would have been keen to know how he was faring on his travels and they were not alone.

During Whaley's absence magazines and newspapers in Britain and Ireland had maintained a keen interest in his affairs. In January the *Town and Country Magazine*, a London society periodical, had run a feature on the 'Jerusalem Pilgrim' making much of his association with a courtesan known as the 'Fille de Chambre' (probably Harriet Heydon). Thriving on gossip and scandal, *Town and Country* had a large circulation and Whaley's appearance in its pages was a marker of his burgeoning celebrity. Its Irish equivalent, *Walker's Hibernian Magazine*, reprinted the article in its February issue.[9] Meanwhile newspapers throughout Britain and Ireland carried regular (and frequently inaccurate) reports on Whaley's progress. Most expressed confidence that his expedition would succeed but there was very little reliable information on his whereabouts and all kinds of rumours floated about. On 2 December 1788 *The Times* stated that he had sailed from Malta for Acre when in fact he was in Smyrna. In January it correctly reported that he had reached Smyrna but on 20 February, before Whaley had even reached the Holy Land, the newspaper asserted confidently that he was on his return journey.[10] Many other reports were equally erroneous: it was mentioned that he had landed in Alexandria, a city he never visited, and in mid-April, with the *Heureuse Marie* still making her away across the Mediterranean, it was claimed that Whaley had reached London and was due in Dublin within a week.[11] The inaccuracies are unsurprising, given the haphazard nature of eighteenth-century journalism, especially in regard to events that occurred overseas. While some articles were based on information in the letters Whaley sent home, many others were drawn from hearsay and the muddled accounts of seafarers and travellers who had encountered, or claimed to have encountered, him in different ports. Yet the number of times Whaley's name appeared in print reflected the strong public interest in his expedition and this would only increase as its conclusion approached.

For his part he longed to be back in Ireland, '*my land of saints*'. Knowing he would soon be released from the lazaretto he wrote to his fellow bettors to inform them he would be in Dublin by July, 'a year sooner than they intended I *should, at least*'.[12] On 27 May, after twenty-one days' detention, Whaley and Moore were permitted to resume their travels.[13] They set out for Paris the next day, passing through a tense and turbulent France. Severe drought and a brutally cold winter had destroyed crops and livestock, bringing many close to starvation. Amid widespread unrest, the Estates General had met at Versailles on 5 May to address lower-class grievances. They had been unable to agree on a programme for reform and the situation had deteriorated until France was on the brink of revolution. A few weeks later Louis XVI would dismiss the popular minister Jacques Necker, provoking riots that culminated in the storming of the Bastille on 14 July. France was about to plunge into years of bloodshed, terror and upheaval. Whaley did not stay around to witness the unfolding crisis but in years to come he would find himself intimately embroiled in the events of the Revolution.

On 2 June he reached Paris and four days later he was in London. His arrival was noticed immediately, with *The Times*, *Ipswich Journal*, *Bath Chronicle* and *Newcastle Courant* among the newspapers to publish a notice of his return. Whaley now had only 'to reach Dublin before the business will be completed … a task of no great difficulty'.[14] However, things were not quite as straightforward as that. When Whaley had sailed from Dublin the previous September he had left a large number of debts still unpaid and the associated negative publicity threatened to tarnish his achievement.[15] It seems that around the middle of June he returned secretly and, with Samuel Faulkner's help, made an effort to discharge some of the obligations.[16] But if so he had limited success because many debts remained unsettled.

***

Whaley's arrival in London had been widely reported in the Irish press and it may have been an open secret that he was back in Ireland. On 19 July 1789 he 'officially' announced his return in Dublin. It was just under ten months since he had sailed from George's Quay amid the cheers of a great throng and now crowds gathered again to welcome him back. St Stephen's Green was ablaze with bonfires and abuzz with revelry, a sign that the lower classes had bought into Whaley's success. Across the city there was a genuine outpouring of goodwill and congratulations for the returning hero, who was praised for the speed and success of his expedition.[17] 'He is to find the rich fruits of his travels in his native soil,' the *Dublin Evening Post* enthused. 'Here golden showers are to rain down on him, in reward of his exertions; sorrow and repentance he leaves to those who doubted the fervency of his zeal, or the ardour of his devotion.' Now those who had bet against him would have to pay what they owed.[18] We do not know how much exactly Whaley won but it seems to have been at least £15,000 (although many newspapers put his winnings at much more than that). When the cost of the expedition, estimated by Whaley at approximately £8,000, was deducted, a profit of £7,000 remained. He later described this as 'the only instance in all my life before, in which any of my projects turned out to my advantage'. (W, 270)

The adulation and financial reward was not undeserved. Whaley had, after all, pulled off something extraordinary. Very few Irish had travelled to the Near East in the early modern period and even fewer made it to Jerusalem. He and Moore may have been the only eighteenth-century Irish travellers to leave accounts of their experiences in the Holy Land. His return to Dublin was indisputably his finest hour. He had survived a multitude of hindrances and dangers including stormy seas, dead calms, rain-soaked roads, hostile janissaries, fever, plague, pirates and bandits, and yet he had made it back within the allotted time and claimed victory. He had shown all those who dismissed him as a feckless wastrel that he could achieve what they thought he would find impossible. More importantly, his experiences on the way to and from Jerusalem had given him, perhaps for the first time, a sense of appreciation for the wealth and privilege he had known since childhood. 'He only, who has encountered dangers and difficulties, and groaned under the pressure of hunger and fatigue, may be said to know the inestimable blessings of personal security, ease and comfort.' (W, 225) Hugh Moore had shared these hardships. In the course of their long and arduous journey together the two men had become firm friends and they remained close in the years that followed.[19]

But what lay in store for Whaley now? Now that he had achieved his great ambition of travelling to Jerusalem, his mother no doubt hoped he would leave his wayward and chaotic past behind. Writing to her son in 1784 Anne had anticipated that within a few years he would be 'settled comfortably in your own country, with a good wife and a child or two … your wild oats I expect will be sown, and you will have reaped such advantages from the knowledge you will have acquired of men and manners, as to make a most delightful companion to the woman of your choice, a comfort to your friends and an acquisition to society'.[20] Similarly, his tenants in Counties Carlow and Armagh must have hoped that their long-absent landlord would take up residence and look after their welfare. There was also speculation that he would marry. Noises were made about 'an intended marriage … between one of the daughters of a late great Law Peer and the *Jerusalem Pilgrim*, which will make a great accession to his fortune'.[21] It was also said that his successful pilgrimage would 'effectively wipe away the sins and transgressions of his youth'[22] and Whaley himself may have believed that he had broken the curse of ill-luck that had dogged him in the past.

But already there were signs that none of this would come to pass. Unlike Moore, who quietly resumed his military career and faded into anonymity, Whaley had no intention of settling down to a normal life. On the very evening he had got out of the lazaretto he had sought out an old acquaintance in Marseilles and gone on a bender 'to make ample amends for the long abstinence and self-denial I had undergone'. (W, 268) While no one would have denied him a bit of self-indulgence in the circumstances, the night had finished ominously with a gambling session in which he had lost £300. A few days later, in Paris, Whaley had spent a further £450 as a result of 'an unexpected event', possibly involving a female.[23] This made a total of £750 expended before he had even reached his homeland. It did not bode well for the future, and there was also the matter of his unpaid debts. He still owed very large sums to Lundy Foot and others. With the success of his wager having received such extensive publicity, his creditors were well aware that he had returned. Now they were about to call in their loans.

PART THREE
DEBT AND DEATH

14

WHIRL AND BLAZE

Built into a stone wall on the Old Bray Road in Cornelscourt, south Dublin, stands an unusual upright marker. It was once a five-mile-stone, marking a distance of five old Irish miles from that place to Dublin city centre, and on 13 September 1789 it was the scene of Whaley's latest wager. The sport of pedestrianism, or racewalking, had become hugely popular both as a pastime and an incentive for gambling.[1] Whaley had been drawn into the craze and on 29 August he and a Mr Ferns had staked 100 guineas (£105) on which of them could walk five miles along the banks of the Grand Canal within an hour. Though Ferns won the race and the bet easily,[2] Whaley was confident his next wager would work out in his favour. Two weeks later he bet an army officer, Arthur Wesley, 150 guineas that he could not walk the five miles from the Bray Road mile-stone to the corner of Leeson Street and Circular Road within an hour. Perhaps Whaley felt he had superior insight into how much distance could be covered on foot in a given time, but if so he was mistaken. Then just 20 years old, Wesley was fit and energetic and he set off at such a fast pace that the gentlemen who accompanied him had to trot their horses to keep up. Despite the poor condition of the road he reached his destination within fifty-five minutes and Whaley had no choice but to shell out the agreed sum.[3]

The equivalent of almost a year's pay,[4] 150 guineas was quite a windfall for Arthur Wesley but much greater successes lay in store for the young officer. In the years that followed he would rise to become one of the British Army's most successful and distinguished generals. In 1798 he changed the spelling of his surname to Wellesley and in 1814 he was made a duke. The following year he took command of the Allied army at the Battle at Waterloo. Whaley did not know it, but within a little over six months he had met the two men who would hand Napoleon Bonaparte his first and last defeats in battle: Ahmad Pasha al-Jazzar and the Duke of Wellington.

In 1789, however, Whaley was much more famous in Ireland and Britain than either of them. When word got out about his interest in racewalking he was acclaimed as a 'celebrated pedestrian' and a myth even emerged that he had completed his journey to Jerusalem on foot 'except so far as it was necessary to cross the sea'.[5] Stories like this served to enhance his allure and his fame spread quickly on both sides of the Irish Sea. London newspapers like *St James's Chronicle*, the *London Chronicle* and *The Times* reported regularly on his doings[6] and doors opened admitting him into the very highest echelon of society. The upper classes in Britain and Ireland knew him as the Jerusalem Pilgrim or 'Jerusalem' Whaley. But the ordinary people of Ireland knew him by another name, one that celebrated his status as a dashing and eccentric gentleman. For them he was 'Buck' Whaley.[7] Over two hundred years later, this is still the name by which he is best known.

Still only 23 years old, Whaley was not the first or last young man to have his head turned by fame and celebrity. Any sense of piety or perspective he had acquired on his travels was soon discarded and once again he embraced a life of expense and excess. In the early autumn of 1789, while his tenants at Fonthill were busy saving the corn,[8] he flitted between Dublin and London, where he 'took a house ... bought horses and carriages; subscribed to all the fashionable clubs and was in a short time a complete man of the *ton* [i.e. high society] at the West End of the Town'. (W, 271) Of course, Whaley could not sustain this lifestyle without large amounts of cash and while he stood to make a tidy profit from the Jerusalem expedition it probably took him some time to gather his winnings. On 21 August the Earl of Grandison paid up the £455 he owed and by the end of the month several other of his 'Jerusalem friends' had also coughed up.[9] Yet many others may not have been so prompt and Whaley found that he needed money fast. He decided to sell some of his property in Carlow and instructed Samuel Faulkner to evict any undesirable tenants and start taking proposals from would-be purchasers.[10] However, the rumour that he would obtain a large fortune by marrying a judge's daughter turned out to be nothing but idle speculation. A match could not have been in train so soon after Whaley's return; indeed, apart from his dalliances on Patmos and Cyprus his romantic life had been on hiatus for nearly a year. Harriet Heydon had remained in London, and while she no doubt still held some affection for her 'dear Tom', they did not renew their relationship.

In any case it was not long before another woman caught his eye. In the weeks after his return Whaley had courted the Prince of Wales's favour, and to celebrate the Prince's 27th birthday on 12 August he set up an impressive display on the façade of his house on St Stephen's Green. 'In the centre of the front [of the house] was an elegant representation of a plume of three feathers, his royal highness's crest, formed by variegated lamps … in addition to a number of other lights the pallisadoes [railings] were stuck thick with flambeaus. Porter and ale were distributed in abundance to the populace about the door.' This impressive tribute was reported in the London press and a few weeks later Whaley made an even grander gesture by giving the Prince the Arabian stallion he had brought home from the Holy Land.[11] Although parting with the horse he had gone to so much trouble to acquire must have been difficult, the opportunity to join the royal heir's circle made up for it. In September the Prince welcomed Whaley into the fashionable society he had gathered around himself in Brighton, where he owned a lavish villa known as the Pavilion.[12] The Prince was no stranger to over-indulgence, and his father George III reprimanded him severely for drinking, whoring, gambling and associating with prodigals and wastrels. However, 'the more he was accused of being such a wastrel, the more he felt inclined to behave like one, and the more, indeed, he did behave like one'.[13]

It was not surprising then that he was interested in a character like Whaley. Probably they saw one another as kindred spirits, which they certainly were as far as their partiality for the gaming tables was concerned. It may have been while gambling with the Prince that Whaley met the woman who became his inseparable companion for the best part of a decade. The tale went that during one of their sessions Whaley won the affections of 'a Favorita' of the Prince, 'whom her ungallant protector had in a moment of desperation staked as his only marketable asset'.[14] The story may be fictitious, but it is worth noting that over a century later one of Whaley's descendants claimed that his ancestor's long-term partner had been one of the Prince of Wales's mistresses.[15] Her name was Maria Courtenay and she was a slender and attractive woman with a calm and balanced temperament. Whaley later praised her as 'a consolation to me in all my troubles' and 'a constant check on the impetuosity of my temper'. (W, 270)

But even the level-headed Miss Courtenay could not have reined him in during the heady autumn months of 1789, when he gambled and spent with abandon. Meanwhile his creditors were clamouring for their money. Most of his long-standing debts still remained unsettled and Whaley was quickly racking up new ones. He was said to have started putting them 'in train for payment' on 15 August[16] but soon afterwards he borrowed £1,500 from the London banker John Hood, probably in order to cover his expenses and gambling losses in London. Although Hood coughed up the money he fretted that 'W. is going too far' and asked Whaley's lawyer Robert Cornwall for advice on whether he should give him further credit. Cornwall felt this to be a matter for the banker's own discretion, but added ominously, 'I fear all is over in that quarter': meaning, presumably, that he did not think it was safe for Whaley to be lent more money.[17]

Caught up in the 'whirl and blaze' of his celebrity, Whaley found himself footing the bill for various flatterers and spongers:

> the wide influence of his name, and the credit of his estate were without reserve communicated to those ephemeral fashionables, who live like butterflies in the sunshine, and derive subsistence as the satellites and seducers of the great, and who sometimes gradually exhaust in their numbers the copious springs that supply their wants! To the unceasing calls of such Mr. Whaley was never deaf.[18]

No doubt these hangers-on encouraged him in many unrealistic schemes, such as a new plan to build a ship, a cutter he named the *Minx*, and set off once again on his travels.[19] This would cost thousands of pounds and to raise the money Whaley decided to sell the house on Stephen's Green, but the plan fell through when his mother, who under the terms of Richard Chapel Whaley's will was entitled to reside there until her death, refused to agree to the sale. Whaley then decided to approach Lundy Foot, a seemingly inexhaustible source of revenue (even though Foot was still awaiting the repayment of previous loans). Here he had more success: with Whaley offering some of the Carlow estate as security, Foot advanced a loan of £4,600 on 24 November 1789.[20] Work on the yacht commenced, but Whaley would not have much opportunity to enjoy it. His gambling was about to spiral out of control.

★★★

Among the luminaries Whaley mingled with in the Prince of Wales's circle was Charles James Fox. One of the greatest politicians of the age, Fox was a renowned campaigner against slavery and oppression. Yet he also led a scandalous private life and was an avid gambler with 'winnings and losses … on a heroic scale'.[21] Whaley probably first made Fox's acquaintance during one of the Spring 1790 meetings at Newmarket, the racing capital of England,[22] and found himself mesmerised by the charismatic politician: 'his abilities as a statesman were not less conspicuous than the dissipation of his manners. He could sit up a whole night at a gaming table, and the next day make the Treasury Bench shake by the force of arguments.' (W, 276) Inevitably he and Whaley sat down to gamble. Although Fox had suffered astronomical losses at Newmarket in the past, in his contest with the Jerusalem Pilgrim his luck was greatly improved. 'I paid a compliment of two thousand guineas to his superior skill,' Whaley recalled, 'and six thousand to several others of the same party: among whom was H.R.H. the Duke of Y[ork], so that the opposition was completely triumphant, and levied a pretty severe fine on my purse.' (W, 276) In total this amounted to a loss of £8,400, the worst Whaley had suffered since returning from Jerusalem. Work on the *Minx* had now finished and she was lying in dock near Dublin,[23] but this misfortune meant it was unlikely he would be able to keep her. He needed to raise money fast.

The quickest solution was to sell his lands in Carlow. Fortunately a would-be purchaser had emerged, one of the richest men in Ireland: Colonel Henry Bruen of Oak Park near Carlow Town. During the American Revolutionary War Bruen had served as the British army's Deputy Quarter

Master, amassing a colossal fortune through shady financial practices. On his return he 'acquired large estates and considerable political influence in Ireland as an insurance against prosecution in Great Britain'.[24] No doubt he believed that purchasing the Whaley estates would enable him to shore up his influence even further. In May 1790 Whaley instructed his attorney Robert Cornwall to offer the property to Bruen for £41,000. Cornwall did as he was asked, but knowing how profligate his client was he feared that even if the sale went through the money would be 'nothing more than a temporary supply'. By the middle of June Whaley and Bruen had agreed terms, but when Cornwall considered the extent of Whaley's debts he was convinced that 'the sum will be inadequate to answer the different demands'. Lundy Foot alone was owed £30,000, and creditors in England also required large sums.[25]

This was only the summit of the iceberg. Early in July Whaley informed Cornwall that he wanted a further £10,000 from Bruen, over and above what had been agreed for the estate. The lawyer was stunned to discover that even if Whaley got this money it would not be sufficient to clear his outstanding debts. When all of his gambling losses and expenditures on the ship and other indulgences were added up, the depth of the trouble his client was in became clear: 'he is undone beyond a possibility of recovery … his debts at this moment I am sure, would amount to near £70,000'. Cornwall believed Whaley's best option now would be to take up some sort of common employment, but the chances of that were less than slim.[26] On 21 August the sale was concluded and Bruen took possession of most of the Carlow lands, with the exception of Fonthill House and the lands of Straboe.[27] Whaley was now keen to be off back to London where, Cornwall supposed, 'he will put the coup-de-grace to the remains of his shattered fortune'.[28] Whaley's decimation of such a large landed fortune, while certainly excessive, was not unheard of. In that same year the Earl of Barrymore had to sell a 140,000-acre estate in County Cork to settle a debt of £60,000. Between 1792 and 1794 the Earl of Belfast racked up gambling debts of £70,000, and his constant betting would greatly reduce the family estates.[29]

As for Whaley, as Cornwall had anticipated the money from the Carlow estate proved insufficient to clear his debts. Bailiffs employed by his creditors were on the lookout for him and he was no safer in London than he had been in Dublin. In September 1790 he decided to relocate to the small port of Parkgate near Chester. Parkgate was the main point of embarkation for Ireland and so allowed for a swift getaway across the Irish Sea in the event that a bailiff or creditor came sniffing around. While it was an attractive town, with elegant red and white houses fronting onto its promenade, these were beyond Whaley's means and he took a small cottage on the beach, hoping to live there incognito while he settled on a plan for the future. 'I dont wish to have it known where I am, or what, I am going to do,' he wrote to Faulkner, 'and the less you say upon the matter the better'.[30] Having removed himself from metropolitan life and all its temptations he was, in effect, going cold turkey: 'play [i.e. gambling] that cruel rock that, I have ever split upon cannot here assail me'.[31]

It is not clear whether Maria Courtenay was with Whaley during this time of bitter self-reflection, but his humble seaside abode was a far cry from the opulent houses he had inhabited in Dublin and London's West End. He sought solace in drink and finding the wine in Parkgate to be 'abominable' he asked Faulkner to send him five dozen bottles of the best claret he could get 'by the first ship that sails'.[32] But bad wine was the least of his problems. Around the middle of October his cottage was almost destroyed in a storm, forcing him to retreat to Chester where he took lodgings for three months.[33] The lonely weeks gave him plenty of time to mull over the change in his fortunes. It was now over a year since his return from the Holy Land and the contrast with that time could scarcely have been greater. Then he had been the all-conquering Jerusalem Pilgrim, feted by the good and great in Dublin and London. Now he was depressed and near-destitute, reduced to a humble existence far from the buzz of the city and abandoned by the 'friends' who had happily relieved him of his money in the good times. 'I know no use [for] nor do I wish to make new acquaintance[s]', he had confided to Faulkner in September. 'I would the dev[i]l had the greatest part of them I ever had.' Three months later, coming towards the end of his time in Chester, he was still of the same mind: 'should it please God that things ... take a turn [for the better], [I'll] keep myself free of many people'.[34] But tragically, he had not seen the last of these 'people'. In the gaming houses of London and Dublin, cardsharps and cheats (known as blacklegs) were waiting in the wings for an opportunity to relieve him of what was left of his estates and fortune. Even greater disaster lurked just around the corner.

★★★

'The French Revolution, at this time, began to make some noise in the world … Amongst the many whom curiosity led to this wonderful scene of action, I repaired to Paris in the year 1791.' (W, 276-7) In his memoirs Whaley gave the impression that his move to Paris was a matter of choice, a premeditated decision to learn more about the causes and course of the Revolution. In fact, it was motivated by something much more forceful than curiosity. By early 1791 he had grown weary of his self-imposed exile in Chester and returned to London. Despite his resolution to avoid certain company, he allowed himself to be enticed into a situation where the 'cruel rock' of gaming could injure him once again. This time it did so almost beyond hopes of recovery.

In London, Whaley normally resided at St James's Coffee House on St James's Street. This happened to be the same street on which two gentlemen's clubs, White's and Brooks's, were situated. 'These two clubs attracted not only the richest men in London but the most brilliant … But it was the extraordinary recklessness of the gaming at these places that most firmly seized the imagination.'[35] Visiting one of these establishments (probably Brooks's) early in February, Whaley was targeted by 'a set party' – a gang of blacklegs. The sequence of events that followed was depressingly familiar. In all likelihood the swindlers first got him drunk. They then enticed him to a private gaming table and 'at one sitting' relieved him of a sum of shocking magnitude: £26,000. It was a scene reminiscent of the Lyons debacle seven years earlier, only this time the damage was much worse, equal perhaps to €10 million in today's money. It was the single biggest financial loss of Whaley's life, and given the already poor state of his finances it was nothing short of a catastrophe. Even the sale of his Armagh property would be insufficient to raise the money and whatever securities he provided were not likely to stand up for long. When it was discovered that he could not pay what he owed he would most likely end up in a debtors' prison. Outside of that his options were severely limited. One loomed large above all. 'I suppose the next accounts will be of his having put an end to himself,' Robert Cornwall mused, 'and I should not wonder at it.'[36]

15

THE BIRD IS FLOWN

He may have been close to despair but Whaley was not ready to end it all just yet. An innate resourcefulness had got him out of scrapes in the past and now he called on it again. He knew he could not possibly pay such a huge sum as £26,000, but succumbing to the horrors of a debtors' prison was out of the question. There was, however, another course of action: to get out of the country as quickly as possible. Having bought a narrow window of time by raising money on securities, he fled to Dover. The bailiffs were soon in hot pursuit. Somehow managing to evade them, Whaley got on board a vessel and was off once more on his travels. The contrast with his embarkation for Smyrna two and a half years before, at Deal just a few miles up the coast, could not have been greater. Then he had been brim-full of enthusiasm, with money in his pocket and seemingly limitless possibilities before him. Now he was fleeing with his tail between his legs, a wretched defaulter who seemed fated to end his days in penury. It seemed unlikely that he would return to either England or Ireland and Robert Cornwall anticipated that what was left of his property 'will be attacked on all sides as the way he raised money lately in England was, by drawing drafts on houses which would not be accepted, so that in short he has been guilty of swindling – I find several of his debts have been sent over here in quest of him'.[1] Yet Whaley did have one thing going for him: no one was sure of his intended destination. Cornwall heard he was headed for Florence, where his friend Lord Hervey was the British envoy to the Tuscan Court, but he may have started this rumour himself in order to throw his pursuers off the scent.

Whatever his initial planned destination, by April he had arrived in the French capital. At the end of that month his mother received 'a very melancholy letter from poor Tom … from Paris', written 'in such wretched spirits that it made me cry'.[2] While Whaley's main source of angst was the shambles he had made of his life, he was also disturbed to find himself at the epicentre of the French Revolution. Nearly two years on from the fall of the Bastille, Paris was in a state of ferment, with the National Constituent Assembly in favour of a monarchical regime in which the king and an assembly shared legislative and executive powers. Meanwhile the working-class *sans-culottes* wanted to abolish the monarchy, the aristocracy and the Church in favour of a republic and there was growing tension and hostility between the two sides. Convinced that the Revolution was the work of a small group of extremists, Whaley sympathised with Louis XVI and his family, then being held under house arrest at the Tuileries Palace. On the night of 20 June 1791 the royal family attempted to flee Paris but were overtaken at Varennes some 140 miles east of the capital. Whaley saw them being escorted back to the Tuileries under guard. Defying a strict order that none should uncover their heads in deference, he raised his hat as the royal carriage went past. 'I should have paid dearly were it not for one of the National Guards, who persuaded the *sans culottes* to do me no injury by assuring them I was a mad Irishman.' (W, 284) It was not difficult for him to pass for a madman: poverty had forced him to pawn his valuables and spare clothes, and he cut a dishevelled and distracted figure. Yet he still hoped to turn things around. In a letter to his mother he claimed to have formulated 'a plan that he will adhere to'.[3] Now he hoped to execute it, but to do so he needed the help of a close family member. He would have to return to Dublin, even though this meant risking arrest. With the king's return having 'restored a temporary tranquillity to [Paris] … I gladly availed myself of this calm, to demand my passport, which was immediately granted'. (W, 285)

★★★

If there was any member of the Whaley family whose troubles could be said to equal, if not exceed, Tom's then it was William. Described by Robert Cornwall as 'the most troublesome rascall I ever met',[4] he was nearly as bad as his brother at managing his finances. He was also hot-tempered and violent and had been lucky to escape punishment after killing a man in a duel on 14 July 1790. The affair, which attracted special attention because one of the principals was 'brother to the celebrated

Mr. W[haley],[5] originated out of a row between William and the lawyer Denis O'Kelly at Kearns's Hotel in Dublin. Owing to some past encounter there was bad feeling between the two men and it flared up when one of them barged in on the other as he was gaming in a private room. They exchanged sharp words, followed by volleys of glasses and candlesticks. A challenge was issued and swiftly accepted and the antagonists met early the following morning at a disused quarry near Merrion Square. O'Kelly was a fiery character, known for having horsewhipped the English tourist Richard Twiss, who had criticised his home province of Connacht in his book *A Tour in Ireland in 1775*. More significantly he had plenty of experience on the duelling field, and William seemed likely to come off the worst in the encounter.[6] Having won the toss to see who would have the first shot O'Kelly took aim and fired, narrowly missing his opponent's head. William then fired and hit the lawyer in the chest, 'the ball piercing between the finger and thumb of Mr. O'K.'s hand, which he held on the lower part of his breast, as if to guard that vital part; and taking effect in his side, through the lobe of his liver; he immediately fell on his back'. O'Kelly managed to reach to his second for another pistol, which he was just about to fire when the strength drained out of his limbs and he died on the spot.[7]

Only sometimes did duels end fatally. Even when they did, participants were rarely prosecuted owing to a widespread tacit acceptance of the 'code of honour' among the upper classes and the authorities. Nonetheless O'Kelly's widow brought charges against William, but when the case came to trial on 13 December 1790 for some reason the prosecutors failed to appear and he was acquitted.[8] Cornwall hoped this experience would be 'the means of settling' the young man, but he was to be disappointed. In May 1791, three months after his brother had fled England, William got into another violent row, and this too ended fatally. On this occasion he argued with a hackney coachman over a fare. Robert Cornwall related what happened:

Whaley unfortunately gave him a blow, the fellow in a few days after took a putrid fever and died and the coroners inquest have brought in a verdict of murder against Whaley, he very luckily escaped being taken ... from every inquiry I have been able to make I am satisfied he has not been guilty of taking the fellows life but then the friends of [Denis O'] Kelly have so spread the contagion of his guilt, that every one believes him to be the perpetrator.[9]

Rather than face the consequences, William chose to follow his brother's example and abscond. He made his way to Wales, probably in order to lie low with his sister Mary Susanna (Susan), who was then living in Carmarthen.[10]

By early August William was in Brecon, having for some reason 'been obliged to come so far into Wales', and with his money almost entirely gone he was getting by on a frugal subsistence. Living in this state he was shocked to receive an unexpected visitor. 'I cannot inform you how his coming ... surprised me', he wrote to Faulkner.

I knew nothing of [it], until I found myself sitting in the same room with him. He really was so disfigured, that I scarcely knew him. Will you then believe that he is not mad; but I think him worse, he is more obstinate, and intransigent than ever, altho' *his cloaths even*, are in pawn in Paris ... all his *trinkets* &c &c are in the same way.

In all likelihood Tom Whaley was not alone. It seems that after arriving in Dublin he had been reunited with Maria Courtenay (who had by now borne him a son, also called Tom) and on finding that William was in Wales they had taken ship for Swansea. The privations of Whaley's life in Paris had clearly taken their toll physically and mentally, but that was the least of his worries as his many creditors remained alert for news of his return. 'If it is found out in London that he is here, all is over,' William insisted. 'I am certain he must go to the [Court of] Kings Bench, nothing could keep him from it.'[11] In setting foot on British soil Tom was taking a great risk, but he hoped it would bring great reward. His plan was to raise £4,000 by offering the lands of Straboe, one of the pieces of property he had retained in Carlow, as security. To do this he needed his brother's consent, as a portion of an annuity held by William was payable out of the income on the lands. The problem was that Straboe had already been committed as security for loans from Lundy Foot and various other parties, and William was sure that no one would be 'mad enough to lend him a guinea on it, as it is security for so many different things'. Still, he agreed reluctantly to the scheme, on condition that the money be raised without any of the property being sold.[12]

Tom sent word to Robert Cornwall asking him to come over and take charge of the legalities. Meanwhile William had to support his penniless brother even though he himself had little money. This seems to have caused a quarrel in which Maria was also involved. Meanwhile Cornwall, for some reason, refused to travel to Wales and instead went to London. Despite the risks, Tom had no option but to set out for the capital. He arrived there around 9 September and met with Cornwall. The two men managed to further the business of securing the loan, but William still had to consent to offering Straboe as security, and as he and his brother were quarrelling there was no guarantee he would do so. Tom wrote to him to beg his pardon and William 'agreed to make friends with him', but resolved 'never more to see his lady'.[13] Tom remained in London for a few weeks. Probably he cut such a beggarly figure that it helped him avoid attention, but even so he narrowly avoided being collared by a bailiff. The Straboe scheme was causing him a great deal of trouble, which he hoped would be worthwhile when he got his hands on the £4,000, but he was in for a shock. Some of the legal documentation needed to finalise the loan could not be obtained and by the time Whaley returned to Dublin in October the scheme had fallen through.[14]

After so much risk and effort, this exasperating outcome drove Whaley to a new pass. Previously he had raised money by selling his Carlow lands, but he had not touched the Armagh estate, seemingly hoping to retain it as security for the future. Now, determined to raise money at all costs, he decided to break this sacrosanct rule and sell off part of the estate. Faulkner and Cornwall were charged with carrying through the sale but Whaley's affairs were in such a muddled state that it could not be quickly achieved. Finally, after a long drawn-out process, they managed to offload some of the Armagh lands to two Church of Ireland bishops, the Archbishop of Armagh and the Bishop of Cloyne, in March 1792.[15] In the meantime Whaley's debt to Lundy Foot was finally paid. This had been transferred to Henry Bruen as part of the purchase agreement for the Carlow lands and early in February Bruen settled with Foot.[16] Somehow, Whaley's financial concerns were being put in some kind of order. He also decided at this time to dispose of the house and lands of Fonthill, where he had once planned to settle as a country gentleman.[17] Everything was in order for the sale when the key to Faulkner's desk, where copies of the tenants' leases were stored, went missing. 'You may easily guess what the consequence was to a man endowed with so little patience as Mr. Whaley', Cornwall observed wearily. With the help of a blacksmith they broke open the desk and got the documents needed to close the deal.

When the proceeds from the Fonthill sale were added to the money from Armagh, Whaley once again had a substantial sum in his pocket and he was keen to return to Paris with Maria Courtenay and his son. Though he owed both Cornwall and Faulkner money he contrived to pay them only some of what was due. All this time he had been evading his creditors, and when he learned that the bailiffs were lying in wait on the Dublin quays 'in anxious expectation of their prey' he decided to embark from Waterford. On the night of 11 March 1792 he set out on a route that brought him through Leighlinbridge, County Carlow, virtually past the doors of Fonthill. There is no way of knowing his thoughts as he rode past the silent fields he had once owned, but Cornwall believed that 'if he had any feeling surely his travelling thro' the county ought to sting him to the soul'. It was indeed a shame: Fonthill had been a productive estate and in the hands of a responsible and improving owner it and the other Whaley lands in Carlow would have benefited both landlord and tenant. But whatever Whaley's feelings were, he was leaving Carlow and Ireland behind, perhaps for ever. 'The bird is at last flown,' Cornwall informed Faulkner. 'He is the most unfortunate young man I ever knew, I think he will not again returne.'[18]

***

Whaley arrived back in the French capital in more confident mood. With typical exaggeration he claimed in his memoirs that he returned with £14,000 (W, 285) when in fact he only had £5,000, but he was still much better off than he had been when he arrived the previous year. However, he found that Paris had sunk into even greater unrest as France moved from a state of uneasy peace to one of conflict. The Revolutionaries believed that the Hapsburg Empire was sheltering their enemies and on 20 April France declared war on Austria. In response the Austrians formed a military alliance with Prussia, hoping to defeat the Revolutionaries and restore Louis XVI to his full authority. Although Whaley followed these developments with alarm, there were plenty of things to distract him from the political situation. Now that he again had money he was determined to keep it and once again he resolved to gamble no more. But he found himself unable to resist the charms of the Pavillon d'Hanovre, a fashionable venue on the Boulevard des Italiens. The Pavillon was a haunt of courtesans, 'perfect mistresses of the art of seduction' (W, 281), and fashionable gentlemen. All of these denizens were interested in one thing only: the contents of his purse. By slow degrees they enticed him to gamble and in early May William Whaley received reports that his brother had lost over £7,000 in Paris.[19] This was an exaggeration, but Tom seemed to have reverted to a depressing and all-too-familiar pattern of gamble, lose, gamble.

He might easily have fallen once more into destitution were it not for a chance encounter with an old acquaintance. The man offered him some salutary advice: instead of trying to profit by gambling, why not profit from gamblers? One way of turning the gaming system to one's advantage was to set up a faro bank. Faro was a card game that required a banker and could have any number of players. The odds heavily favoured the banker but were stacked against the ordinary players, who staked bets on the dealer turning over certain combinations of cards. Setting up a faro bank required a significant amount of capital but anyone who could do so stood to earn a fortune. Despite his losses Whaley still had enough money for the purpose, and he and his acquaintance entered into a partnership and hired a fashionable venue which soon attracted 'the genteelest and most numerous company ever met with in Paris'. (W, 290) Whaley wrote to his friend Lord Hervey in Florence, asking him to send 'any of my countrymen' that he encountered on to him. 'If they are fond of play [they] will be sure of being treated in a *safer way* chez moi than elsewhere in Paris, as I hope to keep away all sort of *bad* company.' He was confident that his latest venture would be profitable – 'I am assured it will not fail of success' – and he was not mistaken.[20] Within a few weeks he had accumulated profits that ran into the tens of thousands. It was a remarkable reversal of fortune, his greatest success since the Jerusalem expedition.

Whaley was now in a position to resume the style to which he had become accustomed, but it was becoming evident that he would have to do it elsewhere. Hostility against the aristocracy and gentry was intensifying in Paris. 'There's an air of ferocity and self-created consequence in the common people very uncomfortable', one English aristocrat noted.[21] By the summer of 1792 the upper classes were fleeing the city in droves. Many of them headed for Lausanne in Switzerland and in July Whaley opted to join them. He seems to have left Paris in a hurry, judging by the fact that he was still owed thousands by the patrons of his faro casino. Even so he brought a great deal of money with him and could afford to travel in style, setting out 'with an immense retinue, not forgetting my cook and thirty led horses ... On my route I was often stopped and examined by the *sans culottes*, who were now the supreme rulers; but at length I arrived without any accident at Lausanne.'[22] (W, 291)

★★★

A picturesque town with panoramic views of Lake Geneva and the Alps, Lausanne was the resort of upper-class exiles from all over Europe. Among them were several Irish expatriates, including the clergyman Robert Fowler, son of the Archbishop of Dublin, and Valentine Lawless, whose sister Whaley would later marry. But despite the vibrant social scene he did not resort to play. Perhaps his experience of running the faro bank had taught him, at last, to gamble only when the odds were weighted in his favour. Instead he took a house, set his French cook to work and kept 'open table for strangers in general, but more particularly for my own countrymen'. (W, 292) He also frequented the residences of other exiles, where he found plenty of opportunities for diversion. 'Scarce an evening passed but we had a tea party and a ball, at which was always present a number of beautiful and accomplished women.' (W, 292) Although Maria and their infant son had travelled with him from Paris to Switzerland,[23] this did not stop him from paying court to the ladies. He pursued a Miss E., but all his efforts to obtain a 'private interview' proved to be in vain, as the lady intended he 'should be indebted to Hymen [the Greek god of marriage ceremonies] for what I hoped to obtain by means of love alone'.

Whaley abandoned the chase but did not 'suffer much pain from the disappointment'. (W, 294) This evoked an increasingly positive mental attitude. Far from the clutches of the bailiffs and buoyed by his financial success in Paris he was starting to rediscover the fearlessness of his early youth. From the northern shores of Lake Geneva he could see the mighty Alpine peaks to the south. One of them, its slopes almost entirely cloaked in snow and ice, was taller and more majestic than the others. The sight of Mont Blanc renewed within him a spirit of adventure that had lain dormant since his Jerusalem trip. Now he resolved to set out on another expedition which, though shorter, was no less daunting: he would climb over 15,000 feet through the snow to the summit of the great mountain. Although the attempt on Europe's highest mountain failed and almost proved fatal, when Whaley returned to Lausanne the news of his latest flamboyant adventure probably only added to his reputation.

Continuing his rounds of expatriate high society he visited some of the area's most famous English residents. The writer William Beckford had taken up residence across the lake at Evian, having fled England following accusations of sexual misconduct with a boy. In late August Whaley called on him, probably on one of his 'public days' during which all comers were welcome.[24] None of the guests cared to mention the scandal that had caused his exile, but another famous English exile did. Whaley also paid several visits to Lausanne's most fashionable noblewoman, Georgiana Cavendish, the Duchess of Devonshire. A charismatic and vivacious character, the duchess had moved to the continent after separating from her husband the previous year.[25] At her home Whaley met the 55-year-old historian Edward Gibbon, who was living a sedate life after completing his great work *The Decline and Fall of the Roman Empire* in Lausanne in 1787. When Whaley mentioned that he had visited Beckford 'the historian observed, with a truly pedantic air, "that it was astonishing any Englishman would visit a man who lay under such an imputation as Mr.

B[eckford] did: that even supposing him innocent still some regard was due to the opinion of the world; and he would venture to say, that I was the only one among my countrymen who had ever paid that man the smallest attention since his banishment.'" Whaley's response was brief and pointed: 'The only reply I made … was, that I did not look upon this little piece of history as any way deserving the attention of so great a man. The duchess complacently smiled: the rest of the company looked grave; my pedant was dumb, and I took my leave.' (W, 298) We do not know if the exchange really happened as Whaley described it, but if so he could take satisfaction from a verbal victory over the man he himself admitted was the most renowned historian of the age.

As summer faded into autumn the fashionable season in Lausanne drew to a close. It was time to leave. With France increasingly disturbed and the French Army about to invade Savoy, Whaley decided to head in the opposite direction and cross the Alps into Italy. As he prepared to depart he could look back on the previous eighteen months with some satisfaction. The catastrophe of February 1791 could have destroyed him but somehow he had got his affairs back on track. Though he had squandered most of his property, he had at last managed to turn the gaming tables to his advantage and now he was experiencing an upsurge in his fortunes for the first time since 1789. He still had cash at his disposal and while many creditors were questing after him in Ireland and Britain, as long as he remained on the continent he was out of their reach. More strikingly, he had rediscovered his gung-ho willingness to attempt what to others seemed foolhardy or impossible. Abortive as the Mont Blanc expedition had been, he had survived it and it is unlikely that he would have had the courage to make the attempt a year earlier. He had recovered his spirits and he was now moving on to new adventures in Italy. The coming months would tell whether his luck would run on or run dry.

★★★

Whaley toured around Italy for two months, visiting Milan, Florence, Rome and Naples.[26] In Florence he spent a number of days with Lord Hervey and again met the Duchess of Devonshire, who had also travelled there from Lausanne. Then he went to Rome, where he found a letter from his attorney waiting for him. It contained alarming news: the time to submit a claim for the money still owed him by the patrons of his faro bank in Paris was about to expire. In a letter written some months later Whaley claimed the amount he was owed was 'above 40,000', while in his memoirs he put it at £25,000.[27] Possibly these were overstatements, but even so it must have been a very large sum. It was an unusual position for Whaley to be in. For once he was not fleeing creditors but pursuing those who owed him money. This was enough to induce him to risk the hazards of Revolutionary Paris once more.

He embarked from Leghorn (Livorno) in 'an open boat', probably a galley, on 17 December 1792. Sixty miles out to sea the ship ran into a gale and was forced to take shelter in Portoferraio, 'a miserable place where I was detained 6 days by the badness of the weather'. This dubious start to the journey proved to be a harbinger of the troubles that lay ahead. Resuming his journey, Whaley landed in Nice around 24 December only to find that the town, then part of the duchy of Piedmont, had been occupied by French troops. It was not long before he became aware of the atrocities they were perpetrating in the name of the Revolution. 'The day before I arrived they had the barbarity to cut [a] prisoners arms off for attempting to make his escape.' Then, on Christmas Day, the soldiers 'broke open the prison where 5 unfortunate Piedmontese prisoners were confined [and] cut them and the gaoler in pieces and drag[g]ed their bodies thro' the town'.[28] If things were this bad in Nice what must it be like in Paris? Undeterred by the warning signs and intent on recovering his money Whaley continued on his way, arriving in the French capital early in the New Year.

Meanwhile his family had no clear idea of where he was. His mother held out little hope of influencing him. On 2 January 1793 she wrote despairingly to Faulkner, 'what will become of him God knows, his end I fear will be a foreign jail'.[29] She believed he was still in Italy and would no doubt have been shocked to learn that he had returned to Paris, especially with the war now well underway. After defeating the Austro-Prussian forces at Valmy on 20 September 1792 the armies of the Revolution had gone on the offensive, overrunning the Austrian

Netherlands (modern-day Belgium)[30] and occupying the Rhineland. Now France was on the brink of war with Britain and a friend informed Whaley that as a British subject he was not safe to walk the streets. But it was not these impending hostilities that raised tensions to fever pitch. The monarchy had been toppled, France was now a republic, and the king was in a perilous position. Accused of colluding with France's enemies, he had been put on trial in December. Most of those who remained loyal to Louis XVI did not dare to reveal their feelings, and the city simmered with anxiety and suspicion. With the trial underway 'all minds were intent upon the issue: but no one dare communicate his thoughts to another. All was distrust, and gloomy silence, in a city once the seat of mirth and noisy festivity.' (W, 311)

On 17 January 1793 the National Convention found the king, or Citizen Capet as he was now called, guilty and condemned him to be guillotined four days later in the Place de la Révolution. Whaley saw the ministers of the Revolution 'mount the carriage pale and trembling, like so many culprits, charged with the awful commission of announcing to the King a sentence which was at once a mockery of justice and a disgrace to human nature'. (W, 312) He regarded the dethroned monarch as a Christ-like figure who had patiently endured all the insults and indignities heaped upon him. Whaley had been in the city the previous June when a mob invaded the Tuileries Palace, forcing the king to don a red Phrygian cap (one of the symbols of the Revolution) and drink a toast to the nation: 'when I saw him for a whole day exposed to [the crowd's] taunts ... [and] forced to wear a red bonnet, the images which had been ever present in my mind, during my stay at Jerusalem, rushed back on my memory, and actuated by a momentary impulse of religious enthusiasm, and the parity of circumstances I exclaimed: Ecce homo'.[31] Now, like Christ, the king faced execution. Later, in the Café de Foix, Whaley saw two men, 'armed with sabres and pistols, exclaiming and repeating many times "Let all join with us who wish to save our unfortunate monarch."' (W, 312) He did not join the men but stayed for some time mulling over their words. He was staying opposite the Pont Royal,[32] a short distance from where the king would face the executioner. Could he somehow rescue the condemned monarch?

16

THE WILDEST GOOSE CHASE

The morning of 21 January 1793 dawned damp, foggy and numbingly cold. The king was taken from the Temple, the fortress where he had been held since the previous August, and placed in a carriage drawn by two black horses. From there over 1,000 guards escorted him to the Place de la Révolution, where a throng was assembling. Hoping to blend in with the Revolutionaries, Whaley attired himself 'like a true *Sans culotte*' and set out to put his plan into operation. Almost immediately he found himself faced with an intimidating show of force. Soldiers lined the streets four deep and when he got to the Place de la Révolution he saw that it was defended by cannon placed at the entrances. A huge crowd filled the square. He pushed his way through 'but when I came to the fatal spot, my resolution failed me'. Rows of blue-coated soldiers surrounded the scaffold ready to crush any disturbance. In typically half-cocked fashion Whaley had given no thought to how he would break through their ranks or, even if he did, how he would get hold of the king and spirit him to safety. Realisation dawned at last: 'fully convinced that there was not the smallest prospect of rescuing the unfortunate victim from the hands of his murderers, I fled with as much precipitancy from this scene of slaughter, this deed of blood by which human nature was so woefully outraged, as I had used before in approaching it'. (W, 312–13)

The king ascended the scaffold and attempted to address the crowd, but most of what he said was drowned out by drumbeats. His confessor, the Abbé Edgeworth de Firmont, an Irishman, offered words of consolation as the executioners seized him and tied him to a plank. As the guillotine fell Firmont cried out, 'Son of St Louis, ascend to Heaven.'[1] The executioner displayed the head to the crowd. A few were heard to cry out for the Republic and the Revolution but most were frozen with horror and 'the deepest silence lay like a pall over the regicide city'.[2] Whaley, meanwhile, had retreated to a coffee house. As he sat there trying to come to terms with what had happened, a group of men entered. One of them, his face stained with blood, began to report the details of the king's death. The scene made a powerful impression on Whaley and he recorded it as it unfolded. 'The unfortunate king is no more,' he wrote. 'I have this moment heard the particulars from a savage (I cannot call him a man) that is at present relating them … and who horrible to tell is all besmeard with the innocent monarchs blood.' He recoiled as the man thrust at him what he called 'the noble relicks of tyran[n]y': some of the king's hair and a handkerchief stained with his blood.

> He has now cut the handkerchief in small pieces and is sharing it with the other bloodhounds [and] I have been forced to partake of some of the hair … The rascal that is my authority and that is besmear[e]d with the kings blood is an Englishman[.] he sais that everyone near the scaffold painted their faces as he did … Oh my lord what a scene of horror in this town.[3]

In his memoirs Whaley claimed that he rebuked the men 'with a sternness produced by a kind of sensation I had never felt before … for the savage pleasure they testified and the mean part they had acted. "These are accursed spots," exclaimed I, with the liveliest emotion, "which not all the waters of the Thames or the Seine can wash away."'[4] (W, 314–15) Such an intense burst of feeling was rare for him and it makes for one of the most powerful moments in his writings. Yet there was a strange irony in his sympathy for the slain monarch: in 1649 his ancestor Edward Whalley had signed the death warrant of King Charles I.

★★★

Whaley also had more pressing matters to worry about. He had not managed to recover the smallest fraction of the money owed to him. 'Every thing is dismay and confusion,' he lamented. 'I can get nothing settled with respect to the business that brought me here nor would I have undertaken the journey for any consideration whatever could I have supposed it possible for me to be a witness to the scenes of cruelty every where committed.'[5] Hoping to make good his loss, shortly before the king's execution he had gone to the Palais Royal, meeting place of the royalist Club des Valois, and played hazard with the army officer Count Arthur Dillon. 'A good-looking man, tall, with receding hair and an aquiline nose, a small mouth and large black eyes', Dillon was said to resemble 'a parrot eating a cherry'.[6] He belonged to a distinguished Franco-Irish family that had 'adopted France for their country ... fighting gloriously for her cause'. When the Revolutionary Wars broke out in 1792 Dillon had been in command of the Army of the North but his royalist sympathies caused him to be demoted. Accused of treachery, he was recalled to Paris following the Battle of Valmy.[7] He shared Whaley's dismay at the king's predicament, which they may have discussed as they rolled the dice. Whaley came off the worst in the game and once again his losses were enormous, totalling 4,000 louis d'ors (around £4,000). He paid Dillon half the money that night, giving his word of honour that he would settle up the remainder in due course. Then he stumbled home, 'perplexed and stupified with my losses, and cursing that infatuation, which was continually involving me in new distresses'. (W, 309)

Whaley was now out of cash. How would he raise the money owed to Dillon, or even provide for his mistress and his little boy? Returning to Ireland or England seemed out of the question, with his creditors remaining alert for any news of him. Instead, he and Maria decided that she should set out for London on her own and somehow raise money there. 'Everything being settled according to this plan, she departed ... I then threw myself on the bed and remained some time overwhelmed with grief and vexation.' (W, 310) To be reduced to penury once again after he had recovered his fortunes the previous year was almost impossible to bear and when an acquaintance, Colonel Wall, told him Dillon had cheated him he was only too willing to believe it. On 1 February he confronted the Count, 'signifying my determination not to pay him'. (W, 316) The outcome was predictable: the two men agreed to settle the matter the following evening in the Champs Elysées.

The Champs Elysées was not then the traffic-filled urban boulevard it is today, but a large wood made up of rectangular groves of trees surrounding a broad central avenue. Wall had agreed to act as Whaley's second and they waited at the agreed spot for half an hour before Dillon appeared along with three companions. Whaley took up his position but Dillon hesitated, indicating a desire to speak to one of his party. Wall refused and as the seconds debated the matter Whaley realised that a troop of soldiers was approaching, seemingly to arrest them. 'I had scarcely time to mount my horse, and apprise W[all] of our danger, when the horsemen came close upon us. We immediately set off full gallop: D[illon] pursued us till we were out of hearing, uttering all the invectives and opprobrious language he could think of.' (W, 316–17) With the duel averted Whaley had lived to fight another day, but his situation had now become extremely precarious. France had just declared war on Britain and as a British subject he was liable to be arrested. Meanwhile Dillon did his utmost to have him locked up and 'at that time, there was from the prison to the guillotine but a regular step, and the interval very short between the one and the other.'[8] (W, 317) He spent the next three weeks 'skulking about like a thief' (W, 318) and moving from lodging to lodging to evade the authorities. Things could not go on like this. The constant anxiety and moving about was taking its toll on his little boy; meanwhile dark rumours reached his ears that Dillon was planning to assassinate him. He had no choice but to get out of Paris.

★★★

Whaley set out for Brussels in late February, hoping to making contact with Maria and arrange a rendezvous. He soon found himself engulfed by even greater turmoil than he had faced in Paris. Having defeated the Austrians at Jemappes in late 1792 the French general Dumouriez was planning to invade the Dutch Republic and his troops were massing in Belgium. Flushed with their recent success these soldiers were insolent and aggressive, as Whaley would find when he met them on the road. After a short stay in Brussels he received word that Maria was headed for Calais. He set out again and, travelling via Dunkirk, arrived in Calais sometime around the middle of March. When a packet boat came in sight his spyglass allowed him to discern Maria among the passengers on board but to his dismay he found that the Calais authorities were enforcing an embargo on British shipping. The packet boat was refused permission to dock and he watched helplessly as the vessel sailed back to Dover. Following Maria to England via another port would prove difficult, especially when he lacked the necessary papers. Luckily he made the acquaintance of an American lady and her two daughters, who invited him to accompany them to Ostend, some fifty-five miles up the coast. 'We availed ourselves of an old passport which the lady had for herself, her two daughters and her son, who was then absent and whom, on this occasion, I was to personate.' (W, 324) With renewed determination Whaley set out with his new companions, but a horrific experience lay in store on the road ahead.

Some eighteen miles from Ostend they stopped for the night in a small village, only to find it overrun by over 1,000 French soldiers. A number of them surrounded him, robbed him of whatever money or valuables he had, 'and strictly interrogated me as to my name and country, backing each impertinent question with a bayonet pointed at my breast'. (W, 325) Worse was to follow. The soldiers forced Whaley to watch the 'mamma and two pretty daughters … undergo the *manual exercise* whilst I was threatened to have my ears cut off if I dared to murmur … the blushes of the poor girls as soon as day light appeared was you may well imagine truly distressing'.[9] Rape was, unfortunately, all too common among the crimes of the soldiers of the Revolution. Only after the belated intervention of some officers were Whaley and his companions permitted to proceed to their destination.

Following a ten-day wait at Ostend they at last managed to get on board a vessel bound for Dover. Whaley had hoped to find Maria there, but he found that she had left for Deal. Over the next twenty-four hours he found himself playing an extraordinary game of chase, as he followed Maria first to Deal (where he managed to borrow money from his acquaintance Admiral Macbride, who was stationed there as commander of a frigate squadron[10]), then to London, then back to Deal, only to find that she had set out in a packet boat for Ostend. He hired a rowboat to follow the packet boat and five hours later they came upon her anchored just nine miles off Ostend. Whaley went aboard and at last 'found my Eurydice, who was then in bed, worn out with fatigue and anxiety'. After so many tribulations it was an especially joyful reunion and soon Whaley

15. Jerusalem from the north. Whaley stated that when he first set eyes on the city on 28 February 1789 'the emotions that took possession of my heart beggar all the eloquence of language'. View by David Roberts, 1839 (New York Public Library).

16. The Rotunda, Church of the Holy Sepulchre, Jerusalem, *c*.1780s–90s. This drawing by Luigi Mayer, whom Whaley met in Constantinople, shows the monks, pilgrims and beggars that crowded the church. From *Views in Palestine, from the original drawings of Luigi Mayer, with an historical and descriptive account of the country, and its remarkable places* (London: R. Bowyer, 1804) (New York Public Library).

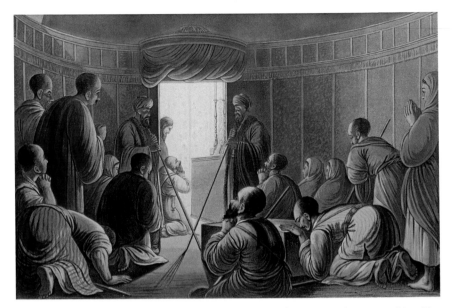

17. Entrance to the Chapel of the Holy Sepulchre, Jerusalem, *c.*1780s–90s. Although Whaley went to Jerusalem for a wager, he was so transfixed when he saw Christ's tomb that he became an actual pilgrim. From *Views in Palestine, from the original drawings of Luigi Mayer, with an historical and descriptive account of the country, and its remarkable places* (London: R. Bowyer, 1804) (image courtesy of the National Library of Ireland).

18. Nablus. On their return journey from Jerusalem Whaley and his companions were attacked and robbed near the town. View by David Roberts, 1839 (New York Public Library).

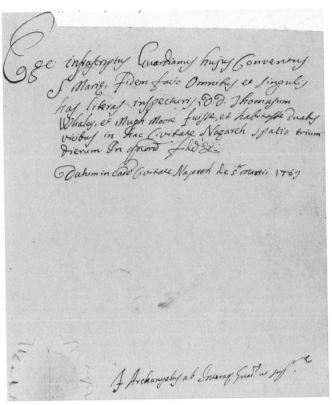

19. Certificate issued by the Guardian of Nazareth's Convent of the Annunciation confirming the visit of Thomas Whaley and Hugh Moore, March 1789. This was one of the documents Whaley brought back to Ireland as proof that he had visited the Holy Land. From manuscript journal of Captain Hugh Moore, 1788–9 (Ömer M. Koç).

20. Arthur Wesley as a young army officer. Following his return from Jerusalem, Whaley bet 150 guineas that Wesley could not walk five miles within an hour, but he proved more than equal to the task. Wesley later changed his surname to Wellesley and enjoyed an illustrious military career. In 1814 he was created first Duke of Wellington and a year later he commanded the Allied army at the Battle of Waterloo. Miniature portrait by unidentified artist, 1787 (Christopher Bryant).

21. Ahmad Pasha al-Jazzar in 1775, the year he became Ottoman governor of Sidon. In this portrait by Thomas Aldridge, 'the Butcher' looks ruthless and implacable (Michael Berreby).

22. Ahmad Pasha al-Jazzar condemning a criminal, c.1799. His advisor Haim Farhi, standing to the left, has had his right eye and nose cut off as punishment for some infraction. From F.B. Spilsbury, *Picturesque scenery in the Holy Land and Syria: delineated during the campaigns of 1799 and 1800...* (London: Edward Orme, 1803) (image courtesy of the National Library of Ireland).

23. The Prince of Wales (later George IV). Following his return from Jerusalem Whaley presented the Prince with an Arabian stallion. By Willem van Senus after George Henry Harlow (Rijksmuseum, Amsterdam: RP-P-1910-446).

24. Charles James Fox. One of the most brilliant statesmen and orators of his day, Fox was also a notorious gambler. In 1790 Whaley lost 2,000 guineas to him at the Newmarket Races. By Samuel William Reynolds (I), after John Raphael Smith (Rijksmuseum, Amsterdam: RP-P-OB-70.968).

25. 'Mrs Whaley' (Maria Courtenay). Described by Whaley as 'a lady of exquisite taste and sensibility', she was his companion for most of the latter part of his life and a steadying influence during trying times. Portrait attributed to George Chinnery (Metropolitan Museum of Art, New York).

26. The town of Lausanne, overlooking Lake Geneva. While staying here in the summer of 1792 Whaley decided to climb Mont Blanc. Late-eighteenth-century view by Daniel Dupré (Rijksmuseum, Amsterdam: RP-P-BI-7252).

27. Louis XVI prepares to ascend the scaffold in Paris on 21 January 1793. Whaley's planned rescue attempt came to nothing and he fled the scene in horror. By Luigi Schiavonetti, after Charles Benazech (Rijksmuseum, Amsterdam: RP-P-OB-73.022).

28. Count Arthur Dillon. This Franco-Irish army officer took exception to Whaley's failure to pay a gambling debt and the two arranged to fight a duel in the Champs Élysées (New York Public Library).

29. Fort Anne, Douglas, Isle of Man, in the nineteenth century. Whaley began building the mansion around 1797 but did not live to see it completed (Frances Coakley).

had even more reason to rejoice. 'She desired me to observe a petticoat she then wore, and which, she said, had not been off for three weeks … she shewed me two thousand pounds sewed in the binding.' (W, 328)

Now that Whaley and Maria were together again and had money, he could have resumed his original plan and headed for Switzerland. After all, London promised nothing but trouble. He owed over £10,000 to various parties there and he knew they would hound him for every penny. On the other hand, France was swarming with hostile troops and he had no desire to be questioned again at bayonet point or to have Maria suffer the same fate as his American friends. London, he decided, was the lesser of two evils. Perhaps he even flattered himself that he could elude his creditors, but if so the illusion was soon shattered. No sooner had they arrived in the city than Whaley ran into an old acquaintance 'to whom I was under the necessity of giving seventeen hundred pounds to stop his mouth and prevent his giving intelligence to the rest'. (W, 328) Once again it seemed that as soon as money came into his hands it flew back out again. Staving off the inevitable he assumed a false name and took up residence in Moorfields, 'never stirring out but on Sunday evenings'. (W, 329) The caution was all in vain. Before long another creditor tracked Whaley down, a waiter from Brooks's Club looking for £400 he had lent him (presumably) at the time of his £26,000 loss there in February 1791. He could not pay and this time there was no escaping incarceration.

For some reason Whaley was sent not to a debtors' prison but to the Bridewell, which was 'solely designed for thieves and murderers'. Maria was not allowed to accompany him and he found himself 'thrust into a common room, amidst wretched criminals of all descriptions'. (W, 330) The desperate situation called for desperate measures.

> I represented to the Jailor, that I was not committed on a charge of any crime, and that I was a gentleman. 'That may be,' said the Jailor: 'but here we make no distinction but according to the money a man can afford to spend. I have excellent champaign and claret, and if you choose to call for either, I can accommodate you with one of my own apartments.' I acceded to the proposal … and invited the Jailor to take a glass of wine with me; an offer which I had no

occasion to repeat; and accordingly I plied him so closely with his own home-brewed champaign, that he was soon in a fit condition for my purpose, which was that of descending from the window into the street ... I had scarce made the attempt when the Jailor's daughter, a stout athletic wench, assisted by two of the understrappers, seized me and immediately conveyed me to the common room, where I should have been very roughly handled were it not for the interposition of ten guineas, which I fortunately had then in my pocket, and with which I appeased the infernal crew there assembled ... (W, 330–1)

By now Whaley was all but at the end of his rope. Since his departure from Italy the previous December everything had gone against him. His plan to rescue Louis XVI from the guillotine had come to nothing, while the chaos of the Revolution had ensured that he never saw any of the money he was owed. Then he had lost another massive sum to a man who, wrongly or rightly, he was convinced had cheated him. He had fled the dangers of Paris only to encounter even worse horrors on the road before eventually returning to England and the fate he had so long eluded: imprisonment for non-payment of debt. 'I wish to God I had remained at Florence,' he wrote later to Hervey, 'and not undertaken what I have since found to be the wildest of my *wild goose chaces*.'[11] Now he was locked in prison, out of money and out of ideas.

17

THE WANT OF MONEY AS USUAL

'No sir, the Devil in hell is not quite as bad as the Devil in human form of whom I mean to speak.'[1] So commented an observer on the politician John Fitzgibbon, who became Lord Chancellor of Ireland in 1789. The remark was not as contentious as it seems, for Fitzgibbon was a man who provoked extreme reactions. He was roundly hated for his opposition to Catholic relief and even his political allies found him hard to get on with. His main ambition was to safeguard the connection between Ireland and Britain while ensuring that the Protestant elite remained in control of the country, but he had no time for the wasteful and self-indulgent members of his class – people like his wife's brother Tom Whaley, who over the years had 'probably made many ... unrecorded demands on his brother-in-law's time, patience and purse.'[2] Now, locked in the Bridewell, Whaley was in hell or near enough to it, and it seemed that only the devil could get him out. It just so happened that Fitzgibbon was in London and Maria, with the help of Whaley's brother, managed to get word to him. Whaley's antics had caused Fitzgibbon some embarrassment over the years and he probably rolled his eyes when he heard about this latest misfortune. Had all things been equal he might have left him to his own devices, but he knew his wife would have wanted him to do something. The next day Fitzgibbon went to the Bridewell and undertook to settle the debt owed to the waiter.

Before Whaley could be freed it was necessary to check if there were detainers for any of his other debts. Luckily the prison office 'happened to be in the county of Surrey. Had it been in Middlesex, there would in all probability have been detainers to the amount of all my debts. As it was [Fitzgibbon] had only four hundred pounds to pay with the costs.' (W, 331) Whaley was free to go, but the number of places to which he could go was fast diminishing. He knew that if he stayed in London he would be relentlessly pursued by the bailiffs. He also owed plenty of money to people in Ireland, but at least there he still had property which could be sold or mortgaged to raise money. His mother and stepfather, however, were in England: with Anne suffering from rheumatism, the Richardsons had relocated to Bath. Around the middle of May 1793 Whaley joined them there to try and put things in order for his return. A fortnight or so later he set out for his homeland.[3]

***

In Ireland Whaley's debts were legion, caused not only by his gambling but also by the prodigal lifestyle he had pursued in the year following his return from Jerusalem. He had piled up expense after expense, giving little or no heed to where the money would come from. When the bills and loans were left unpaid, the suppliers and merchants had resorted to legal action to get their money. In 1790 and 1791 the courts had ordered him to pay a Joseph Dalmer a total of £2,000. Meanwhile he owed a further £2,000 to Robert Clements and over £1,133 to Austin Cooper, not to mention £700 to the Dublin wine merchant John Ferns.[4] His mother and stepfather were themselves in financial difficulties and unable to help him. 'I am very sincerely sorry to find that your affairs in Ireland wear so bad an aspect,' John Richardson informed him, '[but] the distress is general and all those who are best inclined to assist you are entirely disabled. This I assure you is my case.' By now the house on Stephen's Green had been let to a man named Turner Camac, who was allowing it to fall into a dilapidated condition. Whaley hoped to raise money by selling his interest in the property to Camac but Richardson was strongly opposed to this, believing it would be foolish 'to sell such a thing to such a man, [as] to whom it is now let, from only a tempor[ar]y necessity at not more than half its value'. Whaley pressed ahead regardless and at some point in 1793 he raised £2,000 by mortgaging the house.[5] Even this was far from adequate to satisfy his demands. While he had sold some of his County Armagh lands in 1792 he still possessed a sizeable estate there, but this he would sell only as a last resort.

Whaley was also troubled by the disturbed political situation in Ireland. Returning after more than a year's absence, he was alarmed to find the ideals of the French Revolution quickly gaining ground in his homeland. To keep the peace the government had decided early in 1793 to establish a militia, a domestic force to be manned through compulsory service. Most people violently opposed conscription and between May and August riots broke out across the country. Fierce clashes between the rioters and government troops resulted in around 230 deaths. 'Every possible opposition that the wretches are capable of is given by them to the raising of the militia', Whaley complained. Like most of the Anglo-Irish Protestant upper class he was out of touch with the grievances of the majority Catholic population, which fuelled both the anti-militia rioting and the growing support for republican organisations such as the United Irishmen. Reflecting bitterly on these developments, Whaley wished he had never left Italy and declared, 'upon my soul had I the offer for myself of Florence or the Ld. Lieutenancy [of Ireland] I hate Ireland so consummately I wd. prefer the other to it'.[6]

As negative as this sentiment was, it must be taken in the context of the atrocities perpetrated in the name of the French Revolution, which Whaley had first-hand experience of: the slaughter of Piedmontese prisoners in Nice, the guillotining of Louis XVI in Paris, and the rape of his female travelling companions near Ostend. The possibility that a republican regime like the one that held sway in France would be established in Ireland filled him with fear and revulsion. But he did not truly hate Ireland. He never considered himself a dyed-in-the-wool Irishman (he and most Anglo-Irish Protestants thought of themselves as 'English, albeit the English of Ireland'), but he did have affection for his homeland, which he sometimes called his 'dear land of saints'.[7] During his travels he had felt an affinity with those who shared the Irish fondness for warmth and conviviality. Juan de Bouligny, a Spanish diplomat he met in Constantinople, was 'well acquainted with Irish hospitality' (W, 105), while a friendly Greek who lodged him and his party in Cyprus 'seemed to possess the soul of a true Hibernian'. (W, 248)

Although Whaley found himself less well disposed towards Ireland during the tumultuous summer of 1793, his personal financial problems were as much to blame as anything for his resentment. Of course there was one way in which he might recover his fortunes 'or complete my ruin' (W 332): gambling. He was unable to resist the lure of Daly's Club, now installed in magnificent new premises on College Green in Dublin. No expense had been spared and the interior was 'furnished in a superb manner, with grand lustres, inlaid tables, and marble chimney-pieces; the chairs and sofas were white and gold, covered by the richest "Aurora silk". One visitor described it as 'the most superb gambling house in the world'.[8] The splendid surroundings did not soothe Whaley's temperament and he found himself prickly and prone to anger. When he caught a Galway gentleman, Mr Burke, staring at him in Daly's in June 1794 he asked him 'did he learn such manners in his travels'. 'I did,' Burke replied, 'yet I have not been at Jerusalem.' Whaley responded with abusive language, Burke struck him, and a challenge was unavoidable. Agreeing to fight with pistols, the two men met in the Phoenix Park on 19 June. Standing at a distance of twelve paces, they fired simultaneously. Whaley's shot missed, while Burke magnanimously fired his pistol in the air. With neither harmed, the two made up their quarrel.[9]

Added to his confrontation with Arthur Dillon, this was Whaley's second affair of honour within a year and a half. The fact that each of the quarrels originated in a gaming house shows how much 'play' agitated him. He had classic gamblers' syndrome: though terrified of suffering another horrendous loss, he played on in hopes of a windfall that would retrieve his fortunes. 'There is a point in self-made or self-fantasised career when it is harder, perhaps, to face cold financial and professional realities than to struggle on in the dream that some huge win will redeem all past losses and failures.'[10] Time and again this flawed rationale had driven Whaley to stake and lose money, sinking him further into the mire of debt. Various parties continued to pursue him in Ireland, and as usual he could not visit London without risking arrest. His brother William claimed he had been in a position to help him clear his debts there 'but alas! he drew the money back, and I doubt, much, whether the creditors will ever again, come into the same terms'.[11] Yet it was not clear how William could have helped Tom: he himself had only just avoided prison in London for failing to pay money he owed.[12] Meanwhile their mother and stepfather's financial problems persisted.[13] With little or no chance of getting money from any other quarter, in late 1794 Tom

surrendered to the inevitable and decided to sell the remainder of the
Armagh estate.

★★★

The Armagh lands were thought to be worth £10,000 but finding a
suitable buyer proved to be no easy matter. As ever, Whaley turned to
the solid-as-a-rock Samuel Faulkner for assistance. Though Faulkner had
known Whaley and his brothers since they were children he must have
come to rue the association, which had caused him no end of trouble over
the years. He had helped Tom and John out on numerous occasions and
without his intervention William would certainly have wound up in prison
in London. He was now in his seventies, his weakness for fine claret was
causing him to suffer attacks of gout,[14] and the strain of managing the
Whaleys' estates and debts was wearing him out. It was hard to disagree
with Robert Cornwall's assessment: 'they are a most unfortunate set of
men and every one who has dealings with them have [sic] been implicated
in their misfortunes'.[15] Cornwall could not know that for Faulkner, even
greater misfortune still lay in store.

In November 1794 the Armagh lands were out of lease and Whaley
asked Faulkner to advertise for new tenants so they could be made ready
for sale.[16] Things did not move swiftly enough for Whaley's creditors, who
continued to resort to the courts to get their debts paid. For him the best
course of action was to get out of the country until the sale was finalised,
but where could he go? England, for obvious reasons, was not an option.
Nor was the continent, with the French Revolutionary Wars still raging.
But there was another possibility. Surrounded by the Irish Sea and not
properly part of Britain or Ireland, the Isle of Man had always seemed
outside the law. For centuries it had been a centre of smuggling, which
did not abate even after the British Parliament purchased the island in
1765. More significantly from Whaley's perspective, it had been a refuge
for the insolvent since 1737, when its legislative assembly passed an
act exempting debtors from arrest for foreign debts. Man was the ideal
place for him to lie low and he relocated there early in 1795, settling in
the neighbourhood of Douglas. Initially he planned to stay only until

the Armagh lands were disposed of and by June 1795 he was confident that 'every thing now is in a fair way for the sale'.[17] However, the process proved to be more complicated than anticipated. The Archbishop of Armagh emerged as a likely buyer but he refused to commit. Over the course of the summer Faulkner and Cornwall dealt with other would-be purchasers,[18] but legal action taken by Whaley's creditors complicated the process. The antiquary Austin Cooper,[19] to whom Whaley owed over £1,000, succeeded in obtaining a judgement for the Armagh estate to be sold by public auction to discharge his debt.[20] However, parties who had been given to understand that they could make private offers for the estate objected and the auction did not go ahead.[21] Probably in order to sort out the legal mess surrounding this, but also to get Whaley to repay a sum of money he owed Faulkner, Cornwall decided to travel to the Isle of Man to meet him.

The lawyer had a safe journey to the island[22] but his meeting with Whaley was less successful, with the latter failing to stump up what was owed. Meanwhile in Ireland two men, Thomas Prentice and a Mr Wilson, were showing real interest in buying the Armagh lands, but Faulkner was running out of patience with Whaley. He decided that he would not sign over the estate until he received his money. 'I believe I must go to the island to gett a settlement out of this man,' he confided to his brother Hugh. 'Cornwall advises it by all means.'[23] With the stormy autumn season now underway the Irish Sea was often perilously unsettled, as Cornwall had discovered when he sailed from Man for Whitehaven in north-west England on 25 October. The conditions were so atrocious that his ship took seven hours to reach its destination. 'We could not carry a bit of sail and all the gales of wind I ever before experienced was but a trifle to it.'[24] Faulkner decided to press ahead with his journey regardless and travelled to Dublin to take ship for Man. On 16 November he wrote a final word to Hugh: 'nothing new or particular to mention ... but the want of money as usuall.'[25] He sailed the next day aboard the *Bee*. That evening a powerful south-westerly gale sprang up on the Irish Sea. The wind was not believed to be dangerous 'as it does not set upon the Welch or Irish coasts, but leaves an open sea to drive before it.'[26] This confident statement overlooked the fact that the Isle of Man is due north-east of Dublin and any ship heading in that direction would be driven onto the island's coast. Caught in the furious gale, the *Bee* was wrecked on the rocky peninsula of Langness, Man's southernmost point. All crew and passengers were drowned, though Faulkner did not go down with the ship. A wave swept him overboard and the following day his body was washed ashore, a gold watch and forty guineas still on his person.[27]

A few days later the news reached Dublin. Robert Cornwall, who was Faulkner's nephew as well as his business associate, was devastated. He had the unenviable task of informing Hugh: 'the dreadfull tale of woe I have to communicate, will require you to muster up every resolution as a man, to bear the stroke which has been inflicted on us all. you have lost an affectionate brother, and I an uncle dear to me as my own existence'.[28] The timing could scarcely have been worse. Cornwall warned that Faulkner's 'affairs are in such an unsettled state at present, that I know not what will be the consequences'. He had died without reaching a settlement with Whaley and as a consequence the Armagh lands remained unsold. Cornwall asked Hugh to 'keep this matter as quiet as possible … but this I fear cannot be done'.[29] He was correct. A few days later it was reported in the newspapers.[30] Now there was every chance that Whaley's creditors would descend en masse to get satisfaction by means of Faulkner's estate. But the tragedy also may have had a more far-reaching outcome, one that none could never anticipate. It may have moved Whaley a step closer to immortality.

18

WHALEY'S FOLLY

Around the year 1900 the bookbinding aficionado Sir Edward Sullivan visited a London auction room. At the auction he noticed and purchased 'what I recognised to be an interesting example of Irish binding, in the characteristic style of decoration common in Dublin at the close of the eighteenth Century, consisting of two handsome 4to volumes of manuscript bound in red morocco, inlaid and tooled in gold, and lettered on the back "Travels by T. W.".'[1] The volumes were, of course, Whaley's manuscript memoirs and when Sullivan published them as *Buck Whaley's Memoirs* a few years later he thrust the 'Jerusalem Pilgrim' back into the spotlight for the first time in over a century. The publication was popular enough to ensure his lasting fame over the decades that followed. But had the Irish Sea not claimed Samuel Faulkner in the stormy autumn of 1795 Whaley may never have written his life story.

***

No letters or documents have survived to record Whaley's reaction to Faulkner's death but almost certainly it left him badly shaken, perhaps even racked with guilt. He had known him since he was a small child, and the agent had always acted the part of a friend rather than a land agent or business associate. Anne Richardson had praised Faulkner for the 'care and affection' he showed her son and Whaley's own letters contain flickers of his fondness for the bluff old Ulsterman. When absent on his grand tour he remembered the happy days they had spent when he was a child: 'should I live to see you in Dublin we will ride to the county Carlow togather [and] laugh at old times'.[2] He knew that Faulkner had only set sail in order to recover money he should have repaid him, and the realisation that his old friend and helper had died because of him must have affected him deeply. Not long afterwards, in an unmistakeably contrite and reflective mood, he started work on the memoirs. Perhaps for the first time in his life he took a good hard look at himself and saw all of his weaknesses, self-indulgences, frailties and vanities reflected back in harsh light. He did not shy away from the glare and admitted to 'extraordinary levities … an eccentric and exalted imagination and ridiculous pretensions to notoriety'. (W, 3) He also confessed to a neurotic personality that had only made bad situations worse:

> To avoid an impending evil, I have formed plans so wild and extravagant, and for the most part so impracticable, that what I had before dreaded appeared light when compared with the distress I incurred by my own precipitate folly. Added to this, an impatience of all control whatsoever, and a temper always impelled to action in proportion to the resistance which it had to encounter. (W, 10)

Whaley's self-analysis was accurate: he had followed this course all too often, from his scatter-brained attempt to sort out his financial problems by abducting an heiress to his ill-advised decision to return to Paris during the turbulent weeks before Louis XVI's execution. Also, he finally understood just how superficial was the fashionable world he had moved in in Dublin, London, Paris and elsewhere. Having been 'deceived in believing that a life of dissipation could produce enjoyment; or that tumultuous pleasures led to real happiness', he had discovered that 'transient pleasures … are constantly succeeded by pain and languor'. To his credit, he consistently refused to blame others for his failings. His mother, he insisted, had brought him and his siblings 'up in the paths of religion and virtue: and whatever follies any of us may have committed, the cause could never be imputed to her'. (W, 9) He also absolved the inept William Wray from any culpability for the 'follies and eccentricities' of his grand tour, 'which I am willing to take on my own account'. (W, 11) He even refused to name the two Irishmen who had swindled him in Lyons 'because I only wish to impeach myself'. (W, 20)

Whaley now believed that happiness could 'only be attained in a calm and retired life remote from the vortex of fashionable amusements' (W,

7) and, perhaps to his surprise, he had found peace of a kind on the Isle of Man. In March 1796 he and Maria purchased some land near Douglas in Maria's name,[3] probably so as to avoid alerting any interested parties to Whaley's presence on the island, and they settled down to a simple existence, even indulging in a little farming. They now had three children: a second son, Richard, had been born sometime after their return to Ireland in 1793, and a daughter, Anne, arrived a year or two later. Whaley was happy to divide his time 'between the education of my children, the improvement of my small farm, and the writing of these Memoirs, which I hope may prove of some service to youth in particular and to travellers in general'. (W, 8) He clearly intended the memoirs for publication, hoping not unreasonably that the adventures of the renowned 'Jerusalem Pilgrim' would sell well and produce much-needed funds. With this in mind he devoted most of the work to the Jerusalem expedition. While he seems to have kept some notes on his travels, like any autobiographer he relied to a large degree on personal recollection. As it was now around seven years since the expedition he must have been hazy on many details, so he borrowed the journal of Hugh Moore, who was now a captain in the 5th Dragoon Guards, and used it to flesh out his recollections of various events and places, occasionally reproducing Moore's descriptions almost verbatim. Two manuscript versions of the memoirs were produced: the original and a copy. For whatever reason they were not published during Whaley's lifetime and would languish in obscurity until Sullivan unearthed them. Nonetheless his financial situation improved slightly. His account with Faulkner was sorted out posthumously and the Armagh lands were finally sold, allowing him to settle into a relatively comfortable life on the Isle of Man. But this period of restful contemplation would not last. Though Whaley had been sincere about henceforth avoiding the 'vortex of fashionable amusements', in time he would be drawn back into high society with all its snares and temptations. It remained to be seen if he could resist them.

He was not above sitting again for a portrait and at some stage, possibly in 1797, he commissioned George Chinnery to produce full-length paintings of himself and Maria which were later exhibited in Dublin. Whaley was 'represented in a cornfield, with his gun in one hand, the other extended, as if directing his dogs, or determining his path: his servant appears close behind, crossing a stile, with his hand to his mouth, giving the sportsman's whistle.[4] This portrait seems to have been lost around 1902 but the companion likeness of Maria is now in New York's Metropolitan Museum.[5] It depicts a slender figure in a dark, flowered muslin dress, standing in a grove of trees. She has an attractive, sensitive face with somewhat sad eyes and the slight roundness of her abdomen may indicate early pregnancy (see Plate 25).[6] Towards the end of 1797 she gave birth to another daughter, Sophia Isabella, who was baptised near Douglas on 13 December.[7] But even as Maria and Whaley celebrated the new addition to their family they may have sensed that her days were numbered. Perhaps her labour had been difficult and debilitating, but whatever the reason she made her will a few weeks later on 23 January 1798. She left the land she had purchased on the Isle of Man to her four children, naming Whaley as their sole guardian. All her remaining possessions she left to him.[8]

By now Whaley had finished work on the memoirs and there are signs that he was growing restless. Early in 1798 he decided to return to Ireland, at least temporarily, as he had thought of a way to avoid imprisonment for debt. He had not been a member of parliament since 1790 but he knew that MPs were entitled to freedom from arrest in civil matters, a privilege commonly used by those who were liable for unpaid debts. In February he purchased the seat for Enniscorthy, County Wexford, for £4,000, borrowing half the sum from the politician John Colclough. He managed to persuade Colclough to accept a mortgage of the last surviving remnant of his Carlow estate, the townland of Straboe, as security, even though it had already been offered as collateral for numerous loans.[9]

Whaley could not have chosen a more turbulent time to re-enter politics. In the early months of 1798 Ireland was a powder keg waiting to explode. For years the middle and lower classes had been agitating for political reform and in the 1790s the United Irishmen began planning an uprising. The government's response – to violently stamp out sedition – proved counter-productive. In May rebellion erupted in south-east Leinster and quickly spread to Ulster. The Crown forces resorted to increasingly brutal tactics to crush the insurgents, who also committed atrocities. On

9 June the rebel army engaged a government force at Arklow but was beaten back. The commander of the Crown troops, Francis Needham, commended 'the spirited exertions of Mr. Whaley', while also singling out his aide-de-camp Captain Hugh Moore for special praise.[10] It is tempting to imagine the old friends Thomas Whaley and Hugh Moore reunited and fighting side-by-side in the Battle of Arklow, but it is more likely that 'Mr. Whaley' was William Whaley, who was now a major in command of a detachment of government troops. Tom Whaley does not seem to have taken part in suppressing the rebellion, but like most other members of the upper classes he was firmly on the government's side and wanted to see the rebels defeated as soon as possible. During the summer he stayed for a time at St Stephen's Green,[11] but even in Dublin the grim realities of the conflict were starkly evident. The citizens would have been shocked by 'the ghoulish horror of a civil war almost on their doorstep … lamp-posts used as gibbets and bridges across the river decorated with the trophy corpses of rebels'.[12]

Sensibly enough, Whaley had maintained a foothold on the Isle of Man. One never knew when the disturbances in Ireland, or his still precarious financial situation, would again compel him to beat a retreat. He and Maria had started building a mansion on the land they had purchased overlooking Douglas harbour. Whaley named it Fort Anne in honour of his mother and it was rumoured that before he laid out the foundations he had enough soil shipped over from Ireland 'to allow six feet in depth of Irish earth to underly the whole of the house', either to win a bet or fulfil an oath that he would live on the Isle of Man, and yet dwell on Irish soil.[13] But Maria would not live to see the house completed. She had not recovered from whatever was ailing her and by September she had died.[14] The passing of his adored companion, perhaps the only woman he had truly loved, must have hit Whaley hard. For almost a decade he had been devoted to her, calling her 'the principal source of all my felicity'. (W, 270) At some point afterwards he suffered a second devastating blow when his infant daughter Anne passed away. Now there was no telling what turn his life would take.

★★★★

And yet, over the two years that followed his fortunes improved greatly. Work on Fort Anne continued, with the house taking on such a luxurious appearance that the locals dubbed it 'Whaley's Folly'.[15] Such magnificence did not come cheaply. Sullivan believed that 'money must have come to him, and in large amounts too ... If local tradition count[s] for anything, the house would appear to have been built out of the proceeds of successful gambling.'[16] Local tradition must have counted for something because by the summer of 1799 Whaley had been drawn back into the world of wagers. Once again, it seemed that a tired and entirely predictable sequence of events would unfold: he would stake large sums and lose them, and then frantically wager more money, until he lost all of his property and the last vestiges of what was once a formidable fortune. When his last remaining possessions were sold he would end his days in prison. So much seemed inevitable: only this time, things were different. Somehow, Whaley was no longer a loser.

Now, when he gambled he found his luck much improved, even when betting on that most unpredictable aspect of life in Ireland: the weather. On 15 July 1799, St Swithin's Day, it rained. Whaley had enough confidence in the saying 'St Swithin's day if thou dost rain/For forty days it will remain' to lay a wager on its veracity and sure enough, for the next forty days there was 'rain every day, more or less'. His winnings were enormous: £7,000, almost equal to his profits from the Jerusalem expedition.[17] This was a time of success and affluence for Whaley, and it was not down simply to luck or the vagaries of the weather. Somehow he had become a more canny operator, able to turn both private and public affairs to his advantage. Early in 1800 he reaped another windfall, this time from a more reliable source: an inheritance. On 11 January he married Mary Catherine Lawless at St Peter's Church in Dublin. We know nothing of how Whaley met or courted her, but for him the union was undoubtedly one of convenience. It was no accident that the marriage took place only a few months after Mary's father Nicholas Lawless, the first Baron Cloncurry, died leaving a great fortune. Before his death her brother Valentine had stood to inherit between £60,000 and £70,000, but he had been arrested on suspicion of high treason and imprisoned in the Tower of London. His father, afraid that the Crown would confiscate any money inherited by his son, had altered his will to prevent this. As a result much of the fortune had passed to Mary. Whaley was still in considerable debt but under the marriage settlement he secured £3,000 from his new wife to help him meet his obligations.[18]

He also found ways to make money out of politics. By now, Ireland was in the throes of a constitutional upheaval. The devastation of 1798 had convinced the British Prime Minister William Pitt that a Dublin-based parliament could not govern the country effectively and he proposed a legislative union: the Irish Parliament would be abolished and Ireland would be administered directly from Westminster. But it was necessary to get the Irish MPs to vote for the dissolution of their own parliament, and campaigners both for and against the measure had no qualms about offering bribes in return for votes. Whaley decided to take full advantage of this. Having at first supported the Union, he offered his vote to the highest bidder and in January 1800 opposed the measure after being 'absolutely bought by the Opposition stock-purse'. In return he received £4,000, the exact amount he had paid for his seat in parliament. Once he had this money safely in his pocket he switched sides a second time and voted in favour of the Union in return for a further £4,000.[19] The success with which Whaley played the system suggests that he had at last acquired some guile, after having so often been the dupe of others. He now trusted to intelligence rather than blind luck to extract profit from a situation.

The money would have enabled him to pay off his most insistent creditors and perhaps he even contemplated buying back some of his old estate, as he returned to Carlow in the summer of 1800. Early in August he attended the Carlow Assizes, where he met the English philosopher William Godwin (father of Mary Shelley, the author of *Frankenstein*). Godwin was aware that Whaley was the man 'who made himself famous a few years ago by undertaking for a wager to go to Jerusalem & return' but he was also struck by his muddled sense of geography and history: 'This man as a traveller is really a curiosity: he affirmed that Georgia was the capital of Circassia, & that Moesia (a province) was the original name of Byzantium (a city.)'.[20] At this point in time geographical and historical distinctions mattered little to Whaley. With his fortunes on the rise and a new house, new wife and growing family to care for, he seemed to be embarking on a fresh chapter in his life. It must therefore have been all the more shocking when, in November 1800, news reached Dublin and London that he had died.

★★★

Not much is known of the circumstances that led to Whaley's demise. For some reason he decided in the autumn of 1800 to embark on a journey to London. On 2 November he was approaching Knutsford in Cheshire when something happened on the road and 'he was brought in an almost expiring condition to the "George Inn" … then a well known halting place on the mail-coach road, where he died soon after being admitted'.[21] He was buried in Knutsford churchyard and his grave was covered by a stone with a brief inscription: 'Underneath is interred the body of Thomas Whaley, Esquire, of the City of Dublin, who died November 2nd, 1800. Aged 34 years'.[22]

Needless to say the passing of the famous 'Jerusalem Pilgrim' was major news in Britain and Ireland. *The Times*, the *London Gazette* and many other newspapers carried obituaries recalling how 'this gentleman's name had been long celebrated in the annals of the gay and fashionable world'. The *Monthly Magazine* and *Walker's Hibernian Magazine* each ran a lengthy tribute by a writer who had access to the manuscript memoirs and used them to summarise Whaley's life and adventures.[23] The *Freeman's Journal* published a more reflective piece, praising him for his 'liberality and benevolence … His conversation was universally acknowledged to abound in refined sentiments, elegant address, and a convivial disposition.' The obituarist was happy to let others take the blame for Whaley's excesses, noting how numerous scroungers and sycophants had led him astray and how he had suffered 'incalculably … in their manifold lures'.[24] This jarred with Whaley's own admission of personal responsibility for his actions, and indeed most of his misfortunes are to be put down not so much to the influence of others as to his own folly. Either way, those misfortunes were now over. Thomas 'Buck' Whaley, that colourful and ill-starred character, that erratic flame that had burned so brightly, was gone at last. But what had extinguished him? The obituaries ascribed the cause of death to 'a rheumatic fever, which he caught in Ireland'.[25] This seemed plausible: Whaley had always been vulnerable to feverish illness. It had laid him low at Fort Faulkner in 1787 and in Constantinople in 1788–9 and now, it seemed, it had killed him in Knutsford. He had made his will less than ten days before his death, which suggests he was ill and wanted to set his affairs in order.

But as ever with Whaley, nothing – not even his passing – was straightforward. After all, if he was ill why was he travelling? Some twenty years later the author of a popular satirical work, *Real Life in Ireland*, offered an alternate explanation of how he met his end: it was not fever that killed Whaley, but a young girl from Liverpool:

> SALLY JENKINSON was a Liverpool *fair* … At the age of sixteen she was seduced from home by the famous BUCK WHALEY, of *Stephen's Green*: her sister also was seduced by the same man; and, *strange* as it is true, they both lived with him under the same roof 'tis but charitable to say, that one had no knowledge of the other's intimacy for some time with the depraved '*Buck of Ireland*'. When things were brought to light, jealousy ensued, and in a rage the elder sister stabbed WHALEY in the side: he lingered long, and finally died of the wound – no trial ever took place …[26]

The story has the ring of sensationalism about it, and indeed *Real life in Ireland* was written in the style of the journalist Pierce Egan, who was 'always prepared to embellish the truth in the interests of entertainment'.[27] Nevertheless, there is one fact that lends the tale credence. Whaley had indeed been in Liverpool just before his death: it was there that he had made his will on 24 October.[28] Was the explanation of death by fever invented to cover up the actual scandalous circumstances of his demise? The answer, very probably, is no. It is difficult to see the Sally Jenkinson story as anything other than a fabrication. If Whaley did have a mistress or mistresses in Liverpool it seems unlikely that one of them attacked and fatally wounded him on the road near Knutsford. It is equally unlikely that if Whaley *had* been murdered, protecting his reputation would have been given greater priority than having the killer brought to justice.

A sudden and premature death in an inn on the mail-coach road and an unassuming burial in a local churchyard: perhaps not the circumstances that Thomas Whaley would have chosen for his demise. Yet in a way they were oddly fitting. He had sustained so many mishaps, misfortunes, close shaves and illnesses that sooner or later one of them was bound to put paid to him. He had also undertaken so many journeys and stayed in such a variety of lodgings, from the wondrous to the wretched, that a roadside inn somehow seemed an appropriate place for him to end his days. Less than two months later, the Act of Union came into effect. With the emergence of the Sally Jenkinson story and many other tales, Whaley was already passing into the mythology of an older, wilder, pre-Union Ireland. He also loomed large in tales of adventure and derring-do, fuelling the colourful fiction of nineteenth-century writers. He may have helped inspire characters like Barry Lyndon in William Makepeace Thackeray's *The Luck of Barry Lyndon* (1844) and Phileas Fogg (1872). And yet he transcended the world of rakes, gamblers and adventurers. His legacy is greater and more significant than that.

EPILOGUE

'His adventures were much of a piece with those of Sinbad, in the Arabian Nights: one time the persecuted victim of divine wrath; at another the distinguished favourite of a most benign Providence.' (W, 244) So wrote Whaley of a gentleman he met during his travels in Cyprus, but he might as easily have applied the sentiment to himself. In *The Thousand and One Nights* Sinbad the Sailor undertakes seven voyages and in the narrative cycle of each he goes from prosperity to loss and back again to prosperity. Whaley repeated the same cycle many times over the course of his life. After losing thousands of pounds and suffering a dose of the pox on his grand tour, he was restored to affluence and health on his return to Ireland. He then proceeded to squander much of his inheritance, but the triumph of his Jerusalem expedition brought him money, fame and adulation. Over the years that followed he lost almost everything only for him to dramatically rescue his fortunes with the success of his faro bank in Paris. But by early 1793 his affairs had again unravelled spectacularly and he found himself locked up in London's Bridewell prison. This was followed by a desperate period of debt evasion on the Isle of Man until Samuel Faulkner's death jolted him into wisdom and self-awareness and in his final years he managed to turn many things to his advantage.

It was no accident that Whaley had such a topsy-turvy life. His personality had good and bad sides and the conflict between the two helps explain why he continually lurched from success to calamity and back again. The bad points are evident: Whaley was self-indulgent, impatient, thoughtless, rash, vain and, most of all, wasteful. He gambled away a huge fortune, squandering large estates in Carlow and Armagh and many tens of thousands of pounds besides. He also caused untold anxiety and difficulty for Anne and John Richardson, even though his mother's view of her son remained sympathetic to the point of being blinkered.[1] For his close associates Robert Cornwall and Samuel Faulkner he spelt nothing but trouble. Cornwall's letters to Faulkner are a long chronicle of exasperation with Whaley's ongoing financial calamities and other antics, which cost him large sums he probably never recovered.[2] Meanwhile the reward Faulkner reaped for his many years of selfless service was death by drowning. Whaley, however, often exaggerated or embellished the truth in order to portray himself in the best possible light (though he is by no means the only memoirist to have done so). There is a temptation to simply dismiss him as a spoiled and selfish wastrel.

And yet it is not that simple, because Thomas Whaley was also a sympathetic character with many likeable aspects. Conscious of his personal flaws and failings, he knew that chance had bestowed great wealth and opportunity on him and he regretted that he had often heedlessly wasted these advantages. He had undeniable personal courage, whether on the duelling field or when confronted with danger on his travels, and he was resilient in the face of hardship. He could also be compassionate and charitable and Hugh Moore was among those who considered him a valuable friend. Socially, Whaley was praised for his 'convivial disposition'[3] and was probably good fun to be around. He was no snob and happily shared the society of everyone from the Prince of Wales to the humble clerk William Norwood.

Whaley was a true child of the Georgian era, an extraordinary time of eccentrics, chancers and gamblers. To name but a few, Sir Arthur Brooke,[4] the first Marquess of Drogheda,[5] the second Earl of Massareene,[6] the seventh Earl of Barrymore,[7] the second Marquess of Donegall[8] and William Norcott[9] all obliterated their fortunes and family estates at the gaming tables. Whaley stood firmly among the ranks of these notorious gamblers, but he also stood apart from them. There is a reason why he is still remembered long after they and many others have faded into obscurity: he was a far more attractive and compelling character than any of them. One of the things that made him attractive was his sheer unpredictability. Time and again he surrendered to a compulsive urge to undertake madcap plans and enter into dangerous situations. Whether planning to abduct an heiress, leap over a mail coach from a second-storey window, descend into the depths of St Michael's Cave or blunder up the frozen slopes of Mont Blanc, he was nothing if not interesting.

While he did not achieve everything he desired, it was not for want of trying because he was extraordinarily dogged. The sheer lengths to which he was prepared to go to realise dreams and win wagers surprised even seasoned observers of upper-class eccentricity. Few of those acquainted with him expected him to even reach Jerusalem, never mind complete the round trip within the allotted time. After all, he was profligate and seemingly feckless and virtually every enterprise he had undertaken had ended in failure or disaster. But almost no one appreciated the power of the forces that drove him. He proved tough and determined enough to see his Jerusalem odyssey through in the face of all adversity. He was not daunted by storms, pirates, foreign fleets, bad weather, hostile janissaries or the restrictions of the Ottoman regime. Even when a storm threatened to wreck his ship and drown him he did not fear death so much as the possibility that he would be unable to complete his journey and win his wager. Disease was the thing that came closest to killing him but he had the will to survive and continue his journey, even though it meant struggling on for weeks in a weakened condition. By successfully completing the expedition he did something few of his peers would even have contemplated. He also proved that he was much more than just a wealthy spendthrift. He and Moore were among a relatively small group of Europeans to visit Turkey and the Levant in the eighteenth century and their writings stand as a valuable record of the Ottoman Empire during a crucial juncture in its history. Many of their observations had antiquarian merit and they were among the last visitors to record the inscriptions on the tombs of Jerusalem's first Crusader rulers in the Church of the Holy Sepulchre. On a more personal level, the privations of travel and the dangers they faced gave Whaley a better understanding of the world and his place in it, so that when he returned he could appreciate 'the inestimable blessings of personal security, ease and comfort'. (W, 225)

Where does he stand alongside the other westerners who left accounts of their travels in the Ottoman Empire? He was not as brilliant a writer as Lady Mary Wortley Montagu (1689–1762); his understanding of Ottoman politics and society did not match that of the Comte de Volney (1757–1820); he was not as great an explorer as Johann Ludwig Burckhardt

(1786–1817). But, it might be argued, he captures the imagination more than any of these travellers. Not only did he embark for the Holy Land on the back of a wager, the fact that he had such an uninspiring track record and yet succeeded in making it to Jerusalem and back somehow makes him an appealing, even endearing, character. Today, as in the eighteenth century, most people try to live their lives within society's constraints. We work hard, pay our rates and taxes, abide by the law of the land and strive to put aside some money for our future and our children. When we hear about someone who refuses to play by the rules and follows his or her own desires and instincts rather than society's dictates, we may actually feel a sneaking admiration and follow their escapades with fascinated interest. This is the case whether the person is alive today or a historical figure.

Whaley was not a game changer, though he crossed paths with many. He was not a great statesman like Charles James Fox, or an all-conquering soldier like the Duke of Wellington, or a giant of letters like Edward Gibbon or William Godwin. For centuries historians have deemed him unworthy of attention, referring to him (when they do at all) only in footnotes as an exemplar of the wild excesses of the Georgian era. Many believe that an individual such as he pales into insignificance when set against the principal actors in great political events such as the decline of the Ottoman Empire, the French Revolution or the 1798 Rebellion. But Thomas Whaley bore witness to these events, and his life and adventures are as much part of history as any political upheaval. History needs characters like him – characters who bring the past to life through sheer dint of passion, folly and excess. By retracing his steps we watch a micro-history unfold in vivid, atmospheric and visceral colours. We shudder with him in the filthy stables of north-west Turkey, we share his awe at the splendour of an Ottoman palace, and we are fascinated by his religious epiphany in Jerusalem. We feel his fear on the road from Nablus and his horror at the brutal atrocities of Ahmad Pasha al-Jazzar. We know that he has been naive, irresponsible and wasteful in the past and will be again in the future, yet somehow we are with him, rooting for him. Why? Perhaps because, despite his privileged upbringing, he was something of an underdog. A seemingly perpetual loser and dupe, he nevertheless undertook one of the greatest adventures of the age, and won one of the greatest wagers in the history of gambling. In doing so he created an unforgettable story and a history that is as authentic and compelling as any.

WORKS CITED

(Bibliographic details for the works that are not
cited in full in the notes.)

Bailey, Craig, *Irish London: Middle-Class Migration in the Global Eighteenth Century* (Liverpool: Liverpool University Press, 2013).

De Beer, G.R.,'Puzzles', *Alpine Journal*, 55, 272 (May 1946).

Black, Jeremy, *The British Abroad: The Grand Tour in the Eighteenth Century* (Stroud: Sutton, 1992).

Casey, Christine, 'A wax bas-relief by Patrick Cunningham', *Irish Arts Review Yearbook*, 11 (1995).

Casey, Christine, *Dublin: The City within the Grand and Royal Canals and the Circular Road ...* (New Haven and London: Yale UP, 2005).

Clarke, Edward Daniel, *Travels in Various Countries of Europe, Asia and Africa* (6 vols, London: T. Cadell and W. Davies, 1810–23).

Clemit, Pamela (ed.), *The Letters of William Godwin, Vol. 2 1798–1805* (Oxford: Oxford UP, 2014).

Connell, Brian, *Portrait of a Whig Peer: Compiled from the Papers of the Second Viscount Palmerston, 1739–1802* (London: Deutsch, 1957).

Curran, C.P., *Newman House and University Church* (Dublin: University College Dublin, [1953]).

Davies, Brian L., *The Russo-Turkish War, 1768–1774: Catherine II and the Ottoman Empire* (London: Bloomsbury, 2016).

Dickson, David, *Dublin: The Making of a Capital City* (London: Profile, 2014).

Doumani, Beshara, *Rediscovering Palestine: Merchants and Peasants in Jabal Nablus, 1700–1900* (Berkeley: University of California Press, 1995).

Erdem, Y. Hakan, *Slavery in the Ottoman Empire and its Demise, 1800–1909* (Basingstoke: Macmillan, 1996).

Fa Darren and Finlayson Clive, *The Fortifications of Gibraltar 1068–1945* (Oxford: Osprey, 2006).

Green, Henry, *Knutsford: Its Traditions and History* (London: Smith, Elder & Co., 1859).

Hayes, Richard, *Ireland and Irishmen in the French Revolution* (Dublin: Phoenix Pub. Co., 1932).

Johnston-Liik, Edith Mary, *History of the Irish Parliament, 1692–1800: Commons, Constituencies and Statutes* (6 vols, Belfast: Ulster Historical Foundation, 2002).

Kelly, Ian, *Casanova* (London: Hodder & Stoughton, 2009).

Kelly, James, *'That Damn'd Thing called Honour': Duelling in Ireland, 1570-1860* (Cork: Cork UP, 1995).

Lodge, John, and Archdall, Mervyn, *The Peerage of Ireland: Or, a Genealogical History of the Present Nobility of that Kingdom* ... (7 vols, Dublin: James Moore, 1789).

MacGill, Thomas, *Travels in Turkey, Italy and Russia During the Years 1803, 1804, 1805, & 1806* ... (2 vols, London: John Murray, 1808).

Maguire, W.A., *Living like a Lord: The Second Marquis of Donegall, 1769-1844* (Belfast: Appletree Press, 1984).

Mansel, Philip, *Constantinople: City of the World's Desire, 1453-1924* (London: John Murray, 2006).

Mansel, Philip, *Levant: Splendour and Catastrophe on the Mediterranean* (London: John Murray, 2010).

Matthews, Ronnie, *Portarlington: The Inside Story* (The author, c.1999).

Mazzeo, Tilar J. (ed.), *Travels, Explorations and Empires: Writings from the Era of Imperial Expansion, 1770-1835. Volume 4: Middle East* (London: Pickering & Chatto, 2001).

Mishaqa, Mikhayil, *Murder, Mayhem, Pillage, and Plunder: The History of the Lebanon in the 18th and 19th Centuries*. Trans. by Wheeler M. Thackston (New York: SUNY Press, 1988).

Monahan, Amy, 'The Faulkners of Castletown, Carlow' [unpublished manuscript in private ownership].

Montefiore, Simon Sebag, *Jerusalem: The Biography* (London: Weidenfeld & Nicolson, 2011).

Moorehead, Caroline, *Dancing to the Precipice: Lucie de la Tour du Pin and the French Revolution* (London: Chatto & Windus, 2009).

Philipp, Thomas, *Acre: The Rise and Fall of a Palestinian City, 1730-1831* (New York: Columbia University Press, 2001).

Pringle, Denys, *The Churches of the Crusader Kingdom of Jerusalem: A Corpus* (3 vols, Cambridge: Cambridge UP, 1993).

Ross, Charles (ed.), *Correspondence of Charles, First Marquis Cornwallis* (3 vols, London: J Murray, 1859).

Ryan, David, *Blasphemers & Blackguards: The Irish Hellfire Clubs* (Dublin: Merrion Press, 2012).

Shaw, Stanford J., *Between Old and New: The Ottoman Empire under Sultan Selim III, 1789-1807* (Cambridge, MA: Harvard University Press, 1971).

Sullivan, Sir Edward (ed.), *Buck Whaley's Memoirs* (London: Moring, 1906).

Talbot, Michael, 'Divine Imperialism: The British in Palestine, 1753-1842' in Martin Farr and Guégan Xavier, (eds.), *The British Abroad Since the Eighteenth Century, Volume 2: Experiencing Imperialism* (Basingstoke: Palgrave Macmillan, 2013).

Baron de Tott, Francois, *Memoirs of Baron de Tott: Containing the State of the Turkish Empire ... During the Late War with Russia* ... (2 vols, London: G.G.J. and J. Robinson, 1786).

De Chasseboeuf, Constantin François, comte de Volney, *Travels Through Syria and Egypt, in the Years 1783, 1784, and 1785...* (2 vols, London: Robinson, 1788).

White, Jerry, *London in the Eighteenth Century: A Great and Monstrous Thing* (London: Vintage, 2013).

Young, Arthur, *Travels During the Years 1787, 1788, & 1789 ...* (2nd ed., 2 vols, London: W. Richardson, 1794).

ENDNOTES

Prologue

1 Whaley mistakenly believed that de Saussure was the first man to reach the summit of Mont Blanc.

2 John Owen, *Travels into different parts of Europe, in the years 1791 and 1792 ...* (2 vols, London: Cadell and Davies, 1796), Vol. 2, pp. 307n, 308.

3 De Saussure's expedition had used this gear in 1787. See Christian von Mechel's engraving *Ascent of Mont Blanc by Horace-Benedict de Saussure in August 1787.*

4 De Beer, 'Puzzles', p. 409.

5 De Beer, 'Puzzles', p. 409; G.R. de B[eer]., 'Some letters of Charles Blagden', *Notes and records of the Royal Society of London*, 8, 2 (April 1951), pp. 259–60.

6 Quoted in de Beer, 'Puzzles', p. 409.

7 As the historian Jerry White notes, 'there is no satisfactory mechanism for calculating the modern value of old money' but £1 in the late eighteenth century 'might be approximately £350 in today's money': Jerry White, *Mansions of Misery: A Biography of the Marshalsea Debtors' Prison* (London: The Bodley Head, 2016), p. xix. By this reckoning Whaley's inheritance would equal around £17 million sterling or €19 million today.

8 Whaley's claim that he squandered £400,000 may be an exaggeration. However, the amount he lost over the course of his life ran well into six figures. A more conservative estimate might put the total at around £200,000, still an enormous sum for the time.

9 *FJ*, 8 November 1800.

10 The two-volume manuscript was auctioned and sold by Sotheby's in December 1926: *The Irish Times*, 17 December 1926. The purchaser was 'Ellis': *Book-Prices Current: A Record of Prices at Which Books Have Been Sold at Auction* (London: Elliot Stock, 1927), p. 970. I have been unable to find further information on the purchaser's identity or discover the manuscript's present whereabouts.

Chapter 1

1 Sir Edward Sullivan put Whaley's date of birth at 15 December 1766 (Sullivan (ed.), *Memoirs*, pp. vii, 8), but actually he was born exactly a year earlier than that: contemporary documents show that he came of age on 15 December 1786. 'A State

of the Personal Fortune of Thoms. Whaley Esqr. made up and settled according as his Sisters Fortunes were made up and settled by the late Revd. Mr. Bernard Ward his Guardian and Sir Annesley Stewart Bart. an Executor', c.1786: Whaley Papers.

2   Lodge and Archdall, *The Peerage of Ireland*, Vol. 6, pp. 71–2.

3   *The Irish Builder*, 15 December 1894, p. 293.

4   *The Post-Chaise Companion: Or, Travellers Directory Through Ireland* … (Dublin, 1786), p. 278; http://www.countywicklowheritage.org/page/mining_in_west_avoca (accessed 25 March 2018). In 1795 the Hibernian Mine Company 'unwatered that part of the mines of Ballymurtagh, formerly wrought by the late Richard Chappel Whaley, Esq.' (*SNL*, 21 July 1795).

5   Curran, *Newman House*, p. 9.

6   *Town and Country Magazine*, January 1789, p. 9.

7   Myles V. Ronan (ed.), *Insurgent Wicklow 1798: The Story as Written by the Rev. Bro. Luke Cullen O.D.C. (1793–1859)* (Dublin: Clonmore & Reynolds, 1948), pp. 76, 77–8; *Town and Country Magazine*, January 1789, p. 9.

8   Lodge and Archdall, *The Peerage of Ireland*, Vol. 6, pp. 71–2.

9   John O'Keeffe, *Recollections of the Life of John O'Keeffe* … (2 vols, London: Henry Colburn, 1826), Vol. 1, pp. 205–6.

10   Curran, *Newman House*, p. 9; Casey, *Dublin: the City Within the Grand and Royal Canals*, pp. 506, 507.

11   *SNL*, 18 August 1826; *Town and Country Magazine*, January 1789, p. 9.

12   Casey, 'A wax bas-relief', p. 117.

13   Sullivan has it that Richard Chapel Whaley constructed his new abode in order to humiliate his neighbour, John Meade, later first earl of Clanwilliam, who was living at No. 75. Having purchased the plot of ground that lay adjacent to Meade's house, Whaley set about erecting a pile that would make his neighbour's house 'look no better than a pigstye in comparison': Sullivan (ed.), *Memoirs*, pp. x–xi. But this cannot be correct, as Richard Chapel Whaley was living at No. 75 himself when he started work on No. 76. Clanwilliam did not take up residence in No. 75 until much later (1786).

14   Some, envious perhaps of the Whaleys' wealth and ostentation, attempted to have the lion statue taken down. In 1774 a public committee was charged with taking down 'all projecting signs' in the city and a correspondent recommended 'that the noted sign of the stone [*sic*] lyon in Stephen's Green' be removed: *HJ*, 13–15 June 1774. The recommendation was not acted on and the statue is still there.

15   Casey, *Dublin: The City Within the Grand and Royal Canals*, pp. 506, 508.

16   Faulkner rented the house from the Earl of Milltown, paying a half-yearly rent of £15: Cash Book of Samuel Faulkner, 1785–86, NLI, Ms. 19,447. In later years the poet W.B. Yeats took up residence there.

17   SF to Michael Kearney, 27 July 1791: Faulkner Papers.

18 Faulkner was also an amateur architect. Some of his designs, including one annotated by Thomas Whaley, are in the Irish Architectural Archive: http://www.dia.ie/architects/view/2463/FAULKNER-SAMUEL (accessed 25 March 2018).

19 Note of RCW granting power of attorney to SF, 7 March 1765 (PRONI, MIC21/6); RCW to SF, 6 March 1765 (NLI, P. 3500).

20 Writing to Faulkner many years later, William Whaley referred to himself as 'your old friends son' (WW to SF, 2 October 1794: PRONI, MIC21/6).

21 Register of baptisms, St Peter's, Dublin, 1762–1813: RCBL.

22 Casey, 'A wax bas-relief', pp. 117–18.

23 *FJ*, 24–28 January and 14–18 February 1769.

24 Will of Richard Chapel Whaley: NLI, D. 6597.

25 James Joyce, *A Portrait of the Artist as a Young Man* (London: Penguin, 2000), p. 199. Whaley's mansion was later purchased by the Catholic Church and, as Newman House, became the Catholic University of Ireland. Joyce attended college there from 1898 to 1902. Joyce refers to a secret staircase or passage that supposedly led from the house to another residence nearby, but this story does not seem to have any basis in fact.

26 Alison FitzGerald, 'Taste in high life: dining in the Dublin town house' in Christine Casey (ed.), *The Eighteenth-Century Dublin Town House: Form, Function and Finance* (Dublin: Four Courts Press, 2010), pp. 120–7.

27 Hopkins became a fellow of the Royal University of Ireland in 1884. He lived and taught at Newman House from 1884 to 1889.

28 AR to SF, 19 December [year not given]: PRONI, MIC21/7.

29 AR to SF, 28 December 1773: PRONI, MIC21/7.

30 Will of Richard Chapel Whaley, 5 July 1768: NLI, D. 6597.

31 Affidavit of Samuel Faulkner on the Whaley minors, 31 January 1775: PRONI, T1617/6/2.

32 AR to SF, 28 December 1773: PRONI, MIC21/7.

33 *HJ*, 13–15 June 1774.

34 Monahan, 'The Faulkners of Castletown', p. 48.

35 Matthews, *Portarlington*, pp. 53–4; *DEP*, 14 February 1784.

36 TW to SF, 21 October 1775: Faulkner Papers.

37 Matthews, *Portarlington*, pp. 53–4; *DEP*, 14 February 1784.

38 'A new and Correct Map of se Africa dedicated to Mr. Ward by his dutiful Gd. son Thomas Whaley June 25th 1775': Whaley Papers. Tom's map accords closely with Herman Moll's in giving prominence to the old African kingdoms of Monoemugi (roughly equivalent to present-day Zambia and Zimbabwe) and Monomotapa (comprising Botswana and part of South Africa).

39 TW to SF, 21 October 1775: Faulkner Papers; Monahan, 'The Faulkners of Castletown', p. 48.

40   TW to SF, 2 March 1778: Faulkner Papers.

41   List of expenses for funeral of Master Faulkner, 29 September 1782: Faulkner Papers; TW to SF, 7 January 1783: Faulkner Papers.

42   Black, *Grand Tour*, p. 290.

43   Bailey, *Irish London*, pp. 77n, 214; *FJ*, 7–9 June 1781.

44   *WHM*, December 1800, p. 324.

Chapter 2

1   TW to SF, 5 and 7 January 1783: Faulkner Papers.

2   Black, *Grand Tour*, p. 21.

3   TW Manuscript Memoirs, Vol. 1, p. 12.

4   Young, *Travels*, Vol. 1, p. 58.

5   TW to SF, 7 January 1783: Faulkner Papers.

6   RC to SF, 19 May 1785: NLI, P. 4647.

7   The Scottish surgeon John Hunter popularised the transplantation idea in *A Treatise on the Natural History of the Human Teeth* (1771); TW to SF, 5 January 1783: Faulkner Papers.

8   TW to SF, 7 January 1783: Faulkner Papers.

9   TW to SF, 7 January 1783: Faulkner Papers.

10   TW to SF, 31 August 1783: Faulkner Papers.

11   TW to SF, 28 June 1783: Faulkner Papers.

12   TW to SF, 3 August 1783: Faulkner Papers.

13   TW to SF, 31 August 1783: Faulkner Papers. In 1776 William Congreve, suffering from constant pain following the loss of a hand, obtained 'great relief' at Barèges: Black, *Grand Tour*, p. 181.

14   Laurence L. Bongie, *The Love of a Prince: Bonnie Prince Charlie in France, 1744–1748* (Vancouver: University of British Columbia Press, 1986), p. 285. The Rohan family had a habit of courting controversy. In 1785 Henri Louis's uncle, the Cardinal de Rohan, was at the centre of the Affair of the Diamond Necklace, a major scandal at the French court that unfairly discredited Marie Antoinette.

15   Dramatically, Whaley suggested that he could have been in for the same fate as the Chevalier de La Barre, who was tortured and beheaded in 1766 after insulting a religious procession and damaging a crucifix. However, it seems unlikely that he would have suffered such treatment.

16   He left her at the 'Convent of the Tiercelets' (W, 18), probably one of the convents of the Sisters of the Third Order of St Francis.

17   In a letter to his mother in June 1784 Whaley stated that he left Auch owing £1,000 and spent a further several hundred pounds during a visit to Bordeaux (letter from TW to AR, quoted in AR to SF, 25 June 1784: PRONI, MIC21/7). In fact, he was

probably understating the case as in his manuscript memoirs he stated that he left Auch owing £1,800 (TW Manuscript Memoirs, Vol. 1, p. 28). In the published memoirs a figure of £18,000 is given (W, 18) but this is clearly a misprint.

18   TW to SF, *c.* early 1784: Whaley Papers.

19   TW to JR, 20 [June] 1784: Faulkner Papers.

Chapter 3

1   John Ryan may have been related to Michel Ryan or O'Ryan, an Irish physician based at Montpellier and Lyons. O'Ryan published *Discours sur le Magnétisme Animal, lu dans une Assemblée du Collège des Médecins de Lyon, le 15 Septembre 1784* (Dublin, 1784).

2   TW to JR, 20 [June] 1784: Faulkner Papers.

3   TW Manuscript Memoirs, Vol. 1, pp. 51–2.

4   When he checked out a few weeks later (8 July) his bill came to over £164: Samuel Faulkner, Minor expenses book, 1784–1785: PRONI, MIC21/1.

5   As a major crossroads of trade, London was a magnet for middle-class Irish migrants: Bailey, *Irish London*, p. 5.

6   TW to JR, 20 [June] 1784: Faulkner Papers. In Whaley's memoirs the amounts are given as £200,000 and £25,000 a year but this is clearly an exaggeration: W, 28.

7   Bailey, *Irish London*, p. 194. Grove's generosity eventually brought him to ruin. In late 1788 he went bankrupt. 'Everything was lost; his country house in Mitcham, his coach and horses, even [his wife's] jewellery was sold off in a futile attempt to pay off outstanding debts'. He died in prison in Dublin in 1795, 'penniless and forgotten': ibid. p. 195.

8   TW to JR, 20 [June] 1784: Faulkner Papers.

9   TW Manuscript Memoirs, Vol. 1, pp. 51–2.

10   Quoted in White, *London in the Eighteenth Century*, p. 370.

11   TW to JR, 20 [June] 1784: Faulkner Papers.

12   TW to JR, 20 [June] 1784: Faulkner Papers.

13   AR to SF, 25 June 1784: PRONI, MIC21/7.

14   AR to TW, 27 June 1784: PRONI, MIC21/7. This letter to Whaley has probably only survived because it was never sent. Soon after writing it Anne would have discovered that her son was in London and that his situation was far graver than she had anticipated, making the letter redundant.

15   Liza Picard, *Dr. Johnson's London: Life in London, 1740–1770* (London: Weidenfeld & Nicolson, 2000), p. 163.

16   *Gentleman's Magazine*, 138 (December 1825), p. 569.

17   C. Potts to TW, 16 July 1784: Faulkner Papers.

18   White, *London in the Eighteenth Century*, p. 370.

19 The following year Robert Cornwall enjoyed Richardson's company on a journey to London, 'during the whole course of which, it seemed to be my fellow travellers wish to render each hour more agreeable than the past': RC to SF, 12 May 1785: NLI, P. 4647.

20 AR to SF, 28 December 1773: PRONI, MIC21/7; AR to TW, 27 June 1784: PRONI, MIC21/7.

21 Summaries of letters of John Ryan to TW and draft responses, July 1784: Faulkner Papers.

22 List of Whaley's expenses on the road from London to Holyhead: Faulkner Papers.

23 AR to TW, 27 June 1784: PRONI, MIC21/7.

24 Cash book of Samuel Faulkner, 1785–86: NLI, Ms. 19,447; Johnston-Liik, *Irish Parliament*, Vol. 6, p. 534. A newspaper report on the swearing-in mistakenly referred to him as 'Richard Chapel Whaley'. Tom had not yet outgrown his father's notoriety: *FJ*, 12–15 February 1785.

25 Dublin's Parliament House is now the Bank of Ireland building on College Green. The present-day Parliament House at Westminster had not yet been constructed.

26 Peter Somerville-Large, *Dublin: The Fair City* (Rev. ed., London: Sinclair-Stevenson, 1996), p. 157.

27 On 19 April 1786, Faulkner paid a bill of Whaley's 'for painting done at *his* house in Stephens Green' (emphasis added): Cash book of Samuel Faulkner, 1785–86: NLI, Ms. 19,447.

28 Cash book of Samuel Faulkner, 1785–86: NLI, Ms. 19,447 (passim); William Norwood to SF, 22 August 1786; *SNL*, 18 January 1786. Whaley lost Vixen on Capel Street while visiting his shoemaker in January 1786. Faulkner placed an advertisement offering a reward for the animal's return but we do not know if she was ever found: entry for 18 January 1786, Cash book of Samuel Faulkner, 1785–86: NLI, Ms. 19,447.

29 *DEP*, 15 May 1787; Diness [Denis] Lennard to SF, 23 January 1786: PRONI, MIC21/4.

30 Samuel Faulkner's account book records many of the expenses Whaley incurred indulging in these and other activities: Cash book of Samuel Faulkner, 1785–86: NLI, Ms. 19,447.

31 AR to SF, 4 August 1785: PRONI, MIC21/7; *DEP*, 18 October 1785.

32 Whaley claimed in his memoirs that he hired a Plymouth shipbuilder to construct a 280-ton vessel, with twenty-two guns, at a total cost of £10,000. (W, 34) But in fact his ship was built on the Isle of Wight and it seems to have been smaller and less lavishly equipped.

33 WN to SF, 25 October 1785: NLI, P. 1576; entries for October 1785, Cash book of Samuel Faulkner 1785–86: NLI, Ms. 19,447.

34 *Town and Country Magazine*, January 1789, p. 9.

35 AR to SF, 22 November 1785: PRONI, MIC21/7.

36   What exactly went on during these 'midnight orgies' is unknown. Many years later
      it was alleged that Whaley belonged to a 'hellfire club', a type of gentleman's club
      notorious for blasphemy and provocative behaviour: *Notes and queries*, 2nd series, Vol.
      10 (28 July 1860), p. 77; 3rd series, Vol. 2 (23 August 1862), p. 149; *Weekly Irish Times*,
      24 December 1904. However, there is no contemporary evidence to back up this claim.

37   AR to SF, 25 October 1785: PRONI, MIC21/7.

38   AR to SF, November 1785 and 2 December 1785: PRONI, MIC21/7.

39   AR to SF, 22 November 1785: PRONI, MIC21/7.

40   On 23 December Whaley drew on Faulkner for £50 English in favour of a Mr Span,
      but the money was really intended for someone else: 'I only put Mr. Span to hide the
      real name as it is for a woman'. TW to SF, 23 December 1785: Whaley Papers.

41   AR to SF, 27 December 1785: PRONI, MIC21/7.

42   To fit out these apartments Whaley commissioned a furniture maker to fashion
      doors, bookcases, wash stands, an oak press, an oval dining table and a large oak
      guardevine (a chest for storing valuables). Bills of Joseph Dixon, 4 July, 12 August
      and 29 November 1786: Faulkner Papers. Further expenditure in 1786 included £20-
      14-2½ paid to a man named Clark 'for Sundries done for Mr. Whaley at his Boat' (16
      January) and £3-13-1½ paid to Hugh Murphy for a pole and boom (17 April): Cash
      book of Samuel Faulkner, 1785–86: NLI, Ms. 19,447.

43   WN to SF, 12 August 1786: NLI, P. 1576.

44   Ibid.

45   WN to SF, 25 July 1786: NLI, P. 1576.

46   Hugh Faulkner, quoted in Amy Monahan, 'An Eighteenth-Century Family Linen Business:
      The Faulkners of Wellbrook, Cookstown, Co. Tyrone', *Ulster Folklife*, 9 (1963), p. 34.

47   WN to SF, 15 August 1786: NLI, P. 1576.

48   WN to SF, 6 Mar. and 6 May 1786: NLI, P. 1576.

49   WN to SF, 15, 17, 18, 23 and 28 August: NLI, P. 1576.

50   WN to SF, 4 September 1786: NLI, P. 1576; Lord Sandwich, quoted in http://www.
      historyofparliamentonline.org/volume/1754-1790/member/macbride-john-1800
      (accessed 16 October 2018).

51   Headstone inscription for Catherine Faulkner: Faulkner Papers.

52   Michael Caraher to SF, 19 September 1786: PRONI, MIC21/4; SF to WN, 13 October
      1786: Faulkner Papers.

53   John Whaley to WN, 12 October 1786: PRONI, MIC21/6; AR to WN, 20 October
      1786: PRONI, MIC21/7.

Chapter 4

1   Kelly, *Duelling in Ireland*, p. 195.

2   *FJ*, 21–24 October 1786.

3   *SNL*, 24 and 25 October 1786; *FJ*, 21–24 October 1786. Samuel Faulkner's brother Hugh hinted that Whaley issued the challenge: HF to SF, 10 November 1786: PRONI, MIC21/1.

4   *SNL*, 24 October 1786.

5   *FJ*, 21–4 and 24–6 October 1786.

6   HF to SF, 10 November 1786: PRONI, MIC21/1.

7   AR to SF, 28 November 1786: PRONI, MIC21/7. The previous August, while Whaley was away on his voyage to Plymouth, Richardson had spent 'a considerable time' with Norwood 'talking over several matters respecting the young men particularly Tom': WN to SF, 17 August 1786: NLI, P. 1576.

8   'Savings out of the Estates of Thomas Whaley Esqr. from the time of his Fathers Death in 1769. To the 1st. Day of November 1786. as received by Saml. Faulkner Esqr. Agent, accounted for in Chancery and paid over to the Guardians': Whaley Papers.

9   Robert Cornwall alone was owed over £1,865, which was paid to him in January 1787: Account of sums owed by Thomas Whaley to Robert Cornwall, January 1787: NLI, P. 4647.

10   He had tried and failed to borrow £10,000 from Robert Armitage (a relative of his father's first wife) to offset these costs: Robert Armitage to SF, 17 November 1786: Faulkner Papers.

11   TW to SF, 13 March 1787: Faulkner Papers.

12   White, *London in the Eighteenth Century*, p. 339.

13   Dickson, *Dublin: The Making of a Capital City*, p. 279.

14   John Whaley to SF, 10 June 1787: PRONI, MIC21/6. Though he gambled with abandon himself, Tom was not prepared to allow his employees to do so. When he took on an apprentice musician, Thomas Norton, in January 1787 he insisted that he 'shall not play at cards, dice, tables or any other unlawfull games whereby his said master may have loss'. Indenture between Thomas Whaley and Thomas Norton, 30 January 1787: PRONI, T1617/6/3.

15   William Span to SF, 2 May 1786: PRONI, MIC21/4; Cash book of Samuel Faulkner, 1785–86: NLI, Ms. 19,447; Kath[erine] Wray to SF, 5 December 1786: PRONI, MIC21/4; TW to SF, 21 October 1790: Faulkner Papers.

16   TW to SF, *c.* March 1787: Faulkner Papers; Annesley Stewart to TW, 4 May 1787: PRONI, MIC21/6.

17   TW to SF, 6 and 7 May 1787: Faulkner Papers.

18   Fort Faulkner is now an equestrian centre. A carved stone head over the fan-lit front entrance is a said to be a likeness of Samuel Faulkner, though it also resembles the heads on the facade of Dublin's Custom House, representing Ireland's rivers. My thanks to Sue Chadwick and Ruth Hayes for showing me around the house and grounds in March 2017.

19   Monahan, 'The Faulkners of Castletown', p. vii; William Norwood to SF, 28 February, 4 March, 8 March and 28 April 1787: NLI, P. 1576.

20   TW to SF, 23 May 1787; TW to WN, June 1787; TW to SF, 2 June 1787: Faulkner Papers.

21   WN to SF, 22 May 1787: NLI, P. 1576.

22   John Donnelly to SF, 7 June 1787: Faulkner Papers.

23   WN to SF, 6 June 1787: NLI, P. 1576.

24   Peruvian or cinchona bark is the source of quinine.

25   Harriet Heydon to SF, 2 July 1787: Faulkner Papers.

26   Harriet Heydon to SF, 1787: Faulkner Papers.

27   WN to SF, 4 August 1787: NLI, P. 1576.

28   TW to SF, 2 June 1787: Faulkner Papers.

29   AR to SF, 22 October 1787: PRONI, MIC21/7.

30   Robert Cornwall to SF, 30 November 1787: NLI, P. 4647; FJ, 15–18 December 1787.

31   TW to SF, 26 November 1787: Faulkner Papers; RC to SF, 26 November 1787: NLI, P. 4647.

32   Monahan, 'The Faulkners of Castletown', pp. 58–9.

33   Harriet Heydon to SF, 30 December 1787: PRONI, MIC21/4; TW to SF, 31 December [1787]: Faulkner Papers.

34   Harriet Heydon to Messrs Sweeny & Chearnley, 26 January 1788: NLI, Ms. 41,604.

35   FJ, 30 March–1 April 1786.

36   AR to SF, 24 July 1787: PRONI, MIC21/7.

37   Bury and Norwich Post, 9 July 1788. Other sources put the odds at five to one – 'he gives 4000l. to receive 20,000l' (BNL, 7–10 October 1788, DEP, 7 October 1788) – but this is probably an exaggeration.

38   FJ, 13–16 June 1789 (twelve months); Bury and Norwich Post, 9 July 1788 (fourteen months).

39   BNL, 7–10 October 1788.

40   Sir Lewis Namier and John Brooke, The History of Parliament: The House of Commons, 1754–1790 (3 vols, London: History of Parliament Trust, 1985), Vol. 3, p. 586.

41   Agreement between Thomas Whaley and the Earl of Grandison: NLI, Ms. 10,750.

42   See BNL, 7–10 October 1788, FLJ, 3–7 January 1789 and The Times, 6 June 1789 (£20,000); FLJ, 2–6 May 1789 and BNL, 22-26 May 1789 (£30,000); and FJ, 30 April–2 May 1789 and SNL, 25 May 1789 (£40,000).

43   White, London in the Eighteenth Century, p. 342.

44   Quoted in Vic Gatrell, City of Laughter: Sex and Satire in Eighteenth-Century London (London: Atlantic, 2006), p. 128.

45   According to Jonah Barrington, 'leaping out of a window voluntarily was formerly by no means uncommon in the country parts of Ireland:—some did it for fun—others for love: but it was generally for a wager': Jonah Barrington, Personal Sketches of His Own Times (2 vols, London: Colburn and Bentley, 1830), Vol. 1, p. 255n.

46 Those who did make the journey included the Church of Ireland clergyman Richard
Pococke (1738). A small number of Irish Franciscans also served in the Christian
convents of the Holy Land: Con Costello, *Ireland and The Holy Land: An Account of
Irish Links with the Levant from the Earliest Times* (Alcester and Dublin: C. Goodliffe
Neale, 1974), pp. 64, 111–13. Other eighteenth-century Irishmen to visit the Near
East included Lord Charlemont, who in 1746 commenced a grand tour that brought
him to Greece, Turkey and Egypt, and Robert Wood, who also travelled in Turkey
and Egypt and in 1751 was one of the first scholars to study the ruins of Palmyra: *DIB*,
Vol. 9, pp. 1025–6. However, neither Charlemont nor Wood made it to Jerusalem.

47 *FJ*, 15–17 January 1789.

48 Mazzeo (ed.), *Travels, Explorations and Empires*, Vol. 4, p. xxii.

49 Ibid. pp. vii–viii.

50 *DEP*, 7 October 1788.

51 C.-F. Volney, *Travels Through Syria and Egypt, in the Years 1783, 1784, and 1785.
Containing the Present Natural and Political State of those Countries...* (2 vols, Dublin:
Messrs. Burnet, White, Byrne, W. Porter, Moore and Dornin, 1788).

52 See Philip Mansel, *Constantinople: City of the World's Desire* (London: John Murray,
1995), p. 225.

53 *DEP*, 7 October 1788.

Chapter 5

1 *Ipswich Journal*, 16 August 1788.

2 *Ipswich Journal*, 6 September 1788.

3 *Ipswich Journal*, 23 August 1788.

4 In his memoirs Whaley indicated that this episode took place after his return from
Jerusalem: see W, 272–5. However, contemporary newspaper reports show that it
happened in August 1788: *Ipswich Journal*, 16 and 23 August and 6 September 1788.
Whaley identified his friend only as a Mr. C—. The newspaper reports offer a small
bit more in the way of identification (Mr. Cr—r) but the full name remains unknown.

5 *Ipswich Journal*, 6 September 1788.

6 *DEP*, 20 September 1788.

7 *DIB*, Vol. 3, pp. 1043–5; 'Statement of the title of the Honble. Mary Whaley to the
town & lands of Straboe in the County of Carlow', p. 8: NLI, Ms. 8676(1); *DEP*, 20
September 1788.

8 *Both Sides of the Gutter, or, the Humours of the Regency ...* (3rd ed., Dublin: P. Byrne,
[1789]), pp. 167–70. Copy in BL: 11642.f.13. Sullivan identifies several of those
mentioned: Sullivan (ed.), *Memoirs*, pp. xxxi–xxxv.

9 *DIB*, Vol. 2, pp. 344–5; Walter G. Strickland, *Dictionary of Irish Artists* (2 vols, Dublin
and London: Maunsel and Co., 1913), Vol. 1, pp. 154–6.

10   Other journalists also posited imaginary retinues to accompany Whaley on his trip. According to *Finn's Leinster Journal* his companions included 'his lady, a bagpiper, a ducliner [*sic*] player, two French horns, a sadler, a French cook, a friseur [hairdresser], a black-leg [cardsharp], and a poor poet, who is to keep an account of every thing remarkable that may happen during the voyage, and throw the whole into metre'. *FLJ*, 20–24 September 1788.

11   [Henry Joy,] *Historical Collections Relative to the Town of Belfast from the Earliest Period to the Union with Great Britain* (Belfast, 1817), pp. 127–8; Johnston-Liik, *Irish Parliament*, Vol. 6, pp. 542–3; *BNL*, 31 October–4 November 1788.

12   A.P.W. Malcomson, *John Foster: The Politics of the Anglo-Irish Ascendancy* (Oxford: Oxford UP, 1978), p. 282n.

13   *The Times*, 3 October 1788.

14   *Notes and Queries*, Ser. 6, Vol. 11 (January–June 1885), p. 325.

15   In his memoirs, Whaley suggests that he hired the entire ship. (W, 37) However, there would have been no need for such extravagance, and in fact Whaley only hired a cabin on the *London*: Sullivan (ed.), *Memoirs*, p. 339.

16   *BNL*, 7–10 October 1788. A few weeks later another apocryphal report had it that the *London* stopped off in Carrickfergus to pick up 'several holy recruits' before embarking on the voyage proper: *BNL*, 31 October–4 November 1788. However, it would have been impractical for the ship to make a diversion to Ulster, and Whaley's memoirs make no mention of this or the 'holy recruits'.

17   Captain Francis Liardet, quoted in N.A.M. Rodger, *The Command of the Ocean: A Naval History of Britain, 1649–1815* (New York and London: W.W. Norton, 2004), p. 400.

18   *ODNB*, Vol. 13, p. 527; *British Mercury*, 29 September and 13 October 1788. Whaley would have been surprised to learn that one of the Moroccan Sultan's wives was an Irishwoman. Known as Lalla Sargetta, she was mother to the Sultan's eldest son and had sufficient influence with her husband to persuade him to fetch her own mother from Ireland to live with her in Morocco. The son, Mulay al-Yazid, had proved to be more amicable in his dealings with the British. It was reported that 'the Emperor of Morocco's eldest son is half an Irishman … The young Prince is remarkably fond of the British nation. He speaks English tolerably … The father and son hate each other mortally. They seek each other's death with great avidity': *British Mercury*, 24 November 1788. See also Des Ekin, *The Stolen Village: Baltimore and the Barbary Pirates* (Dublin: O'Brien Press, 2008), p. 272.

19   Fa and Finlayson, *The Fortifications of Gibraltar*, pp. 23–30.

20   Don Ignacio Lopez de Ayala, *The History of Gibraltar from the Earliest Period*. Trans. James Bell (London: William Pickering, 1845), pp. 174–5.

21   The actual governor of Gibraltar at this time was General George Augustus Eliott, first Baron Heathfield (1717–1790), who had distinguished himself during the Great Siege. Heathfield had returned to England in 1787 and in his absence O'Hara was the

acting governor. In 1795 he became governor of Gibraltar proper, a position he held until his death in 1802.

22 He was present when the British surrendered at Yorktown in 1781 and in Cornwallis's absence he led the surrender ceremony, offering his sword to George Washington's second-in-command, a scene immortalised in John Trumbull's famous painting *Surrender of Lord Cornwallis*: *ODNB*, Vol. 41, pp. 627–8. The painting is now in the Rotunda of the United States Capitol in Washington D.C.

23 John Ingamells, *A Dictionary of British and Irish Travellers in Italy, 1701–1800* (London: Yale UP, 1997), p. 721.

24 A contemporary anecdote gives a sense of the banter that might have passed between Whaley and the governor. It was said that when O'Hara was governor of St Lucia, a young man 'naturally supposing him as great a man as his Holiness' applied to him for a papal dispensation to let him marry his aunt. O'Hara promptly issued a dispensation in the following terms: 'The bearer hereof has my permission to marry his aunt, or his grand-mother, if he chuses', signing the document, 'Charles O'Hara, Major General and Pope': *British Mercury*, 29 September 1788.

25 Fa and Finlayson, *The Fortifications of Gibraltar*, pp. 23–30.

26 George Le Mesurier Gretton, *The Campaigns and History of the Royal Irish Regiment from 1684 to 1902* (Edinburgh and London: William Blackwood, 1911), p. 88.

27 Ralph Legge Pomeroy, *The Story of a Regiment of Horse ...* (2 vols, Edinburgh and London: William Blackwood, 1911), Vol. 2, p. 151; Alexander Knox, *A History of the County of Down From the Most Remote Period to the Present Day* (Dublin: Hodges, Foster & Co., 1875), p. 520; Sullivan (ed.), *Memoirs*, p. xvii.

28 *FLJ*, 17–20 November 1779.

29 David Ker to Hugh Moore, 3 October 1807: PRONI, D2651/2/85.

30 Whaley described this as an almost perpendicular descent of 50 fathoms or 300 feet. (W, 56) In fact it was probably no more than a hundred feet but still a significant drop. See cross section of St Michael's Cave system in E.P.F. Rose, 'Military engineering on the Rock of Gibraltar and its geoenvironmental legacy' in Judy Ehlen and Russell S. Harmon (eds), *The Environmental Legacy of Military Operations* (Boulder, Colorado: The Geological Society of America, 2001), p. 104.

31 Whaley did not explore the full extent of St Michael's Cave. During the Second World War engineers blasting a new entrance discovered a further series of descending chambers now known as Lower St Michael's Cave.

32 Virgil, *Aeneid*, 1:630. The actual wording is 'Non ignara mali, miseris succurrere disco'.

Chapter 6

1 Thomas Hope, quoted in Mansel, *Levant*, p. 52; Whaley, *Memoirs*, p. 143.

2 Mansel, *Levant*, p. 53.

3   TW Manuscript Memoirs, Vol. 1, p. 161; Biray Kolluoğlu Kırlı, 'Cityscapes and modernity: Smyrna morphing into Izmir' in Anna Frangoudaki and Caglar Keyder (eds), *Ways to Modernity in Greece and Turkey: Encounters with Europe, 1850–1950* (London: I.B. Tauris & Co. Ltd., 2007), p. 222. An early-nineteenth-century traveller, William Turner, noted that 'the streets of Smyrna, like those of all Turkish towns, are narrow, dirty, and ill-paved': William Turner, *Journal of a Tour in the Levant* (3 vols, London: John Murray, 1820), Vol. 3, p. 288.

4   Nadia Manolova-Nikolova, 'Spanish records of Istanbul at the end of the 18th century' in Plamen Mitev et al (eds), *Empires and Peninsulas: South-Eastern Europe between Karlowitz and the Peace of Adrianople, 1699–1829* (Berlin: Lit Verlag, 2010), p. 121.

5   Mansel, *Levant*, p. 42.

6   Although much of Smyrna was destroyed by fire in 1922, many of the merchant families' superb villas can still be seen in the suburbs of Izmir.

7   Quoted in Mansel, *Levant*, p. 30.

8   *FJ*, 8–10 July, 9–12 August and 1–4 November 1788.

9   For information on the Maltass and Lee families of Smyrna see http://humphrysfamilytree.com (accessed 16 July 2018).

10   According to Moore, the official 'gravely laid it [the spyglass] down beside him, imagining, no doubt, that he did us infinite honor by his acceptance of it'. (M, 15) Whaley had in fact brought with him a whole case of spyglasses, intended as presents for the various dignitaries he expected to meet, and not all recipients of this gift would react as indifferently as the customs official. Spyglasses were rare and much sought-after items in the Ottoman lands.

11   Shaw, *Between Old and New*, pp. 4–5.

12   TW Manuscript Memoirs, Vol. 1, pp. 177–8.

13   Letter from Constantinople, 3 December 1788, printed in *FLJ*, 2–6 May 1789.

14   The Ottoman capital had clearly been talked about as a possible destination at the time of Whaley's departure. One publication even claimed that his wager was for a journey to Constantinople, not Jerusalem: *Annual Register*, Vol. 30 (1788), p. 216.

15   'Scala' was a generic name for places of embarkation and disembarkation in Turkey: M, 35n.

16   MacGill, *Travels*, Vol. 1, p. 133.

17   Mansel, *Constantinople*, pp. 220–1.

18   Slavery existed in eighteenth-century Ireland but the legality of the practice was a grey area: Philip McEvansoneya, 'The black figure in Angelica Kauffman's Earl of Ely family group portrait', *History Ireland*, Vol. 20, No. 2 (March/April 2012), pp. 26–8.

19   Both Whaley and Moore mistakenly thought the town was the classical city of Magnesia ad Maeandrum, governed by the Athenian naval strategist Themistocles

in the fifth century BC: W, 89–91; M, 21. However, Magnesia ad Maeandrum was actually situated to the south, near Ephesus. The town Whaley and Moore visited was known classically as Magnesia ad Sipylum.

20　Other subjects included a view of Smyrna, a view of Constantinople, Paulo, the Captain Pasha (the Grand Admiral of the Ottoman navy) and 'A Turkish lady coming out of the bath'. Unfortunately the drawings were lost following Whaley's return to Ireland: W, 6 and 107.

21　Whaley and Moore both called this town Maccatitch; elsewhere it is referred to as Mohalitch and Mikalitza: *A Hand-book for Travellers in the Ionian Islands, Greece, Turkey, Asia Minor, and Constantinople* ... (London: John Murray, 1840), p. 281. Today it is known as Karacabey.

22　Mazzeo (ed.), *Travels, Explorations and Empires*, Vol. 4, p. xxi.

23　Quoted in Ian McBride, *Eighteenth-Century Ireland: The Isle of Slaves* (Dublin: Gill, 2009), p. 277.

Chapter 7

1　Mansel, *Constantinople*, p. 177; ibid. pp. 176–7.

2　Paintings such as Antoine van der Steen's *View of Constantinople from Pera* (*c*.1770) give a sense of the grandeur of the vista (see Plate 12).

3　Mansel, *Constantinople*, pp. 131–2.

4　Quoted in Mazzeo (ed.), *Travels, Explorations and Empires*, Vol. 4, pp. 142, 143. Sometimes impoverished young females voluntarily sold themselves into slavery, in the not necessarily mistaken belief that it would improve their quality of life. Many Georgian and Circassian girls aspired to enter the harem of a Turkish pasha: Erdem, *Slavery in the Ottoman Empire*, pp. 49–50.

5　*St James's Chronicle*, 9 December 1790.

6　Mansel, *Constantinople*, p. 206; Jeremy Black, *British Foreign Policy in an Age of Revolutions, 1783–1793* (Cambridge: Cambridge UP, 1994), p. 123.

7　Letter of Hugh Moore, Constantinople, [15] December [1789]: Faulkner Papers.

8　Ibid.

9　Mansel, *Constantinople*, p. 12.

10　Mansel, *Constantinople*, p. 177. John Cam Hobhouse also saw dancing boys in Galata some twenty years later, dancing 'to the music of guitars, fiddles and rebeks [a three-stringed instrument played with a bow]; and what with the exclamations of the master of the dancers, and sometimes the quarrels of the Turks, so much noise and disturbance ensue at mid-day as to bring the patrol to the spot. Rome itself ... could not have furnished a spectacle so degrading to human nature as the taverns of Galata'. John Cam Hobhouse, *Travels in Albania and Other Provinces of Turkey in 1809 & 1810* (2 vols, London: John Murray, 1858), Vol. 2, p. 262.

11 TW Manuscript Memoirs, Vol. 1, pp. 248–9. In Sullivan's version, part of this description is replaced by a series of asterisks to denote an instance 'where Whaley's language is somewhat too outspoken' to be included: Sullivan (ed.), *Memoirs*, p. xliv.

12 TW Manuscript Memoirs, Vol. 1, p. 184.

13 Mansel, *Constantinople*, pp. 176–7.

14 Letter of Hugh Moore, Constantinople, [15] December [1789]: Faulkner Papers.

15 'Minister of Saxony, banker to the Russian embassy, and personal friend of many Ottoman ministers': Mansel, *Constantinople*, p. 229.

16 Ágoston and Masters, *Encyclopedia of the Ottoman Empire*, p. 6.

17 The Russian attack was so successful that 'it resulted in the destruction or abandonment of every enemy vessel in the harbor: fourteen line ships, six frigates, and fifty smaller vessels burned, while one line ship and five galleys were captured. Only about 4,000 Turkish crewmen made it ashore; the other 11,000 perished'. Davies, *The Russo-Turkish War*, p. 159.

18 Ibid. pp. 156–7.

19 Ágoston and Masters, *Encyclopedia of the Ottoman Empire*, p. 6.

20 Moore indicated that the Captain Pasha was 69 (M, 46) but most sources have it that he was born circa 1714, making him around 74 at the time of Whaley's visit.

21 Ian R. Christie, 'Samuel Bentham and the Russian Dnieper Flotilla, 1787–1788', *Slavonic and East European Review*, 50, 119 (April 1972), pp. 173–97.

22 In November 1788 there were 'two English frigates for sale' in Constantinople: 'the Sybelle and the Count de Nord … His Majesty's frigate the Pearl of 32 guns, commanded by the Hon. Capt. Finch is here, and though in high order – the Sybelle beats her all to pieces': letter from Constantinople, 22 November 1788, quoted in *The Times*, 23 January 1789.

23 Whaley also claimed to have given him 'a pistol which from its peculiar construction could fire seven balls one after another, with one loading' for which he had paid a hundred guineas. (W, 116–17) Although he did possess a weapon of this kind it seems he gave it not to the Captain Pasha but to another Ottoman dignitary, Ahmad Pasha al-Jazzar, the governor of Sidon, whom he met some months later (see Chapter 12). Whaley also stated that following the audience the Pasha sent him a pelice and a bottle of vastly expensive attar of rose (rose oil, used to make scented water, liqueurs and perfumes): W, 116. However, Moore makes no mention of these gifts.

24 MacGill, *Travels*, Vol. 2, pp. 66–71.

25 MacGill, *Travels*, Vol. 2, pp. 66–71.

26 Advertisement for James's Powder in *DEP*, 5 August 1788.

27 *ODNB*, Vol. 29, pp. 732–3.

28 http://www.academie-francaise.fr/les-immortels/marie-gabriel-florent-auguste-de-choiseul-gouffier (accessed 16 October 2018); Léonce Pingaud, *Choiseul-Gouffier:*

La France en Orient sous Louis XVI (Paris: Alphonse Picard, 1887), p. 85 (author's translation).

29 Shaw, *Between Old and New*, p. 31; Mansel, *Constantinople*, pp. 205–6.

30 Letter of Hugh Moore, [15] December [1788]: Faulkner Papers.

Chapter 8

1 Letter of Sir Robert Ainslie, Constantinople, 15 May 1788, quoted in *FJ*, 8–10 July 1788. This outbreak wiped out many of the inhabitants of Pera and the northern suburbs: *FJ*, 8–10 July, 9–12 August and 1–4 November 1788.

2 Mansel, *Constantinople*, p. 225.

3 When they reached the Holy Land a couple of months later Whaley and Moore drank wine to fortify themselves against 'the noxious vapours of the night': M, 301.

4 TW to SF, 7 May 1789: Whaley Papers.

5 TW to SF, 7 May 1789: Whaley Papers.

6 Whaley's account of Hagia Sophia (W, 110–11) is based on that of Moore, who visited it one day while his friend was bedridden. While impressed by the size of the mosque and the gigantic columns supporting its dome, Moore was dismayed by the ruinous condition of the place: 'the symmetry … is now entirely destroyed. Cornices mouldered away, capitals broken and misplaced, columns, which should have been handed down inviolate to posterity, and preserved as the most chaste models of ancient perfection, broken and disfigured': M, 105. However, Hagia Sophia was restored in 1847–9 on the orders of Sultan Abdülmecid I and is in much better condition today than it was in the eighteenth century.

7 M, 65–101.

8 Apart from this, some of Whaley's statements are obvious inventions, such as his claim that he visited the tomb of the Emperor Constantine (W, 131). In fact the whereabouts of Constantine's remains have been unknown since the Ottoman Turks captured the city in 1453. He also claimed to have spent three months in the city (W, 133) when actually he was there for less than six weeks.

9 Lady Mary's letters were first published in 1763: *Letters of the Right Honourable Lady M[ar]y W[ortle]y M[ontagu]e: Written, During Her Travels …* (3 vols, London: Becket and de Hondt, 1763). For her description of the ladies' *hamam* see Vol. 1, pp. 159–64 and Isobel Grundy, *Lady Mary Wortley Montagu* (Oxford: Oxford UP, 1999), pp. 137–8.

10 James T. Boulton and T.O. McLoughlin (eds.), *News from Abroad: Letters Written by British Travellers on the Grand Tour, 1728–71* (Liverpool: Liverpool UP, 2012), p. 3.

11 Shaw, *Between Old and New*, p. 30. For the Hapsburgs 'the war brought only modest reward at enormous cost: 33,000 dead and 172,000 sick and wounded between

June 1788 and May 1789, and major destruction in the recently colonized Banat during the devastating Ottoman raids in the autumn of 1788': Ágoston and Masters, *Encyclopedia of the Ottoman Empire*, p. 63.

12   With customary exaggeration, Whaley claimed that he was ill in Smyrna for a fortnight. (W, 158) Actually the period of his sickness was only five days, as he arrived in Smyrna on 27 January and was fit to travel again by 1 February.

13   Johnston-Liik, *Irish Parliament*, Vol. 6, pp. 542–3.

14   Whaley's claim that he visited Ephesus while convalescing (W, 159–60) can be safely discounted. The great ruined Greco-Roman city lies some fifty miles from Smyrna (Izmir), and a round trip to it would have been extremely difficult to perform in the short space of time between his recovery from his illness on 1 February and the departure of the *Heureuse Marie* two days later, especially when his weakened condition is taken into account. Moreover, his description of Ephesus is extremely pedestrian with no anecdotal information. In all probability it is derived from another traveller's account.

15   Traditionally it was believed that the author of the *Book of Revelation* and John the Evangelist were one and the same. However, many modern scholars dispute this and ascribe the authorship of Revelation to a separate individual known as John of Patmos or John the Theologian.

16   Founded by St John Christodoulos in 1088, the Monastery of St John the Theologian, or Monastery of the Apocalypse is still a functioning Greek Orthodox monastery. It is also now a UNESCO World Heritage site.

17   Known as the Patmias or Patmian School, the seminary was founded in 1713 by a Greek Orthodox deacon monk, Makarios Kalogeras. Rebuilt in the twentieth century, it still functions as an ecclesiastical school.

18   Whaley indicated that Gilly was French, Moore that he was Venetian. Going by his name the latter seems the more likely.

19   By contrast, the famous libertine Giacomo Casanova often graphically described sexual encounters in his autobiography. 'Where he is vague on dates, he is specific on sex': Kelly, *Casanova*, p. 86. Whaley and Moore were much more reserved.

20   Athanasios D. Kominēs, *Patmos: Treasures of the Monastery* (Ekdotike Athenon, 1988), p. 14.

21   Volney, *Travels*, Vol. 2, p. 54n; de Tott, *Memoirs of Baron de Tott*, Vol. 2, p. 97.

Chapter 9

1   Talbot, 'Divine Imperialism', p. 40.

2   See Judith Mendelsohn Rood, *Sacred Law in the Holy City: The Khedival Challenge to the Ottomans as Seen from Jerusalem, 1829–1841* (Leiden: Brill, 2004), pp. 45–7.

3   Philipp, *Acre*, p. 33.

4   The disguise was good enough to fool Europeans. When leaving Smyrna on 3 February the *Heureuse Marie* had encountered a Dutch frigate, the *Castor*, whose captain Moore had known at Gibraltar. When he hailed the frigate, decked out in full Ottoman dress, her duty officer duly informed the captain that 'there was a Turk along side who spoke French and had enquired for him'. (M, 131) The ship had just arrived in the Near East and the crew of the *Castor* stared at the 'Turk' 'with as much eagerness as if the Grand Signior [Sultan] had been on board'. 'Could I have kept my countenance,' Moore declared, 'I am convinced that I might have remained unknown, so great was the difference that the long beard and the change of dress made in my appearance': M, 132.

5   Over a hundred years later T.E. Lawrence observed, 'My burnt red face, clean shaven & startling with my blue eyes against white headcloth & robes, became notorious in the desert. Tribesmen or peasants who had never set eyes on me before would instantly know me, by the report': quoted in Jerrold Seigel, *Between Cultures: Europe and its Others in Five Exemplary Lives* (Philadelphia: University of Pennsylvania Press, 2016), p. 80.

6   There were seventeen Christian convents in the Holy Land, all of which were run by Franciscans who were mainly French, Spanish and Italian: Volney, *Travels*, Vol. 2, p. 313.

7   Philipp, *Acre*, p. 25.

8   F.B. Spilsbury, *Picturesque Scenery in the Holy Land and Syria Delineated During the Campaigns of 1799 and 1800 ...* (London: Edward Orme, 1803), pp. 2–3.

9   Philipp, *Acre*, pp. 1–3. Most of Acre's European merchants were French. They had their own consul and owned six houses in the town: Volney, *Travels*, Vol. 2, p. 228.

10 Probably the Khan el-Franj or Khan of the Franks.

11 Whaley's memoirs, strangely, give a quite different account of the evening. They indicate that at the merchant's house they were met by a dazzling 'assemblage of beauties', a harem that the merchant had 'collected with much taste and expense in different parts of Asia and among the islands'. They danced and played party games like blindman's buff, and Whaley claimed to have enjoyed himself so much that he did not retire to rest until six o'clock in the morning, bemoaning 'pleasures past, never again to return!' (W, 173) Moore's journal makes no mention of any of this. Whaley may have decided to embellish what in reality was a rather unglamorous and uncomfortable first night in the Holy Land.

12 Around twelve miles from Acre. Whaley called it 'Scietamor' (W, 175), Moore 'Sciefamor' (M, 179).

13 Pringle, *Churches of the Crusader Kingdom*, Vol. 2, p. 116.

14 http://www.nazareth-en.custodia.org (accessed 16 July 2018).

15 Mishaqa, *Murder, Mayhem, Pillage and Plunder*, p. 39; Philipp, *Acre*, p. 160.

16 Mishaqa, *Murder, Mayhem, Pillage and Plunder*, p. 39.

17   Doumani, *Rediscovering Palestine*, p. 37. See also Philipp, *Acre*, p. 33. Whaley and
       Moore both referred to the Jarrars as 'the Jaffars': W, 186; M, 199.

18   As his name indicates, Yusuf al-Jarrar was himself a member of the clan. He was
       also a strong leader, capable of galvanising his followers with passionate rhetoric.
       When Napoleon invaded the Holy Land ten years later, Yusuf wrote a fervent
       poem declaring that news of the invasion had brought 'fire to his heart' and urging
       resistance: Doumani, *Rediscovering Palestine*, p. 19.

19   An ill-advised attempt by the besiegers to mine the fortifications 'literally backfired
       and destroyed most of the camp of Ahmad Pasha al-Jazzar'. Al-Jazzar attacked the
       Jarrars again in 1803 but this too ended in failure: Philipp, *Acre*, p. 19.

20   TW Manuscript Memoirs, Vol. 2, p. 7.

21   Doumani, *Rediscovering Palestine*, p. 22; ibid. p. 23.

22   Doumani, *Rediscovering Palestine*, pp. 42–3.

23   'Swearing by the mustache and the beard … [is] one phase of swearing by the head.
       To swear by one's mustache, or beard, means to pledge the integrity of one's manhood
       … Swearing by the beard is supposed to carry more weight because, as a rule, it is
       worn by the older men': Abraham Mitrie Rihbany, *The Syrian Christ* (Boston and
       New York: Houghton Mifflin, 1916), pp. 171–2.

24   This comment alone evokes a sense of separation that is hard to conceive of in the
       present-day age of mobile technology.

25   TW Manuscript Memoirs, Vol. 2, p. 17.

Chapter 10

1   Volney, *Travels*, Vol. 2, p. 303.

2   Ibid. pp. 308–9.

3   *DIB*, Vol. 8, pp. 195–7 and *ODNB*, Vol. 44, pp. 667–9; Rachel Finnegan (ed.), *Letters
      from Abroad: the Grand Tour Correspondence of Richard Pococke & Jeremiah Milles
      Volume 3: Letters from the East (1737–41)* (Kilkenny: Pococke Press, 2013).

4   Thompson and Tyron 'used their travel accounts to expound the truth of Biblical
      history and prophecy based on their interpretations of the contemporary political
      and economic landscape': Talbot, 'Divine Imperialism', p. 41.

5   Quoted in Hunt Janin, *Four Paths to Jerusalem: Jewish, Christian, Muslim, and Secular
      Pilgrimages, 1000 BCE to 2001 CE* (Jefferson, NC: McFarland & Co., 2002), p. 158.

6   Pringle, *Churches of the Crusader Kingdom*, Vol. 3, p. 209; Clarke, *Travels*, Vol. 4, p. 297.

7   Volney, *Travels*, Vol. 2, p. 309; ibid. pp. 306–7.

8   Clarke, *Travels*, Vol. 4, p. 297. During his stay at St Saviour's in 1806 the Vicomte
      de Chateaubriand consumed 'lentil soup, veal with cucumbers and onions, broiled
      kid with rice, pigeons, partridges, game, [and] excellent wine': quoted in Montefiore,
      Jerusalem, pp. 319–20.

9   Clarke, *Travels*, Vol. 4, p. 298.

10   This may have Qasim Bey, who was appointed *mutasallim* of Jerusalem in 1785: Philipp, *Acre*, p. 71.

11   According to Whaley he even offered them the use of apartments in his palace; 'however, we declined, as we were much better *à la Chrétienne qu'à la Turque*': W, 191.

12   Whaley's memoirs include a partially accurate account of the history of the Temple Mount up to the time of the construction of Al-Aqsa Mosque in AD 643: W, 193–6.

13   TW Manuscript Memoirs, Vol. 2, p. 21.

14   Pringle, *Churches of the Crusader Kingdom*, Vol. 3, pp. 64–5.

15   Their transcriptions are fairly accurate and accord closely with what the Franciscan Elzear Horn recorded earlier in the eighteenth century in his *Ichonographiae Monumentorum Terrae Sanctae, 1723-1744*. See http://www.sepulchre.custodia. org/default.asp?id=4171 (accessed 16 July 2018). Godfrey's inscription translates as follows: 'Here lies the famous Duke Godfrey of Bouillon, who acquired this land for Christian worship, and whose soul reigns with Christ. Amen'. Baldwin I's inscription, somewhat longer, compared him to Judas Maccabeus (the Jewish priest who led the revolt against the Seleucids around 167 BC) and stated that 'Kedar and Egypt, Dan and man-slaying Damascus in terror brought gifts of tribute' to him: Sullivan (ed.), *Memoirs*, pp. 198n, 199–200n.

16   Some fragments of the tombs are now in Jerusalem's Greek Orthodox Museum and in the Studium Biblicum Franciscanum: Pringle, *Churches of the Crusader Kingdom*, Vol. 3, p. 64.

17   At the time of Whaley's visit the aedicule was a relatively plain building. In 1808 it was destroyed by fire and later rebuilt in rococo style. It then suffered earthquake damage and is now held together by steel girders.

18   TW Manuscript Memoirs, Vol. 2, pp. 36–7. The manuscript version gives a fuller account of Whaley's feelings at this time than Sullivan saw fit to include in the published version. (W, 201)

19   Many pilgrims to Jerusalem experience religious epiphanies. Some even contract Jerusalem Syndrome, a state of psychosis in which the sufferer becomes delusional and may believe that he or she is a Biblical figure.

20   'Our hero is at present on a journey to Jerusalem,' the *Town and Country Magazine* had reported in January, 'but not from motives of religion': *Town and Country Magazine*, January 1789, p. 10.

21   TW Manuscript Memoirs, Vol. 2, pp. 46–7. Again, the manuscript gives a fuller account of Whaley's feelings than Sullivan saw fit to include in the published version. (W, 210)

22   Suraiya Faroqhi, *Subjects of the Sultan: Culture and Daily Life in the Ottoman Empire* (London: I.B. Tauris, 2007), p. 110; ibid. pp. 101–3.

23 Volney reckoned that there were about 600 men capable of bearing arms in the town, which suggests that it had a population in the thousands: Volney, *Travels*, Vol. 2, p. 313.

24 Pringle, *Churches of the Crusader Kingdom*, Vol. 1, p. 138.

25 The mosaics are currently being repaired by an Italian restoration company. In 2016 the team uncovered a twelfth-century mosaic of an angel that had been hidden under plaster for centuries: http://www.bbc.com/news/world-middle-east-36591434 (accessed 17 June 2018).

Chapter 11

1 Whaley claimed that the bandits administered a bastinadoing (beating on the soles of the feet) to the servants and guides. (W, 226) Moore does not mention this and it is probably an embellishment.

2 Doumani, *Rediscovering Palestine*, p. 22; Henry Baker Tristram, quoted in ibid. p. 22.

3 According to Moore the *mutasallim* had been told in advance about the attack, though Whaley indicated that they brought him the news personally. Either way, he was certainly disturbed by what he heard.

4 TW Manuscript Memoirs, Vol. 2, p. 86.

5 Following his return to Ireland Moore told the story to Thomas Percy, the Church of Ireland Bishop of Dromore, who passed it on to the Welsh antiquary Michael Lort: John Bowyer Nichols, *Illustrations of the Literary History of the Eighteenth Century ...* (8 vols, London, 1817–58), Vol. 7, p. 510.

6 Mazzeo (ed.), *Travels, Explorations and Empires*, Vol. 4, p. ix.

7 Doumani, *Rediscovering Palestine*, p. 203.

Chapter 12

1 Donna Landry, *Noble Brutes: How Eastern Horses Transformed English Culture* (Baltimore: Johns Hopkins University Press, 2008).

2 The document is pasted onto page 318 of Moore's journal. Sullivan's translation reads, 'I, the undersigned Guardian of this Convent of St. Mary, certify to all and singular who may read these presents, that Messrs. Thomas Whaley and Hugh Moore have, on two occasions, been present and resided in this City of Nazareth for the space of three days, in witness whereof – Given in the s[ai]d City of Nazareth, 5th [*sic*] March 1789, Brother Archangel of Entraigues, Guardian and Superior': Sullivan (ed.), *Memoirs*, p. 224.

3 Whaley had purchased the weapon from a famous London gunsmith, Henry William Mortimer. Although different sorts of revolvers had been in use since the seventeenth

century, this type of firearm would not become popular until Samuel Colt patented his version in the 1830s.

4 As previously noted, Sullivan's version of Whaley's memoirs wrongly places the encounter with al-Jazzar at the time of their first arrival in Acre (W, 168–74). The London Library manuscript makes no mention of a meeting with al-Jazzar at this time and indicates simply that they left Acre the morning after their arrival: TW Manuscript Memoirs, Vol. 1, pp. 396–7.

5 Philipp, *Acre*, p. 52. See also Volney, *Travels*, Vol. 2, p. 54.

6 Originally slave soldiers, the Mamluks established ruling dynasties in Egypt and Syria during the Middle Ages. The name derives from the Arabic word for slave.

7 Philipp, *Acre*, pp. 48–53.

8 Doumani, *Rediscovering Palestine*, p. 100. Al-Jazzar's eventual death in 1804 gave rise to celebrations as far away as Damascus: ibid. p. 100.

9 Philipp, *Acre*, p. 54.

10 Volney, *Travels*, Vol. 2, pp. 268–9; de Tott, *Memoirs of Baron de Tott*, Vol. 2, p. 97. Other accounts verged on the pornographic. Guillaume Antoine Olivier, who met al-Jazzar in 1802, reported that he had murdered several of his women after suspecting them of unfaithfulness. According to this no doubt inflated account he had some of them drowned in the sea, while others he tortured and threw into a cistern. He reserved the harshest punishment for his most beloved wife, cutting off her hands and breasts before disembowelling her: Philipp, *Acre*, p. 56.

11 Whaley claimed that al-Jazzar was rewarded for this atrocity with a great honour: being sent the 'Third Tail' by the Porte. This symbolised his elevation to the highest of the three ranks of pashas, who were given the privilege of bearing a standard of three horse-tails. In reality, however, al-Jazzar was awarded this honour for services rendered before the outbreak of the rebellion.

12 Philipp, *Acre*, p. 54.

13 Ibid. p. 50. A present-day descendant of al-Jazzar has confirmed this, indicating that it denoted the Pasha's status as a strongman or enforcer in the region and did not have negative connotations: Sami Malki, Montreal, Canada, interview with the author, 8 February 2016.

14 Renaudot, quoted in Philipp, *Acre*, p. 58. Renaudot later had to leave Acre after falling out with al-Jazzar: Anne Mézin, *Les Consuls de France au Siècle des Lumières (1715–1792)* (Paris: Ministère des Affaires Étrangères, 1997), p. 515.

15 Moore indicates that they were disappointed to be received in the garden, having hoped to see the inside of the palace. This directly contradicts Whaley's statement that 'On our arrival at the Palace, we were conducted thro' several spacious apartments, and thence to a gallery of immense length, from whence we descended by a flight of one hundred steps, when we found ourselves in a delightful garden.' (W, 168) Moore's account feels believable while Whaley's seems exaggerated.

16   Clarke, *Travels*, Vol. 4, p. 92.

17   The ongoing conflict between Russia and the Ottoman Empire had caused the 'total destabilization of the social-economic life of the empire and the continual disruption of administration': Ágoston and Masters, *Encyclopedia of the Ottoman Empire*, p. 6.

18   Al-Jazzar was on similar form when Edward Daniel Clarke met him eleven years later: 'he defied the whole power of *Turkey*, despised the *Vizier*, and derided the menaces of the *Capudan* [Captain] *Pasha*; although he always affected to venerate the title and the authority of the *Sultan*': Clarke, *Travels*, Vol. 4, p. 84.

19   According to Whaley, al-Jazzar described 'his wars against the unfortunate Ali Bey, a Calif of Egypt, whom he conquered and afterwards put to death'. (W, 169) However, this is inaccurate. Although al-Jazzar had disobeyed the Mamluk leader Ali Bey al-Kabir by refusing to kill Salih Bey, there is no evidence that he killed him. It appears that al-Kabir died in Egypt in 1773, long after al-Jazzar had left the country.

20   Whaley's memoirs do not indicate that he gave such a weapon to al-Jazzar. Instead, he maintained that he gave al-Jazzar 'a pair of pistols, beautifully ornamented in gold and silver' and that the Pasha hurt his hand while firing one of them, having loaded it with too much gunpowder: W, 172. Elsewhere he indicates that in Constantinople he presented the Captain Pasha with 'a pistol which from its peculiar construction could fire seven balls one after another, with one loading': W, 116–17. It is not clear why Whaley did not admit to having given al-Jazzar the revolver. Perhaps he felt that the Captain Pasha would have been a more worthy recipient of this unusual gift and therefore he altered the facts accordingly.

21   Clarke, *Travels*, Vol. 4, p. 87. According to Volney, al-Jazzar's greatest extravagances were 'his gardens, his baths, and his white women: of the latter he possessed eighteen in 1784, and the luxury of these women is most enormous': Volney, *Travels*, Vol. 2, p. 269.

22   Montefiore, *Jerusalem*, pp. 315–18.

23   That Whaley did bring back an Arabian horse from his travels is proved by contemporary newspaper accounts: *St James's Chronicle or the British Evening Post*, 5 September 1789; *BNL*, 11–15 September 1789.

24   Although Moore's chronology of events (see Sullivan (ed.), *Memoirs*, pp. 342–3) indicates that they set sail from Acre on 10 March, immediately following the meeting with al-Jazzar, the trip to Caiffa must have added another day to their journey. In all likelihood they did not sail from Acre until 11 March.

Chapter 13

1   Whaley's memoirs indicate that after leaving Episkopi they continued west to 'Achicis' (Acheleia) near Paphos and proceeded from there to Nicosia, completing the journey within a single day. This is simply unfeasible: it is fifty miles as the crow flies from

Acheleia to Nicosia, and the road would have had to circumvent the great massif of the Troodos Mountains (which Whaley did not mention). It seems Whaley wished to give the impression that he had comprehensively toured the island, but in all likelihood they went no further west than Episkopi.

2   TW Manuscript Memoirs, Vol. 2, pp. 114–15.

3   Erdem, *Slavery in the Ottoman Empire*, pp. 48–9.

4   TW Manuscript Memoirs, Vol. 2, pp. 115–16.

5   Ibid. p. 116.

6   It was possibly a narrow escape. Some Tunisians, like their Algerian neighbours, engaged in piracy. In December 1787, William Norwood wrote from Marseilles that 'owing to the Algerines being very numerous on the coasts here it is found very dangerous to go in any vessal except an English Irish Scotch or French but the latter not by any means as secure as the former': WN to SF, 27 December 1787: NLI, P. 1576.

7   TW to SF, 7 May 1789: Whaley Papers.

8   Ibid.

9   *Town and Country Magazine*, January 1789, pp. 9–10; *WHM*, February 1789, pp. 68–69.

10   *The Times*, 2 December 1788; 5 January and 20 February 1789.

11   *BNL*, 25–8 November 1788; *FLJ*, 18–22 April 1789; William Lappan to SF, 28 April 1789: PRONI, MIC21/4; *FJ*, 30 April–2 May 1789.

12   TW to SF, 7 May 1789: Whaley Papers.

13   While Whaley claimed that the period of quarantine was thirty days, Moore indicated that it was twenty-one, and that the latter is correct is suggested by the fact that they arrived in Paris by 4 June.

14   *The Times*, 11 June 1789; *Ipswich Journal*, 13 June 1789; *Bath Chronicle*, 18 June 1789; *Newcastle Courant*, 20 June 1789.

15   It was expected that Whaley's winnings would enable him to 'liquidate' some 'disagreeable demands': *FLJ*, 14–17 January 1789; *FJ*, 15–17 January 1789.

16   He was back in Ireland by 14 June, when he wrote asking Faulkner to come and meet him either at Font Hill or at Commodore Cosby's house, Stradbally Hall in the Queen's County: TW to SF, [14] June 1789: Faulkner Papers.

17   *DEP*, 21 July 1789; *SNL*, 21 July 1789; *FJ*, 21–23 July 1789.

18   *DEP*, 21 and 23 July 1789.

19   Whaley would leave a large sum to Moore in his will, while naming him as one of the testamentary guardians of his children: NLI, Ms. 8676(1).

20   AR to TW, 27 June 1784: PRONI, MIC21/7.

21   *FJ*, 18–21 July 1789.

22   *FLJ*, 18–22 April 1789.

23   TW to SF, 4 June 1789: Whaley Papers.

Chapter 14

1   The Yorkshireman Foster Powell (1734–1793) did more than most to popularise pedestrianism. His feats included covering a hundred miles in a time of 21 hours 35 minutes: *ODNB*, Vol. 45, pp. 90–1. Powell placed bets on the outcome of his efforts and helped fuel the obsession with gambling on pedestrianism.

2   *Diary or Woodfall's Register*, 11 September 1789.

3   *FJ*, 17–19 September 1789; *BNL*, 22–5 September 1789; *London Chronicle*, 22 September 1789; Rory Muir, *Wellington: The Path to Victory, 1769–1814* (New Haven and London: Yale UP, 2013), p. 19.

4   Richard Holmes, *Wellington: The Iron Duke* (London: Harper Collins, 2002), p. 22.

5   *Monthly Magazine*, Vol. 9, 1 March 1800, p. 187; Lord Cloncurry, *Personal Recollections of the Life and Times … of Valentine Lord Cloncurry* (Dublin: James McGlashan, 1849), p. 182n; Ross (ed.), *Correspondence of … Cornwallis*, Vol. 3, p. 182n.

6   *St James's Chronicle or the British Evening Post*, 28 July, 1 August, 12 August and 5 September 1789; *London Chronicle*, 22 September 1789; *The Times*, 15 October 1789.

7   Letter of William Godwin to James Marshall, 14 August 1800 in Clemit (ed.), *Letters of William Godwin*, Vol. 2, p. 162. Upper-class men known for spirited, eccentric and sometimes violent behaviour were called 'bucks': J.E. Walsh, *Ireland Sixty Years Ago* (Dublin: M'Glashan, 1851), p. 17. Others apart from Whaley were to be so designated included Edmund 'Buck' Sheehy, a Tipperary gentleman, was executed for murder in 1766, and William Alexander 'Buck' English (d. 1794), a duellist and gambler said to have been the victim of a practical joke at Daly's Club: Ryan, *Blasphemers & Blackguards*, pp. 125–6.

8   The Fonthill estate consisted of 400 acres and was highly productive. During the 1789 harvest the steward Patrick Hackett had forty people at work in the fields cutting and stacking wheat and insisted he could 'brag of one of the best crops in the county Carlow'. Patt Hackett to SF, 7 September 1789: PRONI, MIC21/4.

9   Agreement between Thomas Whaley and the Earl of Grandison: NLI, Ms. 10,750; AR to SF, 31 August 1789: PRONI, MIC21/7.

10 TW to SF, 16 September 1789: Faulkner Papers.

11 *FLJ*, 15–19 August 1789; *Morning Post and Daily Advertiser* (London), 21 August 1789; *St James's Chronicle or the British Evening Post*, 5 September 1789; *BNL*, 11–15 September 1789. Whaley did not mention the gift in his memoirs, instead claiming that the horse died while under the care of his groom in London, probably as a result of poisoning: W, 270. It is not clear why he gave this version of events. Perhaps the horse died after the Prince took possession of it and Whaley wished to conceal the fact that his gift had turned out to be worthless.

12 Brighton was then a centre of pleasure and health resorts for the upper classes, who hoped that sea bathing and fresh air would cure 'most of the ills they suffered as a

result of over-indulgence at the table and lack of exercise'. E.A. Smith, *George IV* (New Haven and London: Yale UP, 1999), pp. 44–5; ibid. p. 44.

13 *ODNB*, Vol. 21, pp. 857, 859.

14 Sullivan (ed.), *Memoirs*, p. xxvi.

15 T. Humphry Ward and W. Roberts, *Pictures in the Collection of J. Pierpont Morgan at Prince's Gate & Dover House, London* (London: privately printed, 1907), [pp. 106–7]. According to one writer Maria Courtenay was a cousin of Hugh Moore: Mary Stratton Ryan, 'The Jerusalem Pilgrim: Thomas Whaley (1766–1800) of Castletown and Font Hill, Co Laois', *Carloviana* 63 (2015), p. 63.

16 Philip Hay to SF, 25 October 1790: PRONI, MIC21/4.

17 RC to SF, 2 September 1789: NLI, P. 4647. Whaley's mother thought he should pay Hood 'out of the cash he has already received from his Jerusalem friends': AR to SF, 31 August 1789: PRONI, MIC21/7. This does not seem to have happened, possibly because Whaley had already spent the money.

18 *FJ*, 8 November 1800.

19 Bills from Captain William Tatlock for work on the *Minx*, 1789: Faulkner Papers; Receipt from Kenneth McCulloch, Compass-Maker, to TW, 21 November 1789: Whaley Papers.

20 RC to SF, 23 Oct and 6 November 1789: NLI, P. 4647; 'Statement of the title of the Honble. Mary Whaley to the town & lands of Straboe in the County of Carlow', p. 9: NLI, Ms. 8676(1).

21 *ODNB*, Vol. 20, p. 610.

22 There were two spring meetings at Newmarket in 1790, on 19–24 April and 3–8 May: James Weatherby, *Racing calendar: containing an account of the plates, matches, and sweepstakes, run for in Great-Britain and Ireland ... with an abstract of all the matches, sweepstakes, &c. now made, to be run at Newmarket, from the Craven Meeting, 1790, to the year 1795 ...* (London: H. Reynell, 1790).

23 *FJ*, 22–24 April 1790.

24 Johnston-Liik, *Irish Parliament*, Vol. 3, pp. 297–8; quoted in ibid. p. 297.

25 RC to SF, 24 May and 20 June 1790: NLI, P. 4647.

26 RC to SF, 7, 9 and 16 July 1790: NLI, P. 4647.

27 'Statement of the title of the Honble. Mary Whaley to the town & lands of Straboe in the County of Carlow', p. 9: NLI, Ms. 8676(1).

28 RC to SF, 16 July 1790: NLI, P. 4647.

29 Maguire, *Living Like a Lord*, p. 15; *ODNB*, Vol. 38, pp. 916–17.

30 TW to SF, 15 September 1790: Faulkner Papers.

31 TW to SF, 28 September 1790: Faulkner Papers.

32 TW to SF, 30 September and 6 October 1790: Faulkner Papers.

33 TW to SF, 21 October 1790: Faulkner Papers.

34 TW to SF, 18 December 1790 (first of two letters with this date): Faulkner Papers.

35 White, *London in the Eighteenth Century*, pp. 341–2.

36 RC to SF, 10 February 1791: NLI, P. 4647.

Chapter 15

1 RC to SF, 24 February 1791: NLI, P. 4647.

2 AR to SF, 30 April 1791: PRONI, MIC20/7.

3 Ibid.

4 RC to SF, *c.*3 October 1791: NLI, P. 4647.

5 *London Chronicle*, 17 July 1790.

6 *FJ*, 13–15 July 1790, *FLJ*, 14–17 July 1790; Martyn J. Powell, *Piss-pots, Printers and Public Opinion in Eighteenth-Century Dublin: Richard Twiss's Tour in Ireland* (Dublin: Four Courts Press, 2009), pp. 53–5.

7 *London Chronicle*, 17 July 1790. See also Kelly, *Duelling in Ireland*, p. 201; *Hibernian Journal*, 16 July 1790 and *Clonmel Gazette*, 17 July 1790.

8 *FJ*, 19–21 October and 11–14 December 1790; RC to SF, 13 December 1790: NLI, P. 4647.

9 RC to SF, 4 June 1791: NLI, P. 4647.

10 Susan Stewart to SF, 11 April 1791: PRONI, MIC21/7.

11 The risk of imprisonment for non-payment of debt meant that England was a permanent no-go area for some, such as Benjamin Mee, the brother of Lady Palmerston. In August 1792 Mee was at sea and 'his involved financial affairs were to keep him out of England for the rest of his life': Connell, *Portrait of a Whig Peer*, p. 267.

12 WW to SF, 10 August 1791: PRONI, MIC21/6.

13 WW to SF, 28 August and 11 September 1791: PRONI, MIC21/6; TW to SF, 9 September 1791: Faulkner Papers; RC to SF, 12 September 1791: NLI, P. 4647.

14 RC to SF, *c.*3 October 1791: NLI, P. 4647; Lau Pearson to SF, 20 September 1791: PRONI, MIC21/5.

15 William Lappan to SF, 7 March 1792: PRONI, MIC21/5. Part of the lands were sold to the Rev. James Hamilton, in trust for the Archbishop of Armagh, and another part to the Bishop of Cloyne: 'Case for the opinion of Robt. Trench Esq', p. 4: NLI, Ms. 8676(1).

16 On 1–2 February 1792 Bruen paid Foot £32,146 and four shillings to cover the amount of Whaley's debt along with costs and interest. 'Statement of the title of the Honble. Mary Whaley to the town & lands of Straboe in the County of Carlow', p. 9: NLI, Ms. 8676(1).

17 A list of goods of Thomas Whaley, sold by public auction in 1792, includes pots, pans, a sideboard, an oval table, a carpet, a chandelier, a looking glass, bookcases, glass candlesticks, mattresses, bedding, a pair of card tables, a night table, weeding

trowels, ploughs and a harrow. These items seem to have come from or been sold at Font Hill. List of goods of Thomas Whaley, sold by public auction 1792: PRONI, MIC21/7.

18 RC to SF, 10 and 12 March 1792: NLI, P. 4647; Michael Kearney to SF, 13 March 1792: Faulkner Papers.

19 WW to SF, 5 May 1792: PRONI, MIC21/6. Whaley indicated that he incurred his losses at the Pavillon d'Hanovre in 1791, shortly before Louis XVI's flight to Varennes. (W, 283) However, he does not seem to have had any money to lose at this time and it is far more likely that the episode dates from March–June 1792, when he did have money.

20 TW to Lord Hervey, 22 April 1792: Suffolk Record Office, 941/55/2.

21 Connell, *Portrait of a Whig Peer*, p. 262.

22 Whaley's departure from Paris was not to the advantage of William, who had arrived in the French capital by the end of July. Cash strapped once again, he may have travelled there looking for his brother, who was by then in Lausanne: WW to SF, 30 July 1792: PRONI, MIC21/6.

23 Robert Fowler, who dined at Whaley's house several times, records the presence of Whaley's 'mistress'. Diary of Robert Fowler, 28 July 1792: RCBL, No. 79.

24 Guy Chapman, *Beckford* (London: Jonathan Cape, 1937), pp. 239–40; Connell, *Portrait of a Whig Peer*, p. 269.

25 Diary of Robert Fowler, 23 August, 5 September and 8 September 1792: RCBL, No. 79; Amanda Foreman, *Georgiana: Duchess of Devonshire* (London: HarperCollins, 1999), pp. 276–7; Connell, *Portrait of a Whig Peer*, p. 268.

26 Whaley's description of the tour in his memoirs is peppered with exaggeration. He claims to have spent three weeks in Milan before moving on to Bologna ('where I remained some days wholly occupied in viewing the works of the most eminent masters in painting and sculpture': W, 305), Florence, Rome ('for the two months I remained there, I always found something new to admire, though I generally spent eight hours every day in viewing whatever [was] worthy the notice of a traveller': W, 307) and Naples. No doubt he did visit some or all of these places, but he overstated the amount of time spent in each so as to give the impression he had thoroughly admired Italy's most important art and antiquities.

27 TW to Lord Hervey, 30 June 1793: Suffolk Record Office, 941/55/2; W, 291.

28 TW to Lord Hervey, 28 December [1792]: Suffolk Record Office, 941/55/2.

29 AR to SF, 2 January 1793: PRONI, MIC21/7.

30 For the sake of clarity the Austrian Netherlands will henceforth be referred to as Belgium.

31 TW Manuscript Memoirs, Vol. 2, pp. 173–4.

32 TW to Lord Hervey, 28 December [1792]: Suffolk Record Office, 941/55/2.

Chapter 16

1   Firmont recalled that 'as soon as the fatal blow was given, I fell upon my knees, and thus remained until the vile wretch, who had acted the principal part in this horrid tragedy, came with shouts of joy, shewing the bleeding head to the mob, and sprinkling me with the blood that streamed from it: then, indeed, I thought it time to quit the scaffold': Henry Essex Edgeworth de Firmont and C. Sneyd Edgeworth, *Memoirs of the Abbé Edgeworth; Containing his Narrative of the Last Hours of Louis XVI* (London: Rowland Hunter, 1815), p. 109.

2   Quoted in Moorehead, *Dancing to the Precipice*, p. 165.

3   [TW] to Lord Hervey, 21 January 1793: Suffolk Record Office, 941/55/2.

4   The men Whaley encountered were not the only ones to carry away items smeared with the king's blood. Others included two Irish barristers, John and Henry Sheares, both of whom were later executed for their part in the 1798 Rebellion. It was said that John Sheares, 'crossing over to England in the same packet with young Daniel O'Connell, the future Liberator, then a staunch tory, exultantly exhibited a handkerchief dipped in Louis XVI's blood': J.G. Alger, 'The British Colony in Paris, 1792–93', *English Historical Review* 13, 52, 1898, p. 690. Some of these 'relics' are still in circulation. In 2012 an ornate gourd said to have been dipped in Louis XVI's blood was subjected to DNA analysis which showed that it 'almost certainly carries the bloodstains of the fallen king'. https://www.telegraph.co.uk/news/worldnews/europe/france/9773174/Louis-XVI-blood-mystery-solved.html (accessed 14 June 2018).

5   [TW] to Lord Hervey, 21 January 1793: Suffolk Record Office, 941/55/2.

6   Moorehead, *Dancing to the Precipice*, p. 6.

7   Quoted in Hayes, *Ireland and Irishmen*, pp. 116–17; Mary Ann Lyons and Thomas O'Connor, *Strangers to Citizens: The Irish in Europe, 1600–1800* (Dublin: NLI, 2008), p. 18.

8   Dillon would himself face the guillotine just over a year later. On 13 April 1794 he was taken before the Revolutionary Tribunal in Paris and accused, among other things, of conspiring against the republic. That same day he was brought to the Place de la Republique. 'Arthur climbed the steps, calmly removed his cravat and shouted "Vive la Roi" before the blade fell': Moorehead, *Dancing to the Precipice*, pp. 202–3.

9   TW to Lord Hervey, 30 June 1793: Suffolk Record Office, 941/55/2.

10   W, 327; *ODNB*, Vol. 35, p. 71.

11   TW to Lord Hervey, 30 June 1793: Suffolk Record Office, 941/55/2.

Chapter 17

1   Quoted in Ann C. Kavanaugh, *John Fitzgibbon, Earl of Clare* (Dublin: Irish Academic Press, 1997), pp. 2–3.

2   Ibid. p. 204.

3   JR to SF, 23 May 1793, AR to SF, 29 May and 15 June 1793: PRONI, MIC21/7.

4   'An account of the real and personal property whereof Thomas Whaley Esqre was seized possessed of or entitled unto at the time of his decease...', passim: NLI, Ms. 8676(1).

5   JR to TW, 20 June 1793: PRONI, MIC21/7; 'Case for the opinion of Robt. Trench, Esq', p. 5: NLI, Ms. 8676(1).

6   Jim Smyth, *The Men of No Property: Irish Radicals and Popular Politics in the Late Eighteenth Century* (London: Macmillan, 1998), p. 102; TW to Lord Hervey, 30 June 1793: Suffolk Record Office, 941/55/2.

7   James Kelly, *Sport in Ireland* (Dublin: Four Courts Press, 2014), p. 29; TW Manuscript Memoirs, Vol. 2, p. 21.

8   John T. Gilbert, *A History of the City of Dublin* (3 vols, Dublin: J. McGlashan, 1854–9), Vol. 3, p. 39; R.B. McDowell, *Land & Learning: Two Irish Clubs* (Dublin: Lilliput, 1993), p. 15.

9   *SNL*, 20 June 1794; *FJ*, 21 June 1794.

10 Kelly, *Casanova*, pp. 271–2.

11 WW to SF, 6 September 1794: PRONI, MIC21/6.

12 WW to JR, 8 August 1794; WW to SF, 12 and 29 August 1794: PRONI, MIC21/6.

13 Early in 1795 they finally managed to settle a large debt owed to Latouche's bank in Dublin, though it 'distressed us beyond measure'. This did not stop Whaley from trying to offload his obligations onto them. AR to SF, 17 April 1795: PRONI, MIC21/7.

14 Bernard Ward to SF, 2 March 1795 and James Hamill to SF, 14 March 1795: PRONI, MIC21/5.

15 RC to SF, 28 September 1795: NLI, P. 4647.

16 TW to SF, 29 November 1794: Faulkner Papers.

17 TW to SF, 3 June 1795: Faulkner Papers.

18 RC to SF, 10 June 1795 and August 1795 ('Wednesday 2'o clock'): NLI, P. 4647. Cornwall was acting in his capacity as Whaley's lawyer, but he also had a personal interest in seeing the estate sold because he himself was owed £3,018-13 out of it: 'Statement of the title of the Honble. Mary Whaley to the town & lands of Straboe in the County of Carlow', p. 11: NLI, Ms. 8676(1).

19 Cooper held a number of official posts which supplied with him a considerable income. He was also said to have won the huge sum of £20,000 in a lottery. Such great wealth enabled him not only to loan money to the likes of Whaley, but also to purchase a large amount of property, including Abbeville, a house in Kinsealy, County Dublin which in the twentieth century became the home of Irish Taoiseach Charles Haughey: *DIB*, Vol. 2, pp. 822–3.

20 *BNL*, 21–25 and 25–28 September 1795.

21 Thomas Prentice to SF, 24 and 29 September 1795: PRONI, MIC21/5.

22   Initially Samuel and Hugh Faulkner feared the opposite. A few days after Cornwall's departure they received news that he had been shipwrecked and drowned. 'My God how unfortunate a thing it was that Mr Cornwall should have postponed his voyage until the stormy season,' Hugh lamented, 'or that he could not dispense with going untill he was sure that the equinoctial winds were over'. Luckily the report turned out to be false, 'the whole a mano[e]uvre to find out whether Whaley be in the island or not'. His creditors, it seems, were prepared to go to extraordinary lengths to flush him out. HF to SF, 19 and 22 October 1795: NLI, P. 3500.

23   Thomas Prentice to SF, 18 November 1795: PRONI, MIC21/5; SF to HF, 15 November 1795: Faulkner Papers.

24   Cornwall to SF, 28 October 1795: NLI, P. 4647.

25   SF to HF, 12 and 14 November 1795; SF to HF, 16 November 1795: Faulkner Papers.

26   *SNL*, 19 November 1795.

27   Faulkner was buried in the nearby parish of Malew. See http://www.isle-of-man.com/manxnotebook/people/residnts/twhaley.htm (accessed 21 July 2018). This website also contains substantial information on Whaley's connection with Man.

28   RC to HF, 1 December 1795: NLI, P. 4647.

29   Ibid.

30   *FJ*, 5 December 1795.

Chapter 18

1   Sullivan (ed.), *Memoirs*, p. v.

2   AR to SF, 20 January [year not given]: PRONI, MIC21/7; TW to SF, 28 June 1783: Faulkner Papers.

3   http://www.isle-of-man.com/manxnotebook/people/residnts/twhaley.htm   (accessed 20 July 2018).

4   *Critical review of the first annual exhibition of paintings, drawings, & sculptures ... at No. 32, Dame-Street, Dublin. June, 1800* (Dublin: Carey's sale and exhibition rooms, 1800), p. 12.

5   It is possible that the female depicted in this portrait is actually Mary Lawless, who became Whaley's wife in January 1800. However, the tradition that the portrait is of Maria Courtenay remained strong for the century or so after Whaley's death, and on balance I feel she is the most likely subject. Green, *Knutsford*, pp. 140–1; T. Humphry Ward and W. Roberts, *Pictures in the Collection of J. Pierpont Morgan at Prince's Gate & Dover House, London* (London: Privately Printed, 1907), p. 107.

6   The painting is now in the Metropolitan Museum of Art in New York (accession no. 47.138): http://www.metmuseum.org/art/collection/search/436689 (accessed 18 October 2017), Katharine Baetjer, *British Paintings in the Metropolitan Museum of Art, 1575–1875* (New York: Metropolitan Museum of Art, 2009), pp. 185–6.

7   Sophia Isabella Whaley was baptised at Onchan near Douglas on 13 December 1797: Isle of Man, Baptism Index, 1600–1981 (MS10309/1). She may have been named after her aunt Sophia, who had died in 1793.

8   Will of Maria Courtenay, 23 January 1798: Manx Museum Library, Episcopal Wills 1798, E632. My thanks to Frances Coakley for sending me a copy of this document.

9   'An account of the real and personal property whereof Thomas Whaley Esq[ui]re was seized possessed of or entitled unto at the time of his decease ... ', p. 4: NLI, Ms. 8676(1). Colclough was shot dead in a duel in 1807.

10   *FLJ*, 16–20 June 1798.

11   On 3 July he wrote from St Stephen's Green to the acting Chief Secretary, Lord Castlereagh, requesting a passport for a French friend of his who wanted to come to Dublin: TW to Castlereagh, 3 July 1798: NAI, Rebellion Papers, 620/39/13.

12   Dickson, *Dublin: The Making of a Capital City*, p. 257.

13   Green, *Knutsford*, p. 140. On the face of it this is just another legend, one of many that emerged in the years following Whaley's death. But it may not be as far-fetched as it seems: at least one other Irish gentleman did something similar. In the early 1800s Sir Henry Browne Hayes, who had been transported to Australia for abducting an heiress, built Vaucluse House near Sydney. The area was ridden with snakes so Hayes surrounded the house with turf imported from Ireland. This, he believed, would keep the reptiles at a safe distance. http://adb.anu.edu.au/biography/hayes-sir-henry-browne-2172 (accessed 21 July 2018).

14   Her will was proved on 27 September 1798. Will of Maria Courtenay, 23 January 1798: Manx Museum Library, Episcopal Wills 1798, E632.

15   Sullivan described the interior as it was in the early 1900s: 'many traces of the original luxurious fittings are still visible in the solid mahogany window-shutters with silvered plate-glass let in, the Chippendale panels below the windows, and the mahogany doors inlaid with Chippendale work. Especially noticeable is a finely carved Carrara marble mantelpiece, one of the two medallions on which is said to be a likeness of Buck Whaley himself': Sullivan (ed.), *Memoirs*, pp. xxiv.

16   Sullivan (ed.), *Memoirs*, p. xxv.

17   *The Times*, 29 August 1799.

18   'Draft Case of Mrs Whaley for – the opinion of [blank]', p. 3: NLI, Ms. 8676(1).

19   *DIB*, Vol. 9, p. 865; Viscount Castlereagh to the Duke of Portland, 7 February 1800 in Ross (ed.), *Correspondence of ... Cornwallis*, Vol. 3, p. 182; Johnston-Liik, *Irish Parliament*, Vol. 6, p. 534.

20   Letter of William Godwin to James Marshall, 14 August 1800 in Clemit (ed.), *Letters of William Godwin*, Vol. 2, p. 162. Godwin was right to point out Whaley's inaccuracies: in 1800 Georgia and Circassia were separate countries, and the ancient land of Moesia (now divided between Serbia and Bulgaria) was completely distinct from Byzantium (Constantinople / Istanbul): ibid. p. 164n.

21   Sullivan (ed.), *Memoirs*, p. xxviii.

22   Green, *Knutsford*, p. 139; It seems that the stone has since vanished and the exact location of the grave is unknown. Reputedly a bizarre scene took place before the funeral: 'the workmen had just made up the coffin, when Mr. Robinson, an Irishman, who also was a dancing-master of that day, stepping upon the coffin, danced a hornpipe [a sort of jig or solo reel with intricate steps, similar to a sailor's dance] over the body, – a piece of levity, not to call it an indecency, which our best feelings unite to condemn': Green, *Knutsford*, p. 139.

23   *The Times*, 7 November 1800; *Monthly Magazine* 66 (1 December 1800), pp. 469–70; *WHM*, December 1800, pp. 324–5.

24   *FJ*, 8 November 1800.

25   Sullivan (ed.), *Memoirs*, p. xxviii; *The Times*, 7 November 1800; *Gentleman's Magazine*, Vol. 88 (1800), p. 1114.

26   *Real life in Ireland: or, the day and night scenes, rovings, rambles, and sprees, bulls, blunders, bodderation and blarney of Brian Boru, Esq., and his elegant friend Sir Shawn O'Dogherty ...* (London: Methuen, 1904 [first published 1821]), p. 166.

27   *ODNB*, Vol. 17, pp. 984–5.

28   Whaley made his will at Liverpool on 24 October 1800 and it was proved on 23 January 1801. The testator appointed Mary Whaley, the Earl of Clare, Valentine Goold and Hugh Moore as executors, trustees and testamentary guardians of his three children, to each of whom Whaley bequeathed £2,000. He left £1,000 to Valentine Goold, £500 to Hugh Moore, £500 to Thomas Goold, and the residue of his estate, after these payments were made, to his wife. The original will was destroyed by the fire at the Public Record Office in Dublin in 1922 but the particulars are noted in NLI, Ms. 8676(1); *The Irish Builder*, 15 December 1894, p. 293; and Sullivan (ed.), *Memoirs*, p. xxix.

Epilogue

1   In 1795, on learning that he had left yet another unpaid bill at her husband's door, she concluded that it must have 'escaped Mr Whaleys memory, or I am sure he wou[l]d have continued to provide for it without letting Mr R. be called upon for the payment'. AR to SF, 17 April 1795: PRONI, MIC21/7.

2   Letters of RC to SF, passim: NLI, P. 4647.

3   *FJ*, 8 November 1800.

4   'At his death (7 March 1785) the family estates were much reduced and burdened with debt, and the baronetcy became extinct': *DIB*, Vol. 1, p. 865.

5   In 1784 Lord Drogheda was said to be 'ruining his health and fortune through drink and play' and by the end of his life he was virtually bankrupt: Ryan, *Blasphemers & Blackguards*, p. 124; *DIB*, Vol. 6, p. 620.

6   Clotworthy Skeffington. In 1770 he was thrown into a French debtor's prison after accumulating debts of £30,000. After he eventually attained his liberty in 1789 he continued to live extravagantly, undeterred by his long years of confinement, and became the victim of a swindle by William Whaley.

7   Richard Barry, seventh earl of Barrymore. Around 1790 he squandered £60,000 in England and his debts forced him to sell a 140,000-acre estate in County Cork.

8   After losing £30,000 in 1792 and a further £40,000 in 1794 Lord Donegall (then Lord Belfast) was thrown into the Fleet, a London debtors' prison: Maguire, *Living Like a Lord*, p. 15.

9   Barrister and satirist who fled to the Mediterranean in the 1810s after large gambling losses and was beheaded in Constantinople.

INDEX